Palestinians in Kuwait

Palestinians in Kuwait

The Family and the Politics of Survival

Shafeeq N. Ghabra

Routledge
Taylor & Francis Group

LONDON AND NEW YORK

First published 1987 by Westview Press

Published 2019 by Routledge
52 Vanderbilt Avenue, New York, NY 10017
2 Park Square, Milton Park, Abingdon, Oxon OX14 4RN

Routledge is an imprint of the Taylor & Francis Group, an informa business

Library of Congress Cataloging-in-Publication Data
Ghabra, Shafeeq N.
    Palestinians in Kuwait.
    (Westview special studies on the Middle East)
    Bibliography: p.
    Includes index.
    1. Rural Families—Kuwait. 2. Palestinian
Arabs—Kuwait. 3. Family corporations—Kuwait.
4. Palestinian Arabs—Kuwait—sociallife and customs.
5. Immigrants—Kuwait. I. Title. 11. Series.
HQ666.A2 1987   306.8'5'095367   86-10636

ISBN 13: 978-0-367-28220-2 (hbk)
ISBN 13: 978-0-367-29766-4 (pbk)

So that they may recall:

To my daughters, Haneen, Zaina, and their generation.

Contents

vii

ix

Illustrations

Acknowledgments

The research, field work and writing for this study have taken over two years. The book was originally written as a Ph.D. dissertation under the supervision of Professor James Bill of the University of Texas (at Austin). I am grateful to him for his careful and considerate attention to the manuscript at its several stages. I wish to thank Professor Henry Dietz, Robert Fernea, Lawrence Graham, and Robert Hardgrave, who provided important suggestions for the writing of this study. Four more individuals deserve particular mention for their contribution to the writing of the book. Dr. Barbara Harlow who took time to read the entire manuscript and Dr. Michael Fischer who read part. I thank both of them for the valuable suggestions provided to me. I wish to express my gratitude to Dr. Ghassan Salame of the American University of Beirut whose support encouraged me to turn my Ph.D. dissertation into a book. Finally, I would like to thank Barbara Ellington, senior acquisition editor of Westview Press, for her support.

The following people were also instrumental in the making of this book: The faculty of the Political Science Department of Kuwait University gave me constant encouragement; Ahlam Shammas of the Central Statistical Office in Kuwait provided valuable published statistical data; and the staff of the information center of Kuwait's daily newspaper, al-Watan, permitted me to use their files and library. I owe special recognition to the Kuwait University Scholarship Committee for funding my graduate studies, and therefore most of the research and writing for this study. I deeply thank Paul Attie, whose computer expertise helped address many of the technical problems I encountered in producing the final version of this study. I also thank Anaed Samad-Farah for proofreading the final copy of this study. And I extend my thanks to Beverly Olson for typing the manuscript, and Henry Olson for helping to draw the figures.

I am especially indebted to my informants who gave generously of their time and their joyful and painful recollections. I thank all of them, both those cited in this study and those whose interviews provided important background material and insights. No one who contributed directly or indirectly to the study bears responsibility for any of its shortcomings or misjudgements, but whatever merit this study may have is due to them and shared by them.

Finally, I extend my deepest gratitude to my parents, whose memories of Palestine became mine. They have instilled in me the quest for Knowledge, and always insisted on my best effort. Their support and care during my fieldwork in Kuwait made the whole experience gratifying. I also owe a great deal to my wife, Taghreed. First, I thank her for reading the manuscript during a busy time in her own graduate program, and for providing insightful comments. Our fruitful discussions and exchanges, her companionship and support, throughout the research and writing were essential to the completion of the work.

The system of transliteration followed throughout this study is the standard used by the Library of Congress and approved by the American Library Association and the Canadian Library Association. Some of the signs used by the Library of Congress have been omitted to simplify the transliteration. This applies to h2, t, d, z, q2, h, s, and the dash over letters such as ā. I have just used h, t, d, z, q, h, s, and a, without any of the above additional signs. The two most important signs not omitted are the ᶜ (ayn) for ᶜAmer, and the ' (hamzah) for Mir'ah. In the book, a lower case ᶜ has been used to replace the ' and a ' has been used to replace the '.

Shafeeq Ghabra

xiv

Map 1 : Towns and Villages Cited in the Study

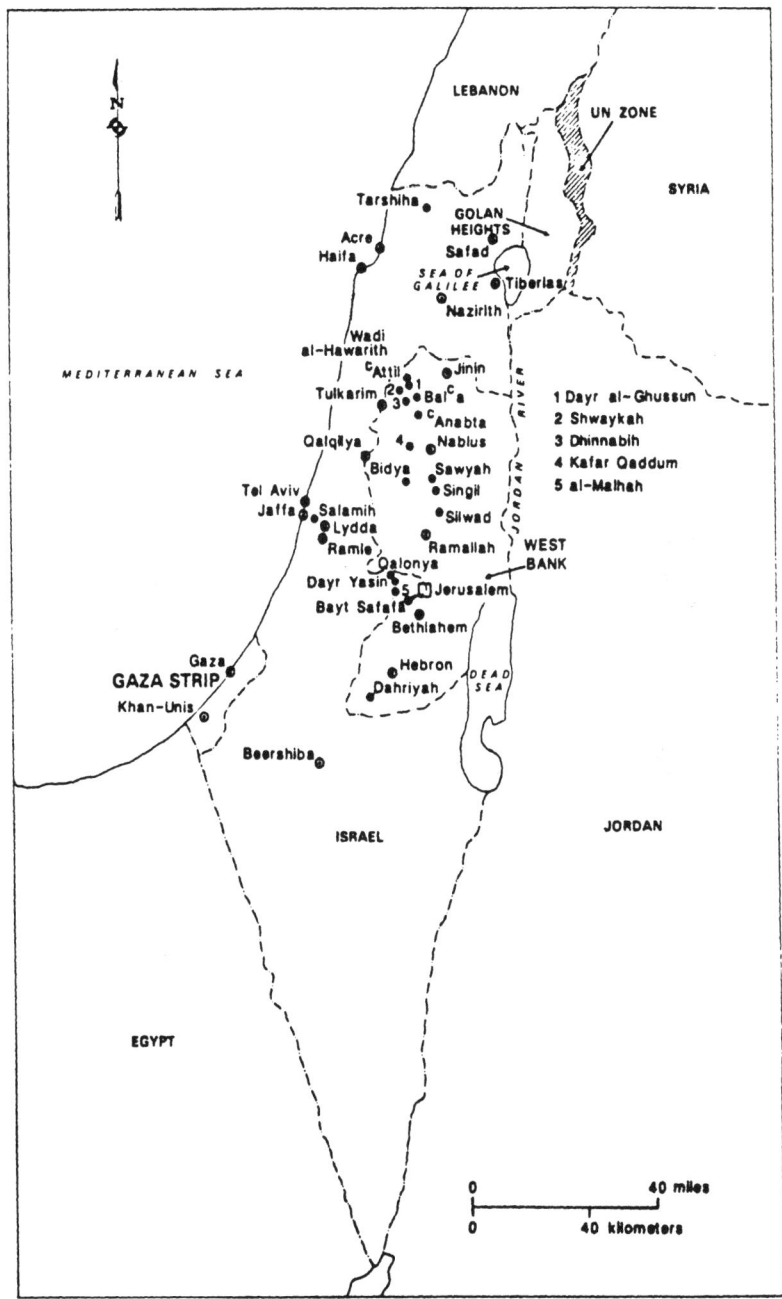

Introduction

This study is an investigation of the strategies of survival and adaptation employed by a displaced population; the Palestinians in Kuwait. Dispersal, uprootedness, and the destruction of many Palestinian villages and neighborhoods in 1948 shattered the old networks and bonds of solidarity that revolved around the town's mosque or church, its families, economy, and way of life. Nevertheless, the Palestinians who were dispersed in the 1948 and 1967 wars, employed a whole set of tactics and strategies of adaptation that have enabled them to preserve the microbonds of their society. Although the Palestinians have established formal organizations to help them meet their educational, cultural, and political needs, my study deals with the more basic dynamic prerequisites that contributed to their survival.

This study will concentrate on one of the most important prerequisites of survival, that is, the reconstruction of the social bonds of solidarity. Without such ties, the stateless cannot exist as a group and would gradually disappear through dispersal, fragmentation, and assimilation. I shall try to explain how the Palestinians used informal relationships (such as kinship and former village and town ties) after the destruction of their formal socioeconomic institutions to regroup and to reestablish their solidarity units. In other words, this book will investigate the strategies by which a dispersed people have preserved, rebuilt, and reshaped their bonds of solidarity, their networks, and their very existence as a group.

1

This inquiry was triggered by a question addressed to me during my graduate course work: What kept the Palestinians from being assimilated into the Arab milieu? What held them together as a separate subculture? Even though they are 85 percent Sunni Muslim Arabs from similar physical and cultural environments. At the time, I was unable to explain the inner mechanisms that usually make solidarity among persecuted groups a natural outcome of their experience. I was only able to explain how external causes and forces, such as the encounter with Zionism, had led to Palestinian solidarity.

Thinking about these questions and searching for a better answer motivated me to study the available literature on stateless groups, ethnicity, and peasant migration in the Third World. Theoretical studies in comparative politics that focused on group politics, informal relationships, and interest groups were also included in my investigation. The Committee on Comparative Politics of the Social Science Research Council stressed in 1957 the role of informal structures in Third World political systems in performing functions similar to those of Western formal structures. Could social solidarity and social reconstruction of the Palestinian diaspora have resulted from different structures (family and village) performing functions similar to those of other institutions found in the Jewish, Armenian, or Nubian experiences?

This study of the politics of family survival is intended to fill one gap in the literature on the Palestinian diaspora. It brings to light an undocumented and important side of the Palestinian diaspora.[1] It is the first study to focus on the role of family, village, and town ties in the preservation, rebuilding, and reshaping of the Palestinian social fabric. It is also the first to examine how these ties have shaped the Palestinian experience in Kuwait.

The cross-national aspect of Palestinian family and village ties and of town, village, and family associations makes this study relevant to Palestinians in other communities. Although every Palestinian's experience in every Arab state or under occupation is unique in some ways, many of the issues discussed in this study are easily generalizable to other communities. Furthermore, I hope this case study will add to the literature on the strategies of adaptation and survival of displaced diaspora societies, and will enrich studies on peasant migration and peasant societies elsewhere.

By focusing on "group" (family, village, and town ties and networks) rather than "class" as a unit of analysis, this study brings to light aspects, experiences, and issues that could not have been reflected if a "class" approach had been followed. Group politics is still very significant in the Middle East, and class, though important, tends to be cushioned, blurred, and diffused by family, village, town, and other kinds of informal ties.

The Palestinian community in Kuwait is the third-largest Palestinian diaspora community.[2] In 1948-1949, it comprised a few exiled men and women. The community now totals approximately 350,000, of a combined Kuwaiti/non-Kuwaiti population of 1.7 million.[3]

The Palestinians who came to Kuwait did not simply migrate from rural to urban areas. They participated in a mass exodus that uprooted urbanite and peasant alike. Thus the Palestinian community in Kuwait is representative of the overall Palestinian community; that is, the Palestinians in Kuwait originate from all parts of Palestine, from all social classes, from different religious backgrounds, and from all major families, villages, and towns.

It is important to note that traditional migration patterns move from less-developed to more-developed areas, but in the case of the Palestinians in Kuwait, the migration pattern was from a more-developed to a less-developed socioeconomic structure. This defined at the very outset their role in the economy and development process. The Palestinians who came to Kuwait did not immediately come as refugees, as happened in Egypt, Jordan, Syria, and Lebanon. The migration to Kuwait, therefore, was a decision individual Palestinians made while in refugee camps or in countries where they sought haven during the war.

The Fieldwork

This study is based on three months of fieldwork conducted in Kuwait during the summer of 1985. This fieldwork involved approximately 110 open-ended interviews (250 hours of tape). Each life history-type interview extended from one to eight hours. Another close-ended survey of 100 individuals was also conducted.

To determine the validity of my interests and the importance of the topic I was about to pursue, I conducted some preliminary fieldwork in Kuwait during the summer of 1984. During that time, I conducted a few interviews which helped me evaluate the significance of my study and provided valuable first hand experience and data. I was also able to acquire most of the relevant, though limited, published and unpublished material written in Arabic (see bibliography). I was surprised to realize, through the initial interviews, that an informal superstructure--an unseen framework based on the power of human relationships--formed a system of overlapping and intertwined social networks that protected and solidified the Palestinian people.

3

Realizing my own very personal reactions to the situation I was studying, I wondered whether a native should attempt a scholarly treatise on his own community. After all, I am, like my informants, a product of a certain socialization process, of the same memories of similar loss, and roots. Like my interviewees, since childhood I had spent considerable time and energy searching for my roots to shape the expression of my identity. Would sharing features of political identity, personality, culture, and past experience with my informants prevent me from dealing with my biases?

I discovered the answer during my fieldwork experience. I learned that personal involvement can contribute significantly to the understanding of important social and political phenomena. Insiders have a special and valuable perspective to offer, one usually out of the reach of outsiders. Our common background helped me understand my informants in a way that would not be possible with a non-native. Common culture and language helped me analyze the data directly without the cumbersome frustrations of translation and assumption. Lengthy discussions with my informants helped me develop my own insights. I attempted to keep the role of a scholarly investigator, but I am aware of my potential idealization of Palestinians and their culture. I made considerable effort to compensate for this bias by attempting to analyze my study with the eyes of an outside observer. Whether or not I have done this, I believe my eyes as a participant have observed interesting and relevant phenomena for others, and I believe my analysis to be critical to the situation.

In the field, I first interviewed the earlycomer intelligentsia. They were the first Palestinian refugees to come to Kuwait and, by and large, were easily identifiable in the community. The material presented in chapter 3 describes their early experiences in Kuwait. Their articulate reports and detailed knowledge of that period were vital to my understanding.

The interviews were not intended to document every role of the earlycomer intelligentsia. I intended only to explain the incipent patterns of survival strategies of this stratum. The size of my sample was not a function of the size of the available population; I stopped interviewing members of this class when I felt I had a representative sample, that is, when new interviews added very little to the picture of their collective experience.

The next step was to evaluate the interviews. As I replayed the tapes, new insights about the situation emerged. These led to further investigation. For instance, while interviewing the earlycomer intelligentsia during my second week in the field, I discovered that the peasantry had been the second group to arrive in Kuwait. This piece of information was confirmed during subsequent interviews. I had been aware

4

of the existence of the underground railroad, but not of its scope or even of how it affected the history and development of the community.

The former peasantry was a harder group to identify. They were no longer peasants but were now distributed throughout Kuwait's public and private sectors. The best way to acquire knowledge about their experiences was through identifiable village associations and funds. By interviewing village fund members, I was able to learn more about the migration of Palestine's peasants to Kuwait and was referred to other individuals from Palestinian villages who could explain their experiences.

While seeking data on the origins of Palestinian peasant migration to Kuwait, other important avenues of investigation were opened to me. While interviewing leading members of village associations, I discovered heretofore unknown but important dimensions to these associations. Prior to these interviews, I had thought I would only briefly discuss the role of such funds in the community in a chapter on the peasantry. I came to realize, however, that these funds have far more important functions than I previously thought.

The study of village funds led me to the study of the village and town solidarity in Kuwait. In fact, further interviews demonstrated that village and town solidarity turned out to be, as explained in chapter 7, a prerequisite for the establishment of village and town funds.

During the conduct of the interviews, every village network led to another. When I interviewed members of the village of al-Malhah, they referred me to members of the village of Qalonya; my investigation of Qalonya led to Bayt Safafa and Dayr Yasin.

After I interviewed a sizable sample from the villages in the Jerusalem area in Kuwait, I sought out refugees from other areas represented in Kuwait. I chose Tarshiha from north Palestine, the Hawarith Bedouin tribes from the coast, and several other samples representing the different kinds of villages that had existed in Palestine. To balance my sample of villages, I decided to search for associations established by Palestinians of town or city origin. Once I felt the sample was diversified enough and once I started gaining little from new interviews, I terminated my interviews.

All through the period of my fieldwork, I received considerable support and assistance from the community. The "networks" I encountered led me to expand my sample. Each interviewee in Kuwait told me about others who might be helpful to my research. In many cases, people would call others and tell them about my work which helped the contacting process and increased cooperation of informants. The Palestinian society relies so heavily on personal ties and contacts that people usually are quite knowledgeable about others in their neighborhood or former village. Each

5

individual knew details of the settlement, such as who came first to Kuwait or who came via the underground railroad.

In every interview, I included questions related to family and the role it played in solidifying the community. Thus, every interview was used for the general Palestinian family sample from which I constructed the chapters on the family (Chapters 5 and 6). I also conducted particular interviews just to get further information about the family. Again, as I interviewed, I discovered aspects I had not considered before I began the study. For example, although the cross-national context of the Palestinian family was envisioned in the original design of the study, the level and intensity of cross-national communication were not foreseen.

In the final analysis, the 110 interviews were not separated by rigid categories. Every interview added something to my understanding of the family, of the earlycomers, the solidarity system, and the politics of survival. Each interview overlapped the others. Hence the peasantry was asked questions about the earlycomer intelligentsia; the intelligentsia was asked about the peasantry. Every interviewee was asked to respond to questions derived from data acquired from other interviewees.

Although many interviews did not find their way into the text, they helped validate my data or helped explain important environmental factors. For example, at least twenty interviews with members of Palestinian mass institutions (unions) and with social workers were not used in the text. Yet these interviews helped me understand the relationship between the host country and the stateless community and the role of Palestinian political institutions in Palestinian society.

I usually conducted two interviews a day, although sometimes I interviewed three or four persons. All interviews were open-ended and flexible. Before each interview I explained what I was doing and asked permission to use the tape recorder. Most people granted permission. In every interview I asked if there was anything the interviewee wanted to add off the tape.

I usually began each interview with a question concerning the displacement experience of the interviewee. The answer I received determined the direction of the interview. I might ask about village life and relationships before the war. I might ask what had happened to the village and to relatives after the war, or how the interviewee came to Kuwait. Further questions might probe the interviewee's first experiences in the country. After discussing a more recent experience, such as that with a village or family fund, the responses often shifted to past experiences. In most cases, I did not have to ask more than a few questions; my informants' recollections often touched spontaneously on issues and aspects I intended to ask about later. At other times, areas which I had not intended to touch were brought out during an interview and added a new, unforeseen dimension. The interviews covered the lifespan of those interviewed as they tried to reconstruct past and present. On several occasions, I was able to interview three to five individuals at the same time, each adding to the insight, or correcting the information of another. This cumulative style of collecting data, with some collective corroboration, proved a good way to reconstruct undocumented events.

Through these interviews, I was able to reconstruct past experience and to look for common experiences shared by people from different backgrounds but having common roots, conditions, goals, and motives. Because almost all interviews were tape recorded, I was able to concentrate on the interview and direct attention to any aspect that might need further illumination.

Although my attention was high during this fieldwork, many aspects remained vague in my mind almost until the end. Difficult decisions characterized the entire field experience. I had to decide daily which interviews to continue and which to stop, which issues to pursue and which to drop as irrelevant to my study.

The tension between time constraints and daily selection of the most relevant material was one of the most serious pressures I experienced in the field. No matter how well prepared I thought I was, I had difficulty making quick daily decisions which I knew would affect the course of my study. I depended on a clear understanding of the theoretical framework to make good decisions in the field. I tried to replace doubt and confusion with confidence and purposeful intent.

As I interpreted the data and began writing, the meaning of my field experience became clearer. By comparing and contrasting the interviews, weeding irrelevant or singular information, and focusing and editing my own analysis, I was able to understand the data at a more abstract level. By writing and rewriting, the data slowly took on a shape and size I felt comfortable with. I hope this book reflects the communicative strength which I discovered as I compiled and analyzed the information received from the interviewees whose experience is the flesh of this study.

Summary of Chapters

Several sociopolitical characteristics make up the post-1948 Palestinian society. Chapter 1 is about these components. In it, I discuss statelessness, family in the Middle East, the Palestinian pre-1948 society, and the type of Palestinian family and social networks that emerged as a vehicle of survival since 1948. It is basically a chapter about important

7

concepts that are relevant to the entire study. Chapter 2 explains how Palestinians became refugees.

Chapter 3 investigates the incipient patterns of survival that the displaced Palestinian intelligentsia employed and attempts to piece together the role this group played in Kuwait and how family networks came to be central to the Palestinian attempt to face the challenges of their post-1948 situation.

Chapter 4 focuses on a different stratum, the peasantry. It treats the incipient patterns of survival the peasantry employed and includes a section on peasant survival as aided by the underground railroad (1951-late 1950s), which brought most of the earlycomer peasants to Kuwait. Peasant adaptation to city jobs, the role of the Palestinian intelligentsia in this adaptation, and the incipient forms of a new rising peasant society centered around village and family are explained.

In chapters 5 and 6 the Palestinian family itself is studied. Chapter 5 is an attempt, through three case studies, to capture the cross-national character of the Palestinian family networks that evolved out of the dispersal experience. Chapter 6 discusses the most important components of the family network in its effective and extended forms. It elaborates on the previous chapters by explaining and analyzing the overall functions of the Palestinian family in Kuwait and in the diaspora. It brings to the forefront the role of the family network in Kuwait and across the diaspora in the rebuilding of the Palestinian social fabric and its role as a unit of social, cultural, national, and economic survival.

In chapters 7 and 8 the study shifts to village and town survival. Chapter 7 explains the major informal mechanisms of the survival in Kuwait of former villages and neighborhoods. Chapter 8 provides case studies of such survival and of village and town associations. These associations contribute significantly to the survival of former Palestinian villages, towns, and neighborhoods in Kuwait.

Chapter 9 opens by analyzing the relationship between the host country (Kuwait) and the Palestinian community. It is also about the reaction of the family, village, and town networks to the crisis situation in the context of present and future roles and trends. The relationship between the microstructures of solidarity on the one hand and diaspora formal macro institutions are addressed. The conclusion, chapter 10, is a brief summary of the study and points to the possible role of family and social networks in the years to come.

NOTES

1. For literature on the Palestinian diaspora, or on the Palestinian in Kuwait and the Gulf, see the bibliography.

2. The total number of Palestinians in each community and all over the world is impossible to determine accurately. This is a result of dispersion and the lack of a census. The following estimate by Abdul Salam Massarueh is the closest to the demographic distribution of Palestinians:

A.	Palestinians living inside	
	Palestine:	2,075,000
	--Pre-1967 Israel	650,000
	--West Bank (including Jerusalem)	875,000
	--Gaza Strip	550,000
B.	Palestinians living outside	
	Palestine:	2,902,000
	--Jordan	1,127,000
	--Lebanon	400,000
	--Kuwait	320,000
	--Syria	245,000
	--Saudi Arabia	250,000
	--Other Arab Countries	220,000
	--Rest of World	<u>340,000</u>
	TOTAL	4,977,000

(Abdul Salam y. Massarueh, "The Palestinians: Exiles in the Diaspora," <u>Middle East Insight</u> 4, no. 6 [1986]:27.)

3. In Kuwait, out of a total population of 1.709 million, 1.025 are non-Kuwaiti (<u>Monthly Digest of Statistics</u>, Ministry of Planning, Central Statistical Office, Kuwait, April, 1985). The last published census of the Palestinians in Kuwait was in 1975. At the time, they numbered 204,178.(<u>Population Census: 1975</u>, Kuwait Ministry of Planning, Central Administration of Statistics, 1976, p. 187). They are estimated to have reached 350,000 by 1985.

9

1

Statelessness in Context

The Palestinian diaspora subculture that emerged in the wake of the displacement experience can be categorized as stateless and family-oriented. Family patterns since 1948 have become more flexible as have Middle Eastern families in general. A non-family social network has also developed and become basic to Palestinian diaspora survival. How do these characteristics interrelate?

Palestinians: A Stateless Society

"Statelessness" in the twentieth century usually describes the political condition resulting from forced mass migration. It springs primarily from laws that allow for the revocation of the citizenship of a naturalized person.[1] Statelessness becomes quite serious when such revocation is targeted against an ethnic or religious minority.[2] In many cases, though, the naturalized citizen and the native-born citizen undergo similar experiences, so statelessness may be defined as any loss of citizenship and the rights associated therewith.

Emphasis simply on the loss of citizenship ignores the problems of many people who lose citizenship as a by-product of forced mass expulsion due to the disintegration of their states during a time of crisis or war. Statelessness may result in perpetually seeking refuge, or a continuing state of dispossession with regard to the original homeland and all rights associated therewith.

11

A state may organize to expel a group of indigenous citizens for many reasons. In some cases, intolerance toward nonconformist groups is enough to justify expulsion. In other cases, war between two states makes each persecute and expel those among its own population whose ethnic identity is similar to that of the "enemy" state. Systems sometimes need a scapegoat to blame policy failure on, and one-sided ideologies often force many into statelessness.

Statelessness is one of the most serious international problems of the twentieth century. Stories of the interwar period and World War II are filled with stateless people seeking refuge. In 1939 Germany introduced laws to revoke the citizenship of its naturalized Jewish population, and even of Jewish citizens by birth.[3] The Jews of Romania and Poland faced a similar fate. The Armenians are another group who were driven from their lands during this century, as were the Palestinians in 1948 and 1967. The number of stateless people is vast, particularly if we include examples drawn from Latin America, Asia, and Africa.[4]

The problems of the stateless are multiple. Because of being rightless, they are vulnerable and insecure wherever they go. The stateless discover that, as long as they are fragmented and weak, they exist as political scapegoats and international victims. At one level or another, problems of residence, travel, employment, property ownership, enfranchisement, opportunity, and education become part of the package of insecurity. Even when naturalized, they continue to feel insecure because naturalization can be revoked simply by changing the law. In her book, Hannah Arendt described the many problems faced by the stateless. Chief among them is the loss of their homes, which means "the loss of the entire social texture into which they were born and in which they established for themselves a distinct place in the world."[5] The stateless suddenly find no place on earth they can "go to without the severest of all restrictions."[6] Even their acceptance by the indigenous populations of the countries they migrate to is problematic and poses problems for sociological, economic, and cultural reasons.[7] In other words, "once the stateless had left their homeland they remained homeless, once they had left their state they became stateless; once they had been deprived of their human rights they were rightless, the scum of the earth."[8]

It is quite important not to confuse the environment of the stateless with their inner dynamics. Though the stateless have difficulty in finding security, shelter, and respect, many stateless communities have rejected mere assimilation and a substitute homeland. To them such attempts, particularly when instigated by international agencies or by other states, are an attempt to get them to surrender their historical rights to their homeland--often seen as providing the enemy the moral victory it seeks. In the Palestinian case, for instance, many clashes took place

12

between the refugees and the local Arab authorities in Jordan and Egypt during the 1950s and 1960s, when these governments attempted to create permanent settlements. The Palestinians have sought to keep their attachment and loyalty to the original homeland. As time passes, the yearning to return becomes even more powerful.

The historical experience of the Jews indicates that only after Babylonian captivity did they develop a special sentiment toward Palestine.[9] Their music, prayers, and hymns developed noticeably during captivity.[10] The experience of the Armenians and the Palestinians is analagous. It seems that in exile the stateless create institutions and practices that help them survive the hardships of dispersion. Statelessness becomes a state of mind, a continuous process of survival.

Traditional Palestine: A Family-Oriented Society

The Palestinians who were exiled in 1948 were a highly family-oriented society that gave precedence to informal and personal ties. As an important socioeconomic unit, the family settled, through its elders, inter- as well as intrafamily disputes. It also provided occupational security for family members, organized working the land, distributed its fruits, and entered into common entrepreneurial ventures. Marriage and divorce, death and burial, were all family issues, part of the sacred domain of uncles, grandparents, and paternal blood relatives.[11]

For example, in the village of Dayr Yasin during the 1930s and 1940s, each of the five major families of the village of six hundred individuals--the Sammurs, Shahadahs, Radwans, Zaydans, and Hamidahs--owned a stone quarry. Economic production in Dayr Yasin rested primarily on stone portering, which was arranged according to family.[12] In the nearby village of Qalonya, however, the family occupation was largely in the government bureaucracy. Two families from Qalonya during the 1930s and 1940s, for example, became predominantly employees in the government-owned telegraph and postal service in Palestine.[13] One family member attracted another until the institution became full of family members.

Housing patterns provide another example of the family as a basic socioeconomic unit. The process of settlement in pre-1948 Palestine would start with a family founder who chose to live in a certain location. With every marriage, a new room would be built; as the family got larger, new houses were built. After a century or so, the quarter would become known by the family name. This pattern was established in the villages of Palestine and in many of its cities. After World War I, many Palestinian cities experienced rapid urbanization, which changed the housing patterns

13

of several Palestinian urban centers, but family settlements remained a dominant feature of Palestinian urban and village life until 1948.

Even in education, family played an important role. For example, many family houses in Hebron, Tulkarim, or Jerusalem became known as centers of learning. This is a function of a culture that was able, through the family, to protect and pass down family occupations from father to son. Houses that produced religious figures usually did so over generations. Although this continuity has survived somewhat, the rigid lines of the past in terms of family and specialization have definitely ceased to exist.

In pre-1948 Palestine, the more functional family unit was the extended (patriarchal) family, or, as Tannous calls it, the "joint family," composed of "parents, their children, the paternal grandparents, the paternal uncles and their families, and unmarried paternal aunts,"[14] in addition to the possible addition of a son-in-law, an orphaned nephew or niece from the husband's side, or any other close paternal cousin. Next in significance was the larger family unit, composed of several extended households that shared the same patrilineal line and bearing the same family name.[15] In many cases, this entire unit, which might range from a few dozen people to several hundred, was linked to a larger, more distinct unit called the hamula. The hamula, which is a descent group, cuts across a set of villages and towns. Its members believe they have a common biological ancestor. Thus, family and all its functions in pre-1948 Palestine were composed of a set of circles, each of which interchangeably performed several functions.

Although the Palestinians have experienced traumatic socioeconomic changes since the 1850s , when, for the first time a system of village/city dependence was created,[16] and despite deeper socioeconomic changes under the British, the family has continued to be an influential unit. Therefore, due to the historical nature of Palestinian family and society prior to 1948, the process of economic development, institutionalization, leadership, and political party-building could not be divorced from family and family alliances. The leadership of the Husaynis and the Nashashibis in the pre-1948 Nationalist Movement is simply a manifestation of the role of family. Even when the Palestinians confronted the British mandate, both at the village and city levels, they sought protection in the family as a socioeconomic political unit. They found it available, and used it as an indigenous means to resist occupation. The working Palestinian population in 1936 went on strike for six months by depending to a large extent on the family to provide food and many necessities. Even during the 1936-1939 rebellion in Palestine, the family played an essential role by providing food, clothing, protection, sanctuary, and information to the rebels.

14

On the eve of their exodus, the Palestinians had a variety of political, social, cultural, and economic institutions that were developing at a very rapid pace. These challenged the family and forced it to give up many of its functions to other, more superior forms of organization. But the family, as it stood in 1948, remained a strong and viable socioeconomic institution.

The nature of Palestinian society and family determined at the outset, particularly after the destruction of all formal institutions, the form Palestinian survival would take. It is clear that social ties and group existence would have had no chance to be reconstructed without the family. This particular reality determined my entire theoretical approach and my research focus on the family as the central agency of Palestinian continuity in the diaspora.

Family in the Middle East

A study of the family is a critical part of the understanding of informal politics in the Middle East. In the Middle East, "the dominant group structure" has been the informal group.[17] However, "informal groups are noncorporate, unofficially organized collectivities that articulate their interests in a relatively diffuse manner. This category includes kinship, status, and regional groups."[18]

At the center of the informal group is the family, which is "the basic unit of social organization [and] the focus of the social change currently in progress throughout the area."[19] The family, which is "the basic unit and building block of groups in the Middle East,"[20] is "at the center of social organization in all three Arab patterns of living (Bedouin, rural, and urban) and particularly among tribespeople, peasants, and urban poor."[21] As Janet Abu-Lughod stated in 1961,

> Middle Eastern culture places a high value on personal relationships, even at a sacrifice of privacy and internal development. This combined with a system of relationships based on the extended kinship group, serves to increase the number of primary ties far beyond what western sociologists, reasoning from their own experience, dare to assume possible. This network of personal associations enmeshes not hundreds but thousands of individuals.[22]

Despite social change, the family persists as a cohesive system of relationships. It remains functional economically, socially, culturally, and

15

politically.[23] It continues to get the support it needs for survival from its members in return for what it can provide them. For the majority of the people in the Middle East, "nothing yet has replaced the family as a source of support and alliance."[24]

The Middle Eastern Family: A Comparative Context

The Middle Eastern family is not fundamentally different from the families in the transitional societies of Africa, Latin America, and Asia, nor is it different from the European family during the Industrial Revolution. The European family during the Industrial Revolution, like the family in today's transitional societies, was not a passive body. On the contrary, it acted as an active, independent agent that absorbed the changes coming from the socioeconomic environment while affecting the outcome of those changes. It fostered social change and facilitated the "adaptation of its members to new social and economic conditions."[25] Whereas in today's Western society family has become primarily an emotional tie,

> in the nineteenth century (among all classes) [it was] heavily weighted toward economic needs and tasks....Family members were valued not only for the way they related to each other and for the degree of emotional satisfaction and nurturing they offered, but also for the contributions they could make to fulfill familial obligations and maintaining continuity and stability in the family's daily existence. Family and kin were particularly valued for providing assistance during periods of crisis and need, with the understanding that their help could be reciprocated in the future.[26]

The conception of the nineteenth-century European family as an active rather than a passive agent only developed among scholars in the late 1950s.[27] Previously, the family was conceived as a passive agent that broke and collapsed in the face of the great industrial urban changes. This concept spilled over into the tradition/modernity dichotomy in the modernizing societies of the world. Many scholars predicted the fall of the family in the Third World alongside religious and primordial ties. Evidence has shown, however, that the family adapted, changed, and hung together to protect itself from the changes brought about by the Industrial Revolution.

16

The new literature argues that the changes in the European family were not sudden. It slowly adapted as it participated actively in molding the new environment. However, it was not a one-way process. The new dynamic model conceived of the family as both an independent and a dependent agent.[28]

The Post-1948 Palestinian Family: Increased Flexibility in Family Patterns

The loss of resources and of all formal institutions in 1948 left the Palestinians with no other single viable protective institution. The informal fundamental apparatus, the family, became the center and the survival core, and the diaspora became a web of families.

Like family in the rest of the Middle East, the Palestinian family proved "impossible to rupture or break."[29] It also proved, in many respects, similar to other Middle Eastern families in that it provided "the element of permanence needed to offset the importance of the other informal group interactions."[30] This "invisible skeleton" became the Palestinians' motivator.[31]

The post-1948 era has seen a changed, more modern role for the Palestinian family. The essence of such a role stems from the fact that the exodus laid the groundwork for family reconstruction on the basis of new conditions. The Palestinian family, since 1948, has acted more as an active, independent agent as it absorbed the changes coming from the socioeconomic environment while affecting the outcome of those changes. It has also helped adapt its members to new conditions. In fact, the exodus and the dispersal changed the extended Palestinian family into a conjugal family. In Kuwait, as throughout the Middle East, the traditional extended family, which lived in one house, disappeared, particularly among the peasants.[32] As the experience of the Arab family suggests, the survival of characteristics of the traditional extended (patriarchal) family in the modern, conjugal family made possible the continuity of the spirit of family role and solidarity.[33] The family became the means by which the Palestinians were able to respond to the conditions of the diaspora.

As the literature on the Arab family suggests, family characteristics are usually expressed in terms of economic, social, and political cooperation.[34] The family is strengthened by "repeated intermarriage, residential proximity, and continual visiting,"[35] and in the continued honoring of family wajib (obligation) to each other.[36] This aspect of the family proved basic to the ability of the Palestinians to preserve their society in the aftermath of 1948.

17

Another highly important trend since 1948 is the emerging flexibility of the family in a situational context. It has been correctly noted in studies on the contemporary Middle Eastern family that no patterned genealogical chart can determine who is or is not family in the absolute sense.[37] What counts is "actual social ties, obligations, attachments, and loyalties, and the networks built up out of these."[38] This makes kinship "situational." It also makes family a practical and realistic concept, regardless of how close or distant members are in blood terms, or whether these ties are through marriage or birth. Hence, as the Egyptian proverb says, "Your kin are those who stand with you when battle lines are drawn."[39]

Family has become, therefore, a web of close and distant relationships, some daily, others only occasional. It is, in actual reality, a combination of patrilineal and matrilineal relationships. "One's cousin is also one's brother-in-law, one's ex-husband has married a woman next door, one's uncle is one's father-in-law, one's husband is a former playmate, and one's child seemingly is shared by everyone."[40]

After 1948, the Palestinian family discovered through experience that to adapt to the new conditions and to face the challenges surrounding it, it needed less rigid borders between households. The family had to become a more flexible unit comprising wider and more cohesive relationships to maximize its chances for survival.

Two types of family networks developed out of this flexible style of family determination among the Palestinians after 1948.[41] These networks are basic to the type of solidarity emerging after the war and are essential to the understanding of the theoretical framework of this study. The first is the effective family netowrk, a set of obligatory relationships and responsibilities that are called on in times of crisis by a group of individuals who consider themselves family. Usually, intensive interaction is basic to such a network, but because the diaspora separated family members, the network has become in most cases cross-national in nature. In the diaspora and in Kuwait, in particular, this effective family network incorporates members of the original extended family in addition to patrilineal and matrilineal relatives. Since 1948, the wife's immediate family has become incorporated into the close effective family network in a way not known before, as a result of the changing status of women in post-1948 Palestinian society.

Every individual is part of an effective family network, and this network is flexible, with borders that often change. It can shrink to incorporate only the original extended family, or expand to include a wider variety of people. This is a function of the circumstances and the people involved in the network. The family network can change because of a dispute, for example, and may exclude or include relatives, depending on

18

need, geography, interest, and immediate concerns. It is, therefore, a set of important close relationships based on family that may differ proportionately in level of interaction from one Palestinian family to another, from one stratum to another. Every Palestinian is at one level or another part of such a network.

A more extended family network stems from each effective family network.[42] This second type of network basically includes relatives from patrilineal or matrilineal lines living in Kuwait or the diaspora. They are potential members of the effective family network, particularly if they live in Kuwait. Usually, they interact with the effective family network on important occasions, particularly at death, marriage, or birth. None of these relationships are as obligatory as those in the effective family network, nor are they based on daily interaction if in the same city or geographical location. However, support in times of need and crisis does increase significantly in the extended family network, which begins then to act as an effective family network. Furthermore, new effective family relationships continue to be recruited from this general extended family network.

The borders between the two family networks, effective and extended, are elastic. Family, therefore, has come to mean a structure with the individual in the middle, encircled by the effective and extended networks. The wider the circle, the more distant the relation. With decreased crisis and more stable environment, responsibilities are less and more relationships become part of the extended family network. As crisis increases, the effective family network is enlarged to include new responsibilities. In other words, the more severe the crisis, the more effective the extended family network, or the more the extended network functions like an effective family network.

The 1948 displacement experience was not the only crisis the Palestinians have faced. Crisis involves, rather, day-to-day experiences, such as problems of residence, travel, employment, property ownership, enfranchisement, opportunity, and education. These problems, a result of statelessness, at times may ease (improved economic conditions, prosperity), at other times the tension may tighten (worsened economic and security conditions). The cyclical nature of crisis since the beginning of the Palestinian diaspora, as this study demonstrates, has recharged family with the strength of an effective network. The dialectic between crisis and family network is basic to any understanding of the relationships between Palestinian family members in Kuwait and the diaspora. During certain periods of prosperity, many relationships, except those of the core family, may become extended. In fact, in each family, several effective networks are formed. Each becomes a reservoir, that is, an extended family network, for the other effective networks.

19

Figure 1: Networks and Crisis

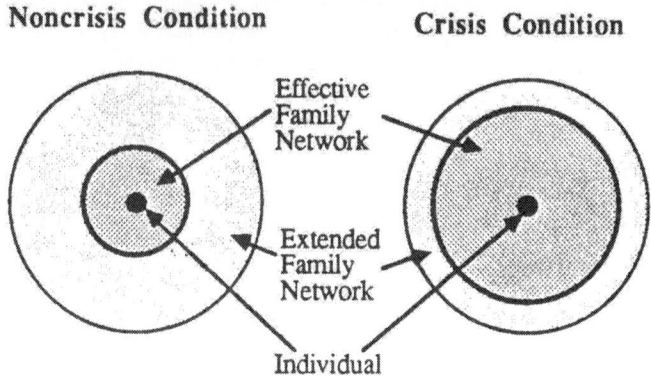

Noncrisis Condition   **Crisis Condition**

Effective Family Network

Extended Family Network

Individual

Palestinian Social Networks

This flexibility of the family context makes nonfamilial village, neighborhood, and friendship ties very significant. Whereas many former village and neighborhood acquaintances have become family through marriage, many others have not. In the Palestinian case after 1948, and in the literature on the contemporary Middle Eastern family, we find that home-boy ties, acquaintances, old schoolmates, colleagues at work, old and new friends, old and new neighbors, are, in many cases, very close to the individual. Many of these relationships become incorporated into the family. Thus, family overlaps with friendship, patronage, and neighbors.[43] These relationships are part of the wider social network. The question, therefore, is how do they fit our definition of the family network?

In practice, every individual has an effective and extended family network. At the same time, everyone has an effective and extended social network. Figure 2 demonstrates the overlap between family and nonfamily networks, that is, friends, neighbors, and village ties.

20

Figure 2: Family and Nonfamily Networks

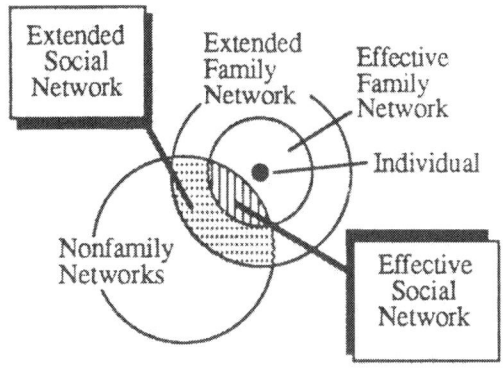

NOTES

1. John Hope Simpson, The Refugee Problem (Oxford: Institute of International Affairs, 1939), p. 231.

2. See Hannah Arendt, The Origins of Totalitarianism, 5th ed. (San Diego: Harcourt Brace Jovanovich, 1973), pp. 275-290.

3. Ibid., p. 277.

4. On the millions of stateless refugees and the dilemmas they face, see Hugh C. Brooks and Yassin El-Ayout, eds., Refugees South of the Sahara: An African Dilemma (Westport: Negro Universities Press, 1970); Louise W. Holbern, Refugees: A Problem of Our Time. The Work of the United Nations High Commission for Refugees, 1951-1972, Vol. 1 and 2 (Metuchen, N.J.: Scarecrow Press, 1975); and Gilbert D. Loescher and John A. Scanlan, "The Global Refugee Problem: U.S. and World Response," Annals of the American Academy of Political Science 467 (May 1983):1-253.

5. Arendt, Origins, p. 293.

6. Ibid.

7. Ibid.

8. Ibid., p. 267.

9. Abba Eban, Heritage: Civilization and the Jews (New York: Summit Books, 1984), pp. 68-69.

10. Ibid.

21

11. Rosemary Sayigh, <u>Palestinians: From Peasants to Revolutionaries</u> (London: Zed Press, 1979), pp. 19-20.

12. Interview with Dr. Zuhdi Sammur of Dayr Yasin, Kuwait, summer 1985.

13. Interview with Dr. Raja Sumrayn of Qalonya, Kuwait, summer 1985.

14. I have taken Tannous's definition of the extended household in Bishmizeen, Lebanon, as applicable to the pre-1948 Palestinian extended household. See Afif I. Tannous, "Group Behavior in the Village Community of Lebanon," <u>Readings in Arab Middle Eastern Society and Cultures</u>, ed. Abdulla M. Lutfiyya and Charles W. Churchill (1942 reprint; The Hague: Mouton, 1970), p. 100.

15. Ibid.

16. Abu Manneh, "The Rise of the Sanjak of Jerusalem in the Late 19th Century," in <u>The Palestinians and the Middle East Conflict</u>, ed. Gabrial Ben-Dor (Ramat Gan: Turtledove Publications, 1978), p. 28.

17. James Bill and Carl Leiden, <u>Politics in the Middle East</u>, 2d ed. (Boston: Little, Brown and Company, 1984), p. 77.

18. Ibid., p. 76.

19. Elizabeth W. Fernea, "A Mirror Image," <u>Discovery: Research and Scholarship at the University of Texas at Austin</u> (Spring 1984):18.

20. Bill and Leiden, <u>Politics in the Middle East</u>, p. 90.

21. Halim Barakat, "The Arab Family and the Challenge of Social Transformation," in <u>Women and the Family in the Middle East: New Voices and Change</u>, ed. Elizabeth Warnock Fernea (Austin: University of Texas Press, 1984), p. 28. For an overview of personal and family relations in the Middle East, see Dale Eickelman, <u>The Middle East: An Anthropological Approach</u> (Princeton, N.J.: Prentice-Hall, 1981), pp. 105-134.

22. Janet Abu-Lughod, "Migrant Adjustment to City Life: The Egyptian Case," <u>American Journal of Sociology</u> 67, no. 1 (July 1961):31.

23. Robert Springborg, <u>Family, Power and Politics in Egypt: Sayed Bey Marei--His Clan, Clients, and Cohorts</u> (Philadelphia: University of Pennsylvania Press, 1982).

24. Fernea, <u>Women and the Family</u>, p. 26.

25. Tamara K. Hareven, "Family Time and Historical Time," <u>Daedalus</u> 106, no. 2 (Spring 1977):59.

26. Ibid., p. 64.

27. Ibid., p. 58.

28. Ibid., pp. 57-70. See also Michael Anderson, <u>Family Structure in Nineteenth-Century Lancashire</u> (Cambridge: At the University Press, 1971); Virginia Y. McLaughlin, "Patterns of Work and

Family Organization: Buffalo's Indians," <u>Journal of Interdisciplinary History</u> 2 (Autumn 1971):299-314. The most pioneering work on the subject is Neil Smelser, <u>Social Change in the Industrial Revolution: An Application of Theory to the British Cotton Industry</u> (Chicago: University of Chicago Press, 1959).

29. Bill and Leiden, <u>Politics in the Middle East</u>, p. 90.

30. Ibid.

31. This term was used by John Gulick in another application in <u>Social Structure and Cultural Change in a Lebanese Village</u> (New York: Wenner-Gren Foundation, 1955), p. 104; Quoted in Bill and Leiden, <u>Politics in the Middle East</u>, p. 90.

32. K. el-Daghestani, "The Evolution of the Muslim Family in the Middle Eastern Countries," in <u>Readings in Arab Middle Eastern Societies and Culture</u>, ed. Lutfiyya and Churchill, p. 557.

33. Ibid., p. 558.

34. Bill and Leiden, <u>Politics in the Middle East</u>, pp. 91-92.

35. Hildred Geertz, "The Meaning of Family Ties," in <u>Meaning and Order in Moroccan Society: Three Essays in Cultural Analysis</u>, ed. Clifford Geertz, Hildred Geertz, Lawrence Rosen (Cambridge: At the University Press, 1979), p. 336.

36. Andrea B. Rugh, <u>Family in Contemporary Egypt</u> (Syracuse, N.Y.: Syracuse University Press, 1984), pp. 89-101.

37. This recent trend in the literature is expressed in the following works. David N. Schneider, <u>American Kinship: A Cultural Account</u>, Modern Societies Series (Englewood Cliffs, N.J.: Prentice-Hall, 1968); Daniel Bates and Amal Rassam, <u>People and Cultures of the Middle East</u> (Englewood Cliffs, N.J.: Prentice-Hall, 1983); Dale F. Eickelman, <u>The Middle East: An Anthropological Approach</u> (Englewood Cliffs, N.J.: Prentice-Hall, 1981); Rodney Needham,"Polythetic Classification: Convergence and Consequences," <u>Man</u> (N.S.) 10, no. 3 (September 1975): 349-369; Hildred Geertz and Clifford Geertz, <u>Kinship in Bali</u> (Chicago and London: University of Chicago Press, 1975); and Hildred Geertz, "The Meaning of Family Ties," pp. 315-379.

38. Hildred Geertz, "The Meaning of Family Ties," p. 335.

39. Bates and Rassam, <u>Peoples and Cultures</u>, p. 194.

40. Hildred Geertz, "The Meaning of Family Ties," p. 333.

41. I have adapted Epstein's effective and extended network concept to apply particularly to my definition of the Palestinian family and its scope. I use effective and extended "family" network rather than effective and extended network, which is an abstract concept that applies to a wider set of relationships than family. A. L. Epstein "The Network and Urban Social Organization," in <u>Social Networks in Urban Situations: Analysis of Personal Relationships in Central African Towns</u>, ed. J. Clyde

Mitchell (Manchester: Manchester University Presss, 1969), pp. 110-111. For literature relevant to networks, family, and migration which bears on the conceptual framework used in this study see the bibliography. For a review of the literature on migration and networks, see Shafeeq al-Ghabra, "Palestinians in Kuwait: The Family and the Politics of Survival" (Ph.D. Dissertation, University of Texas at Austin, Spring 1987).

42. A. L. Epstein, "The Network," pp. 110-111.

43. Hildred Geertz, "The Meaning of Family Ties," p. 315.

2

Palestinians Become Refugees

By October 1948, of 1.4 million Palestinians, almost 900,000 had been driven from Palestine and had become refugees in neighboring Arab states.[1] Just prior to the outbreak of the fighting, the Palestinian Arabs (the indigenous inhabitants of Palestine) made up two-thirds of the population and still owned 89 to 91 percent of the cultivable land in the country. Total Jewish property, by the end of the British mandate[2] over Palestine, did not exceed 180,000 hectares. This represented around 7 percent of Palestine. By the end of the fighting and after the Rhodes agreements of 1949, "Israel was left in occupation of 20,850 square kilometers, or 77.4 percent, of the land and water surface" of Palestine.[3] The Palestinians have not been allowed to return to their homeland, and the new state of Israel has claimed all of the refugees' property.

The First Stage of the Exodus

Early in April 1948, Zionist organizations in Palestine waged a military offensive in which they successfully captured most of the coastal areas of Palestine located between Jaffa and Acre, in addition to West Jerusalem and the villages to the west of it. This offensive, known as Plan Dalet, included many areas not allotted to the Israelis in the United Nations Partition Plan, such as the city of Jaffa or even Dayr Yassin itself and the villages surrounding it. The offensive began forty days before the official declaration of the State of Israel and the subsequent Arab military intervention of May 15, 1948.[4] During this initial wave, which lasted

25

until May 15, approximately three hundred thousand Palestinians were displaced.[5]

The Palestinian inhabitants of the coast and the area west of Jerusalem, where most of the military action took place, suffered from lack of arms and defense systems.[6] This prompted their leaders, particularly those from the towns being attacked, to seek support from the surrounding Arab states. In every case, they returned empty-handed, but assured of the strength of the Arab armies and promised future support.[7]

An example of this response was reported to me by Salwa Abu-Khadra, daughter of Hilmi Abu-Khadra, who was present at a meeting between her father, a Palestinian leader in Jaffa, and his friend the Syrian defense minister, Ahmad al-Sharabati. At this meeting, which took place in Syria one month prior to the Zionist offensive, Abu-Khadra explained to al-Sharabati that the Palestinians were unarmed and defenseless. He urged al-Sharabati to provide arms and ammunition so that the Palestinians might defend their towns and villages. The minister, ignorant of the situation in Palestine, told Abu-Khadra, "In one strike, we can take it over." He repeatedly asserted that the Syrian army could defeat the Zionists and totally rejected the idea of providing arms to the Palestinians.[8]

Similar responses by the other Arab countries had a pacifying effect on the Palestinians.[9] Despite the realities of Zionist superiority in weapons, training, and organization, the Palestinians felt sure of the help promised when the British mandate over Palestine ended.[10]

The Dayr Yasin massacre of April 9, 1948, which took place during the operations of Plan Dalet, came as a shock. In fact, during the worst conflicts between Palestinian Arabs and Jews in Palestine, Dayr Yasin had maintained strong economic ties with the nearby Jewish settlements. Not a single incidence of violence had involved Dayr Yasin members and the Zionists.[11] The massacre filled every Palestinian village and town with fear and panic--increased by the realization that Arab support would not be forthcoming. The Palestinians were, by and large, unarmed, undefended, and untrained. According to Khalid al-Hasan, PLO leader and one of the earlycomers to Kuwait after the war, the effects of the Dayr Yasin massacre on the Palestinians were quite dramatic:

> The Jews always say that unless you are a Jew you cannot begin to comprehend how they felt after the Nazi holocaust. I am sure that is true. But we Palestinians have a saying which is also true. Unless you are a Palestinian, you cannot begin to comprehend how we felt after the massacre at Dair Yassin. Because of what happened there, we really did believe we would all be

26

killed when the Jewish forces entered our cities and towns.[12]

Dayr Yasin was not the only attack involving civilians. In Jaffa, where seventy thousand Palestinian Arabs lived, Zionist shelling and attacks were released on the largely unarmed population during April 1948. The situation further deteriorated as Menachem Begin's Irqun attacked the Manshiya quarter of Jaffa on April 24. This siege, which lasted for four days, was followed by the Haganah's Operation Chametz, which successfully encircled Jaffa and cut off most of the land routes of escape.[13] By April 26, tens of thousands of Jaffans had "fled by boat to Gaza and Egypt, scores were drowned."[14]

The intensive attacks on Jaffa, Safad, Tiberias, Haifa, and Acre in April and early May of 1948 caused several hundred thousand to flee to the north, south, and east. Many went by boat to Lebanon, hoping to find a temporary haven. They were so panic-stricken, they did not bother to take anything with them. As any unarmed civilian population, the Palestinians had to seek safety in areas free of battle.

Most Palestinians believed that in a matter of days the ordeal would end and they would be allowed to return to their towns and villages. Everyone thought the Arabs or the British would put an end to the unfolding crisis. None of the displaced Palestinians believed they would have to remain in Egypt, Jordan, Syria, or Lebanon permanently. It shocked them to see the new state of Israel claim all their villages, towns, and personal property.[15] They were not aware of the extent of the Zionist project, nor of the weakness of the Arab world. Every Palestinian, like all other nationalities, took the right to Palestinian passport, citizenship, and birthplace for granted.[16]

Very few Palestinians realized that an extended diaspora had begun, although some of the young may have understood the events better. Salwa Abu-Khadra, a Jaffan who was nineteen years old in 1948, remembers how saddened she was after Dayr Yasin when her father decided to take her with her mother and younger brothers to Damascus. He returned to participate in the defense of the city. She recalls:

> I walked to school, to every corner that had meaning for me in Jaffa. I recalled my childhood, stared at everything in the neighborhood with my tearful eyes. I knew I should never see it again. Everyone in the family was sure of return in a matter of days. I was not. As I sat with my parents and brothers in the car that was to take us to Damascus, I turned yellow and almost fell unconscious. For the last time ever I looked back to see Jaffa as the car

27

sped away. Since then, the memory has never left me and I became obsessed with returning.[17]

The Continued Displacement of Palestinians

The Israelis prevented the three hundred thousand Palestinians who had become refugees after the initial Zionist offensive of April 1948 from returning.[18] A cease fire took effect on June 11 between the outnumbered Arab armies, which entered the battle May 15, and the newly proclaimed state of Israel. The majority of Palestinians were still on their land when the first ceasefire collapsed on July 9. Beginning in July, the civilian Palestinian population of Galilee and the rest of nonoccupied Palestine took more chances regarding their security. They chose to stay regardless of the dangers. Many got in touch with local Jewish leaders, and some villages and towns raised white flags. But this made little difference to the advancing Israelis. With few exceptions, the Israelis ordered the population of the town or village out after assembling them in the town center. Numerous civilians, including dozens of youths, were shot as an object lesson to those who stubbornly planned to stay. This often resulted in the flight of clusters of populations near the targeted town or village.[19]

The expulsion of the people of Lydda and Ramle on July 12 and 13, 1948, is a clear example. The two towns housed eighty thousand Palestinians. Ramle's captured leaders formally surrendered and allowed Israeli forces to enter the city peacefully. In nearby Lydda, on July 12, after the Israeli army entered the town, a massacre claimed 250 Palestinian civilians. Despite the massacre, the inhabitants of the two towns stayed. This resulted in David Ben Burion ordering their expulsion. The two towns were first looted by the Israeli army, then by the surrounding Jewish settlements, and the majority of those expelled were robbed by the Israeli army. Several dozen children died on the way as they walked to safe areas held by the Arab armies.[20] According to Sayigh, "There should have been a Tolstoy at hand to describe the Hijra [exodus], a leaderless trek of thousands of dazed and panic-stricken villagers, their bundles of bedding dropping by the wayside, families separated, old people dying of exhaustion, children carrying younger children, babies dying of dehydration."[21]

This dispersal of Palestinians marked the beginning of an extended period of homelessness that has touched every Palestinian family. The new reality of refugee life left deep scars. Life had been prosperous in Palestine and the majority had enjoyed a fair standard of living, including a plot of land, a stone house, and a support network of relationships. In addition, the growing public sector had begun to cover social welfare, health, and educational needs by the 1930s and 1940s.[22] Those who fled to Jordan, Lebanon, Syria, or Egypt had an endless set of sad lessons to learn in their new environments. Ahmad Rabih, one of those refugees who poured into Syria, said,

> My father died when the village fell to the Zionists. My mother, five brothers and sisters, and myself walked for three days to get to Arab defenses. We often hid from Jewish forces we encountered on the way. In the refugee camp in Damascus, my mother was helpless. I was the eldest at nine years of age. We had no choice. Most of our family was scattered. My mother and I became beggars. For several months before we found my uncles, we went from house to house to get food, clothes, and other necessities. My mother often took the names of those who gave her food and clothes. She used to tell them, "When we return, we will pay you back." Later, she died, still dreaming of return.[23]

Myassar Shahin, a Palestinian teacher who was displaced to Damascus, never forgot how she woke up every morning during the months following the "catastrophe," as Palestinians called it, to the voices of the relief workers in Damascus calling repetitively, "Righif al-Falestiniya," "Bread for the Palestinians." They were reminding people in Damascus to give away food to the Palestinian refugees.[24]

Many refugees refused relief for days. Relief symbolized the new dependency, the loss of the means of economic production, and the collapse of national existence. With growing social, cultural, economic, and political dispersal, the Palestinians were in the worst position possible: they were dismembered as a people; they were reduced to absolute political, economic, and social marginality; they were leaderless, they were without resources; and every family was dispersed into different areas. In sum, they had ceased to exist in any collective sense.

NOTES

1. Janet Abu-Lughod, "The Demographic Transformation of Palestine," in The Transformation of Palestine, Essays on the Origin and Development of the Arab-Israeli Conflict, ed. Ibrahim Abu-Lughod (Evanston, Ill.: Northwestern University Press, 1971), pp. 156, 161.

29

2. The British mandate over Palestine was a commission granted by the League of Nations to Great Britain. It lasted from 1922 to May 15, 1948. In fact, Palestine fell to the British in 1917. This marked the end of nearly 1300 years of Islamic rule over Palestine.

3. John Roudy, "Dynamics of Land Alienation," in Abu-Lughod, The Transformation of Palestine, pp. 134-135.

4. See Nafez Nazzal, The Palestinian Exodus from Galilee, 1948 (Beirut: The Institute for Palestine Studies, 1978), pp. 14-17; Rosemary Sayigh, Palestinians: From Peasants to Revolutionaries (London: Zed Press, 1979), pp. 73-75; Walid Khalidi, "Plan Dalet," The Arab World (October-November 1969):15-20

5. Erskine B. Childers, "The Wordless Wish: From Citizens to Refugees," in The Transformation of Palestine: Essays on the Origin and Development of the Arab-Israeli Conflict, ed. Ibrahim Abu-Lughod (Evanstan, Ill.: Northwestern University Press, 1971), p. 193.

6. Sayigh, Palestinians, pp. 77-78.

7. See Geoffrey Furlonge, Palestine Is My Country: The Story of Musa Alami (London: Murray, 1969), p. 152.

8. Interview with Salwa Abu-Khadra, Kuwait, summer 1985. Ms. Abu-Khadra is at prcsent the general secretary of the General Union of Palestinian Women.

9. Sayigh, Palestinians, pp. 64-68; David Hirst, The Gun and the Olive Branch: The Roots of Violence in the Middle East (London: Futura Macdonald and Co., 1978), p. 135.

10. When the Arab armies did finally enter the war on May 15, 1948, Egypt could field only 10,000, Jordan 4,500, and Iraq 3,000, a total of 17,500, no match for the 55,000 of the Hagnah, 3,500 Palmach, and 4,000 of the Irqun, or 62,500 all together. See John Bagot Glubb, Peace in the Holy Land (London: Hodder and Stoughton, 1971), p. 307.

11. Interview with Zuhdi Sammur and other members of the village of Dayr Yasin, Kuwait, summer 1985.

12. Alan Hart, Arafat: Terrorist or Peacemaker? (London: Sidgwick and Jackson, 1984), pp. 141.

13. Before Their Diaspora: A Photographic History of the Palestinians: 1876-1948, ed. Walid Khalidi (Washington, D.C.: Institute for Palestine Studies, 1984), p. 336.

14. Ibid., p. 338.

15. John Ruedy, "Dynamics of Land Alienation," in Transformation of Palestine, ed. Ibrahim Abu-Lughod, pp. 134-138.

16. On Palestinian citizenship rights and acquisition, see "A Survey of Palestine," vol. 1, Anglo-American Committee of Inquiry (Palestine: The Government Printer, 1946), pp. 206-208.

17. Interview with Salwa Abu-Khadra, Kuwait, summer 1985.

18. See Benny Morris's study based on newly released Israeli archives, "The Harvest of 1948 and the Creation of the Palestinian Refugee Problem," Middle East Journal 40, no. 4 (Autumn, 1986):671-685.

19. For a new and challenging study on the Palestinian exodus based on Israeli archives, see Benny Morris, "Operation Dani and the Palestinian Exodus from Lydda and Ramle in 1948," Middle East Journal 40 (Winter 1986):82-109. For further references, see Sayigh, Palestinians, pp. 81-92; Nazzal, The Palestinian Exodus; Walid Khalidi, "What Made the Palestinians Leave?" Middle East Forum in Beirut, 1959 (London: Arab Office of Information, 1963); E. Childers, "The Other Exodus," The Spectator (May 12, 1961):672-675; Illyas Shufani, "Laji' fi Baladi" ["A Refugee in My Country"], Shu'un Philistiniyah 84 (November 1978):95-111.

20. For details, see Morris, "Operation Dani," pp. 82-109.

21. Sayigh, Palestinians, p. 104.

22. A Survey of Palestine, vol. 2 (Palestine: The Government Printer, 1946), pp. 609-730; Ylana N. Miller, Government and Society in Rural Palestine, 1920-1948 (Austin: University of Texas Press, 1985), pp. 47-118.

23. Interview with Ahmad Rabih (pseudonym), Kuwait, summer 1985. For similar accounts, see Sayigh, Palestinians, pp. 103-110.

24. Interview with Myassar Shahin, Kuwait, summer 1985.

31

3

The Displaced Intelligentsia

As the war of 1948 came to a close, Palestinian society had ceased to exist. The educated and the uneducated, the rich and the poor, the urban dweller and the peasant, men and women, young and old, Christians and Muslims, suddenly became equal in a shared statelessness. The bonds and networks around which the country's social, economic, and political structures revolved were physically dislocated in the process of dispersal.

The Palestinians' natural response to the politics of dispersal and statelessness was the beginning of the politics of survival. The rebirth of society started even as the war's dust was settling over the refugees. They immediately began to develop tactics and strategies that would maximize their ability to endure the crisis.

Early Migration of Intelligentsia

The first step was to find a new place to live. The most logical place to move because of geographic proximity and similarity of culture and language was to Arab countries. But to find employment and be generally welcome in a foreign country required having something to offer which the host country needed.

Therefore the earliest response of finding a new place came from the exiled Palestinian intelligentsia, composed predominantly of bureaucrats, teachers, doctors, engineers, accountants, army and police officers, businessmen, and academics. Expertise and education provided this class with the keys to survival most needed in the Arab world at that

33

time. Because they carried their skill in their minds, it was easier for them to relocate and immediately offer a needed service to the host country. Thousands of Palestinian professionals and businessmen moved at once into every corner of the Arab world; by doing so, they took the first necessary steps toward long-term survival in exile.

Several hundred pioneers drawn from the Palestinian intelligentsia moved to Kuwait between 1948 and the early 1950s.[1] They laid the groundwork for the Palestinian experience in Kuwait. What follows is an account of the circumstances surrounding the arrival of a sample of earlycomer Palestinians to Kuwait. The individuals represented in this chapter are members of the Palestinian intelligentsia who moved to Kuwait during the period in question.

Goals and Responses of Earlycomer Intelligentsia

Within the context of the reconstruction of the Palestinian social fabric, the incipient sociopolitical relationships that characterized their early response and therefore their politics of adaptation will be the focal points of this chapter. Several major goals developed among the intelligentsia after 1948. First, to survive, they needed to find employment. In Jordan, Lebanon, Syria, and Egypt, the places to which most of them were driven, work opportunities were limited. This prompted them to seek employment in the newly developing Gulf region.

Once the intelligentsia refugees arrived in Kuwait, a second response emerged. Palestinians started to seek each other out and to create ties that laid the foundations of a new Palestinian society. Even as they met each other on the way to Kuwait, such ties began to take shape.

Once employed in Kuwait, a third response developed: the intelligentsia became obsessed with high professional standards. By providing high quality services, by being of value to their employers, they were able to maintain jobs which provided economic support to their families and fellow refugees. This obsession laid the base for another obsession, the deep concern for education and educational attainment. The need to achieve thus became associated with basic survival.

The fourth response was aimed at ameliorating physical dislocation, by reuniting or reconnecting with immediate family and relatives. The major concern of every earlycomer was to rescue his or her immediate family from suffering. Their decision to come to Kuwait had been a function of their family responsiblities. As this was the major concern of every Palestinian refugee, the fourth response was, in essence, the central response.

34

At the same time and in accordance with the earlier responses, a fifth response emerged. The displaced Palestinian intelligentsia, like all Palestinians, reclaimed their personal and political identity--a reflection of pride in who they were and in their roots.

The significance of these incipient patterns of social and political interaction lies in their ability to shape and influence the development of Palestinian family networks and of furthering group survival. As will become apparent, these responses were adopted by the rest of the Palestinians still in the refugee camps, or in the West Bank, Gaza, and Jordan. They also helped to mold, in the years to come, the whole diaspora structure.

These incipient patterns can best be understood as the first step in transforming exile into diaspora. "Exile" (manfa) implies a compulsory movement, whereas "diaspora" (shatat) signifies adjustment to a new environment.[2] According to Webster's Third New International Dictionary, "diaspora" is "a dispersion (as of people of a common national origin or of common beliefs)." It is also defined as "the people of one country dispersed into other countries," such as Jews and Armenians. On the other hand, exile is "to banish or expel from one's own country or home: drive away." In the Palestinian case, as well as in the earlier Jewish and the present Armenian cases, both exile and diaspora were experienced. But, with the passage of time, exile is painfully and slowly transformed into diaspora.

The persistence of the conditions that created forced banishment (exile) makes the diaspora an evolving long-term process of survival and adjustment to the new environment. The process of finding a secure position in the geographical area in which the diaspora peoples find themselves, as both the older Jewish experience and the more recent diaspora of the Palestinians demonstrate, is challenging, complex, and frustrating.

Finding Employment: The Crisis Network in Action

By all accounts, severe poverty engulfed all Palestinians after the 1948 war. The same poverty and unemployment struck the Palestinian intelligentsia.   To ensure physical survival, employment became paramount. The importance of the Gulf, particularly Saudi Arabia and Kuwait, stemmed from the increasing work opportunities available there. Kuwait, in particular, was the choice of many.

Before it became a modern populated country, Kuwait was a small town that had been inhabited since the 1700s by Arabian tribes that had migrated there from Nejd in the Arabian peninsula. It was relatively

35

ignored during Ottoman times and developed slowly during the first half of the twentieth century.[3] During the 1930s, its population did not exceed seventy thousand.[4] The people of Kuwait struggled in the 1920s, 1930s, and 1940s to meet their needs, but were limited by their relative isolation from the main centers of change and events in Baghdad, Cairo, Jerusalem, and Damascus. Just as 1948 witnessed the dispersal of the Palestinians, who had one of the relatively more developed countries in the Arab world,[5] it witnessed the discovery of oil and therefore the beginning of Kuwait's active development.

Since the normal employment channels were not open at the time, personal ties, old friendships, and family ties were useful in finding employment. Whereas credentials and degrees were prerequisites for employment, personal ties, even when by chance, were the entry to it. A few examples should demonstrate the employment process which resulted in the migration of many Palestinians to Kuwait.

Khayriddin Abuljubayn, a teacher who was forced out of Jaffa, took refuge in Egypt on April 27, 1948.[6] To his total dismay, he and his family, his fiancee and her family, and many friends, relatives, and acquaintances, were all put in an Egyptian concentration camp called the ᶜAbasiyah. His father, who traveled to Egypt by sea, was incarcerated in another camp called the Qantarah. Almost all the Palestinians coming from the Jaffa area and south Palestine were placed in such camps under the pretext that they need not go to Cairo, since they could return to their villages and cities shortly.[7] The actual reason rested in the government's fear of an angry reaction if the refugees reached Cairo and told the Egyptians there of the events in Palestine.

While in the camp, Abuljubayn realized certain facts. First, he was now a refugee, and his return to his native city was blocked by the victorious Israelis. From now on, he had to cope with statelessness and exile. His first priority while in the camp was to get out. After ten days, he escaped and was able to find help that resulted in the release of his family. Once free, he received a letter from a friend, Muhammad Najim, who had also been a teacher in Jaffa. Najim was in the Qantarah concentration camp. In the letter, he asked Abuljubayn "to go to the director of the Kuwaiti house in Cairo, Mr. ᶜAbd al-ᶜAziz Husayn, and tell him Muhammad Najim needs help to get out of the camp and wants to go to Kuwait." Abuljubayn immediately went to meet Mr. Husayn.[8] Through this contact, Najim was released. When he arrived in Kuwait in the fall of 1948, he immediately sent visas to Abuljubayn and other Palestinian teachers.

Muhammad Najim's connection to Kuwait went back to the first modern links established between Kuwaitis and Palestinians. He was a member of the first foreign educational team, composed of Palestinian teachers, which came to Kuwait and instituted the modern educational system in 1936.[9] He joined the team in 1938 and stayed in Kuwait until 1942. He is credited with the production of the first stage play in Kuwait.[10]

During this stay in Kuwait Muhammed Najim established good relationships with the Kuwaiti populace and their officials. His particular involvement, as well as the involvement of the Palestinian educational team, fostered among the Kuwaitis a positive attitude toward the Palestinians who came to Kuwait in time of need. They remembered the Palestinians as good teachers, straightforward and reliable.[11] The president of Kuwait's Council of Education, Abdullah al-Jabir al-Sabah, and Nisif al-Nisif, a leading member of the council, and other leading Kuwaitis actively worked to open the way for Palestinian refugee teachers to come to Kuwait.[12] Their efforts turned out to be an opening not only for teachers, but for Palestinians from all walks of life.

The importance of these relationships and social networks, is derived from their function during severe crisis. During stress dormant links become, at least while the crisis is acute, part of an effective social network. The extended social network is compressed and condensed in times of severe crisis to include family and nonfamily. Distant friends and acquaintances as far away as Kuwait (and Kuwait was quite far away in 1948) became part of the effective social network. Networks, no matter how fixed certain segments may be, are relative in the situational context.[13] In this case the context is the relationship between crises and social network.

An example of the crisis network in action is the case of Hani al-Qaddumi, another Jaffan, and an employee in the Department of Travel and Immigration in Palestine, who was displaced with his family to the West Bank town of Nablus.[14] Unemployed and suffering from the loss of property and home, he heard that a representative of Kuwait's Department of Education was in Amman recruiting teachers to work in Kuwait. Prior to 1961, the year of Kuwait's independence from Great Britain, the department carried out the functions of a ministry. Al-Qaddumi realized the representative was a Lebanese friend who used to work in Palestine. Though al-Qaddumi could not make it to Amman in time for the interview, he realized an avenue may have opened for him. Counting on a reference from his Lebanese friend, he wrote a letter directly to the Amir of Kuwait to request employment in the Department of the Interior. Al-Qaddumi, still in his mid-twenties, was appointed as the first director of residence (iqamah) and passports in Kuwait. He arrived to fulfill this position during the fall of 1948.[15]

Many members of the intelligentsia found employment in the states surrounding Palestine before deciding to seek employment in

37

Kuwait. One of these is Khalid al-Hasan, a cofounder of Fatah. His experience is quite revealing.[16]

When Haifa fell to the Zionists on April 22, 1948, al-Hasan decided to stay while his family (mother, four brothers and a sister) moved to Sidon in Lebanon after the Dayr Yasin massacre. After two months of living under Israeli occupation with his safety constantly at stake, he decided to leave on a British ship that was headed to Egypt and then to Kenya. Disappointed by the lack of support from the Arab world, and frustrated at what had befallen his people, he wanted to emigrate to Kenya. As he was passing through Port Said, the Egyptian authorities arrested him and put him in a concentration camp in Sinai. Camp conditions were very poor. He was not accused of anything and had a valid visa to enter Egypt on his way to Kenya. For a year, al-Hasan stayed in the camp, until he arranged an escape that took him to Jordan in June of 1949. Many of the earlycomers experienced similar treatment. Since the exodus, arresting or deporting Palestinians or even forcing them to wait for long hours at airports and borders needed no justification. Simply being a stateless individual or born in Palestine was enough to invite such ill treatment.

After his imprisonment, al-Hasan realized that he could not evade the reality of exile. This prompted him to look for his four younger brothers, his sister, and his mother. He found them all in Lebanon. Because, like all Palestinians in Lebanon, he was forbidden to work, the family moved to Syria, where he worked as a teacher and a secretary for the deputy of the chairman of the Syrian House of Representatives.

Al-Hasan tried in vain during 1950-1951 to establish a commando organization dedicated to the recovery of Palestinian rights, but every Palestinian was preoccupied with day-to-day survival tasks. When basic needs were not satisfied, it was hard to think of political activism and change. And there were, of course, no funds available to instigate or carry out such organization.[17] Once again, al-Hasan realized his priorities lay in working as hard as possible to satisfy the basic needs of the family. Palestinians had no other choice at that point; survival was utmost in their minds.

One day, a chance incident changed the direction of al-Hasan's life. A Palestinian friend came to Damascus and proposed that he go to Kuwait to work with a Kuwaiti merchant. At the time, al-Hasan did not even have the funds to send a telegram of acceptance; his friend paid for it. When he got to Kuwait in June 1952, he did not have one cent in his pocket.

Similar circumstances led several hundred members of the Palestinian intelligentsia to move to Kuwait immediately following 1948. In every case, the need to obtain employment was supreme. Personal ties, in all cases, were basic to the ability to find employment.

38

This early response centered around employment need marke only a first reaction to the displacement experience. It was the first step i.. adapting to a long diaspora. The fact that the majority of the earlycomers who migrated to Kuwait were in their twenties is a sign that the spirit of survival in exile emerged in the young. The Palestinian exile demoralized most of the generation over forty-five years old. For example, eighteen individuals from this age group died in the family of Abu-Khadra of Jaffa from 1948 to 1953.[18] Chronic illness, disability, and death resulting from deep grief beset this group, many members of which simply lost hope.

The Formation of a New Palestinian Society

An example from Khayriddin Abuljubayn's trip to Kuwait demonstrates how the earlycomer society was formed, even before arrival in Kuwait. Palestinians from the same neighborhoods, friends and cousins, met each other on the way to Kuwait. Such meetings were usually the first after the 1948 trauma. Therefore, those who became exiled in Jordan, the West Bank, or Egypt and Lebanon, met again for the first time on the way to Kuwait or just after arrival. The significance of such meetings stems from their being the first post-exile context wherein ties were instantly established. These connections provide another example of how crisis activates dormant relationships and transforms them into instrumental relationships that form an effective and extended network.[19]

When Khayriddin Abuljubayn, the teacher displaced from Jaffa who helped Muhammad Najim out of the concentration camp, decided to leave Egypt in November, 1948, the only possible route to Kuwait was to fly to Beirut and connect from there to Baghdad. Abuljubayn, his sister Iʿtidal, and his younger brother Faruq flew from Cairo to Beirut. In Beirut Airport they met another Jaffan, Hani al-Qaddumi, who was going to Kuwait after being appointed head of immigration and passports there.[20] Al-Qaddumi had been a classmate in the exclusive Rashidiyah Secondary School in Jerusalem in the early 1940s. It was their first meeting after the 1948 disaster. The meeting was emotionally charged, and sadness stemming from the loss of Jaffa and Palestine was evident throughout the trip. They knew very little about what had happened to individuals and families forced to take refuge in other areas. Al-Qaddumi had some information about Jaffans who were in the West Bank and Jordan, but Abuljubayn had information only about those who were in Egypt, and who had survived of those who were held with him in the ʿAbasiyah concentration camp.

39

When Abuljubayn, his sister, brother, and al-Qaddumi reached Baghdad and went to the train station to leave for Basra, Abuljubayn's younger brother Faruq disappeared in the crowd. It was the Hajj season and thousands of pilgrims going to Mecca were there. Abuljubayn started calling to his brother. His voice was recognized by cousin Yusif Abuljubayn who happened to be traveling to Kuwait too. Yusif Abuljubayn, was an automobile repair garage owner in Jaffa. He was on his way to Kuwait as director of al-Ghanim's garage, one of the largest garages in the country.

The group slowly enlarged. Accompanying Yusif was Sa^{c}di Abu-Dhayr, a friend of Khayriddin from Jaffa. He was on his way to Kuwait as an accountant for a large department store. In Basra, the seven Jaffans met other Palestinian teachers on their way to Kuwait. The group now numbered eleven. They were all going in the same direction and for the same reasons. A new society was emerging from these encounters between people who had suffered the same trauma. It was in these chance encounters that the origins of the diaspora solidarity may be found.

In a few years, a society of earlycomer intelligentsia was formed in Kuwait. It was comprised of a few hundred individuals who, because of the nature of their common tragedy and their history, developed the best relationships possible. "Like one big family," as Myassar Shahin, an earlycomer teacher, described them; they helped one another, looked after one another, knew each other by name, celebrated religious feasts together.[21] Shahin uses the kin phrase "one big family" to describe a nonkin relationship that is durable. The use of such terms incorporates the extended social network into the ideology of kin, thus demonstrating the extent of support or solidarity of these nonkin relationships.

This new society included Palestinians from every Palestinian town and city. They were mixing in a way that had never happened before. They were fighting the same struggle for survival, facing the same dilemmas. This common ground of experience provided the foundations of a new Palestinian society in the diaspora.[22]

Kuwaiti attitudes were very important to the Palestinians' ability to form their new diaspora society. By employing Palestinians, welcoming them, and facilitating their adaptation to Kuwait, Kuwait contributed significantly to the ability of the Palestinian earlycomers to respond to post-1948 conditions.

Professional and Educational Standards

Ahmad al-Shukayry (chairman of the Palestine Liberation Organization from 1964 to 1968), during a visit to Kuwait in the early 1960s, addressed the former Amir of Kuwait Shaykh Sabah al-Salim al-Sabah, who was still foreign minister: "I can't but be thankful to you and to Kuwait's leaders for the services and treatment accorded to the Palestinians in Kuwait." Shaykh Sabah replied,

> I cannot accept your praise. We did not bring Palestinian families and offer them charity. Look at them. Among them is the best surgeon, the best doctor, and the best administrator. Without these skills, they wouldn't have been appointed to these positions. They would have been appointed as garbage collectors.[23]

Once employment was available in Kuwait, the earlycomer intelligentsia set a standard for the Palestinians' post-1948 commitment to the achievement of professional goals. To succeed and to withstand the consequences of statelessness, the Palestinians had to be competitive. Without a work ethic, they could have remained a marginal group in constant need of charity. The intelligentsia's professional standards became a basic strategy of adapting to exile.

The Palestinians who moved to Kuwait from 1948 to the early 1950s had a very important developmental effect on Kuwait. Their counterpart in Saudi Arabia, the Gulf, and Jordan, among other Arab countries, had similar influence. In almost every phase of development, be it economic, military, administrative, or educational, the Palestinians had a tremendous effect, particularly during the 1948-1965 period.

This period was characterized by the laying of Kuwait's modern economic infrastructure. In this, the Palestinian role in the work force was crucial. In 1965, for instance, 48 percent of all employees in Kuwait's public sector were Palestinian (15,512 male, 1,477 female). In the private sector, Palestinians composed 41.4 percent of all employees.[24] Not until the mid-1960s was there a balance in employment percentages, between the Palestinian, Egyptian, and Kuwaiti roles in infrastructure development. The following cases will demonstrate the work ethic of the employed Palestinian intelligentsia, but will also put into context the role of this group and its contribution to the country of Kuwait.

Khayriddin Abuljubayn of Jaffa came to Kuwait as a teacher in 1948. From 1953 until 1957, in addition to his teaching job, he was secretary of the Kuwaiti sports union. From 1957 to 1964, he was secretary of the Kuwaiti soccer union.[25] Several others joined Khayriddin in such sports efforts, among them Zuhayr al-Karmi and Jamil al-Salih. Both men had exceptional careers in Kuwait's Ministry of Education. Mr. al-Karmi, for instance, during the 1960s, and for over a decade, simplified science through a popular television program called "Life and Science." Mr. Al-Salih, on the other hand, became chief math inspector for secondary schools. He became the author of the high school mathematics curriculum and was instrumental in the introduction of modern math to Kuwaiti high schools.

Hani al-Qaddumi was the founder of Kuwait's first modern Department of Residence and Passports in 1949.[26] In that same year, he was appointed secretary to the deputy of the Amir of Kuwait, Shaykh Abdullah Mubarak al-Sabah. He coordinated all the diverse agencies under the jurisdiction of the deputy to the Amir, including the embryonic army, the civil aviation organization, the Departments of General Security and the radio station. Kuwait's first modern radio station was founded and directed by Muhammad al-Ghussayn of al-Ramle (Palestine). al-Ghussayn was a senior staff member of the British Near East Broadcast. He worked with it in Jaffa from its start during World War II. After the 1948 war, the company was transferred to Cyprus. In 1956, during the Suez War, al-Ghussayn and all the Palestinian and Arab staff members resigned. In 1958, Kuwait asked him to found and direct its first radio station. Within a year, with the help of Kuwaiti, Arab, and Palestinian employees, Kuwait's first modern radio station was founded. One of the Palestinians who joined the Kuwait radio station as a translator for Reuters in 1959 was Ahmad ᶜAbd al-ᶜAl.[27] He became one of Kuwait's most distinguished radio and television anchormen.

In 1962, when another Palestinian, Ashraf Lutfi of Jaffa, then director of the Office of the Amir of Kuwait, had a stroke, Hani al-Qaddumi substituted for him. In 1965, he resigned and started a successful private business. His company became a leader in marketing medical equipment and drugs. Ashraf Lutfi had previously been director of the office of Abdullah al-Mullah. Al-Mullah was secretary of the government of Kuwait in charge of relations between the Amir of Kuwait and the oil company. Upon the death of Al-Mullah, Lutfi became director of the Office of the Amir of Kuwait. Later, he became the general secretary of OPEC while representing Kuwait. He was highly knowledgeable about the oil industry.[28]

From 1948 to1953, several other Palestinian earlycomers joined the Departments of General Security as administrators. Among them were Anwar al-Hnaydi, Ziyad Zᶜaytar, Zakarya al-Kurdi, and Abdulkarim al-Shawwa. They all were to have remarkable careers in Kuwait's private and public sectors.

A particularly remarkable contribution to Kuwait's infrastructural development came from Abdulmuhsin al-Qatt_ first came to Kuwait in 1951 where he taught in the secondary school which, at the time, was the only second Kuwait. He then went to Jordan where he was in charge c commercial education until 1953. When he was hired by the Kuwaiti government in 1953, the Department of Electricity was just starting as the result of the government's taking over a small private company that generated limited electricity.[29] By the time al-Qattan resigned in 1963, he was general inspector of the Ministry of Electricity, the second-highest position in the ministry.

Alongside al-Qattan, another earlycomer engineer, Dr. Zaki Abu-ʿId, from a village near Jaffa, and one of the few Palestinian engineers to graduate from a university in Great Britain before 1948, participated in the efforts to create a modern, efficient department of electricity. Abu-ʿId, the first Arab engineer in the department, rose to ever higher-ranking positions in the new ministry (chief engineer) until his death in the late 1970s.

But, al-Qattan, like Hani al-Qaddumi and many other high-ranking Palestinians, believed by the mid-1960s that it was time to resign. Native-born Kuwaiti graduates were looking forward to filling the high-level government positions. To al-Qattan and the other high-ranking Palestinians, the time was right. This movement toward resignation coincided with a slow, but long-term government policy of "Kuwaitinization." In this context, many high-ranking Palestinian government employees realized the limits to their growth posed by such a policy. Their concern was with the long-term implications of the slow process of Kuwaitinization. Despite Kuwaiti rejection of such resignations, quite a number of high-ranking Palestinians did resign at the time and during the decade that followed independence. In return for their services, a sizable percentage of the earlycomer intelligentsia was granted citizenship.

Like most of the Palestinians who worked with the government of Kuwait, al-Qattan decided that the only way to realize his potential was through the private sector. This mentality, which later became widespread in the diaspora, was another revival of a centuries-old practice in urban Palestine.

Early in the 1960s, al-Qattan started the Al-Hani Corporation. In a few years, he was able, with little capital, to establish one of the best construction companies in Kuwait and in the region. It encompassed several companies and its operations extended into Lebanon, Saudi Arabia, the Gulf, and North Africa.

The Palestinian role in the private sector of the Gulf expanded tremendously during this period, starting with the first oxygen factory in

.e Gulf founded by Salim al-Hunyadi in the late 1950s. According to Ibrahim Dabdub, the director of Kuwait's National Bank, during the 1950s the Palestinians in Kuwait were primarily individuals working in the public sector. Due to the existance of laws restricting nonindigenous free enterprise in Kuwait, few Palestinian businesses emerged. By the mid-1960s, as Kuwait embarked on an ambitious development program, and as Kuwaiti laws governing free enterprise were reformed, privately owned large Palestinian businesses arose. That era as well produced skilled managers, bankers, and investors such as Khalid Abu al-Saᶜud, manager of the investments of the Amir of Kuwait. Palestinians had come to have, in a very short time, an essential role in the engineering, construction, commercial, food, service, investment, management, and manufacturing businesses of Kuwait.[30]

In education lies another contribution to Kuwait, a reflection of the Palestinian obsession with professional standards. Many of those who came as teachers were assigned as principals and educational investigators. Many wrote textbooks for the Ministry of Education or introduced additional scientific material into the curriculum. Several women pioneers founded modern private schools in the country. One of them, Salwa Abu-Khadra, founded the first nursery school in Kuwait.

The experience of Abu-Khadra, who was born in Jaffa in 1929, is quite revealing. In Damascus, where she and her family took refuge, both of her parents died. As a result, she decided to join her closest surviving family members in Gaza (grandmother and aunt). Since Palestinian refugees encountered enormous difficulties in their movement from one Arab state to another, she had no other means of reaching Egypt except via the underground railroad operating at the time between Syria and Egypt. She sailed from Syria to Gaza in 1954 with her younger brother. She worked as a teacher and married in 1955.

In 1957 she and her husband came to Kuwait. After staying at home with her son for 3 years, Salwa, like many of the pioneering women of her generation decided to join the work force. After a brief work experience in the ministry of health, she realized that one of the serious problems affecting working mothers was the lack of a nursery for their children. Most women were cut off from their family and support networks in Syria, Jordan, or Lebanon, so there were no local relatives to rely on for child care. Abu-Khadra, who had no nursery school experience, wrote a letter to the United States Department of Social Welfare requesting information and references. She received pamphlets, journals, and lists of training programs which put her on a strict program of self-study which lasted over a year. In 1963, she opened a small nursery school which expanded after a few years to become the 12 year school of Dar al-Hanan.

Through her dedicated work and determination, she provided a mod[...] many Palestinian women in Kuwait.

Another influential personality in the development of education in Kuwait was Darwish al-Miqdadi.[31] Because of his exceptional organizational and educational skills, al-Miqdadi was assigned the job of director of education in Kuwait in 1950. During the 1930s, he had founded the Iraqi scout movement and was the president of Iraq's Higher Teachers' College (the highest educational post in the country at the time). After the war of 1948, Kuwait's Department of Education sought out al-Miqdadi, who took up residence in Damascus. From 1950, when he became director of education in Kuwait, until his death in 1962, he contributed greatly to Kuwait's educational advancement.

Dozens of Palestinian doctors also entered Kuwait between 1948 and the early 1950s.[32] Dr. Sami Bsharah, for instance, a surgeon who worked before 1948 in the Jaffa hospital, was one of the first Arab doctors to come to Kuwait. There were only two or three doctors in the country at the time.[33] In 1942, Dr. Yihya al-Hadidi, a Syrian doctor and the first Arab doctor to enter Kuwait, established the Amiri Hospital, the first national hospital in Kuwait.[34] Dr. Bsharah later became the director of this hospital.

Several other Palestinian doctors practiced in the clinics opened in Kuwait in the early 1950s. They participated in the early medical efforts in Kuwait alongside the few British and Arab doctors practicing at the time.

To take just two examples, both Dr. Nazim Ghabra and Dr. ᶜAli al-ᶜAttawnah have had remarkable careers. When they came in 1952, there were no more than thirty-two doctors in Kuwait. They were immediately assigned tasks in clinics and the Amiri hospital. In the late 1950s, they were among several doctors sent to Great Britain at the expense of Kuwait's Department of Health to specialize and gain work experience. On their return, both held important posts at the only major national hospital in Kuwait at the time, the Amiri: Dr. al-ᶜAttawnah as a surgeon and Dr. Ghabra as a cardiologist. In 1964, Dr. Ghabra resigned and started a private clinic for heart disease. In December 1965, Dr. al-ᶜAttawnah decided to go to the United States to further specialize and to learn to perform vascular surgery. Upon his return, for several years, he became the only doctor in Kuwait capable of performing such surgery. He stayed with the government to become, in 1977, director of the military medical administration in Kuwait and the assistant deputy chief of staff for medical services, a post he continues to hold.

In 1965, Dr. al-ᶜAttawnah and Dr. Ghabra were members of the four-doctor team that supervised the medical treatment of the former Amir of Kuwait Shaykh Abdullah S. al-Sabah. Dr. Ghabra was for a long time

45

the personal doctor of former Amir Shaykh Sabah al-Salim al-Sabah and became a member of the committee that supervised his medical treatment.

The Palestinian medical contribution was primarily in the area of general practice, nursing, and administration. On arrival, most Palestinian medical personnel worked outside clinics. In the late 1950s, the majority of them added training and experience, which qualified them to enter surgery, cardiology, and other specializations. Among several Palestinian medical facility administrators was ᶜAdil Jarrah, from Acre, who became general inspector of the Amiri Hospital from 1953 until 1962, when he became first director to the Office of the Foreign Minister.[35]

In nursing, most practitioners came from Christian Palestinian women graduates of the missionary nursing schools in Palestine, such as Saint Luke's Hospital. They headed most of the nursing departments of the Amiri Hospital up to the early 1960s.

These cases are examples of a growing obsession with education. Many earlycomers, whether doctors, engineers, pharmacists, or accountants, at some point in their careers sought further specialization and education. My studies show this behavior to be a response to the insecurities created by the displacement experience, and the consequent desire to keep commitment to the work ethic at a high level.

Among the earlycomer Palestinian urbanites, there were many who were performing essential functions in Kuwait, but the lack of a degree and the necessary experience for a high-ranking appointment required them to start as junior government employees. However, through a combination of an obsession with education and the philosophy of the work ethic, they experienced a high level of social mobility in the private and public sectors of Kuwait.

A good example is ᶜAdil Rishiq of Hebron. Rishiq's father died in 1948 in the battle for Palestine. Rishiq, who was twelve years old, had to quit school and take full responsibility for a family of eight. Until 1953, he worked as an electrician in the West Bank. He then moved to Kuwait, where he was employed as an electrical worker. Whatever jobs he held, however, he kept pursuing his formal education. He even took correspondence courses from RCA (Radio Corporation of America) and from an American school for radio and wireless. His enhanced skills qualified him to work in the Ministry of Education in 1958. He was hired in its audio visual administration, where he increased the use of audio-visual aids in education. He also held workshops for teachers from all over the country. In 1961, he founded the Electronic Appliances Corporation. By the 1970s the company had grown into twelve companies operating across the Arab world, Japan, and France.[36] Meanwhile, Rishiq earned his B.A., M.A., and a Ph.D. through correspondence courses.

46

A similar case is that of Bakri al-Tabba[c], who was employed as a draftsman in the Department of Public Works in Kuwait during the early 1950s.[37] With savings, he went to the United States to obtain a degree in engineering. He is now one of the most outstanding engineers in Kuwait.

Palestinians even became involved in Kuwait's municipality. Khalid al-Hasan, another earlycomer, made an outstanding contribution to the municipality of Kuwait. In September 1953, one year after his arrival in Kuwait at age twenty-five, he was appointed assistant general secretary of the Development Board. The board directed the planning and construction of modern Kuwait. Every construction project was accountable to it and could not even start if the board did not approve it. The board comprised all the members of the municipality of Kuwait, all assistant ministers, and every department in government with relevant projects. When the board was dissolved in 1959 and its jurisdiction transferred to the municipality of Kuwait, al-Hasan was appointed general secretary of the Municipal Council Board. He remained in this position until 1969, when he was granted Kuwaiti citizenship in recognition of services rendered. In 1969, al-Hasan, who is a founding member of Fatah, the mainstream Palestinian guerrilla organization, was elected to the executive committee of the Palestine Liberation Organization (PLO). Since then, he has been one of the major figures in the Palestinian nationalist movement.[38]

Before al-Hasan, another Palestinian earlycomer, Tal[c]at al-Ghussayn, was the assistant general secretary of the Development Board. Later, in the 1960's he became Kuwait's ambassador to the United States. He is at present Kuwait's ambassador to Yugoslavia. He is one of three ambassadors of Palestinian origin who have represented Kuwait.[39]

Another pioneer, General Wajih al-Madani of Acre made his contribution to Kuwait through the Army. Al-Madani, who was born in 1921, participated as a corporal in the joint Arab-Jewish force during World War II. During that time, no Palestinian army officers existed in the ranks of the British Army. Al-Madani's performance in the war provided him with the opportunity to enter the Sarafand British Military College in Palestine. In 1946, he graduated as a second lieutenant. From 1946 until 1947, he trained the embryonic Saudi Army. With Hazim Khalidi, he also trained the eighty-five Palestinians who were recruited to become lieutenants and lead the Palestinians in the defense of Palestine. Many future Palestinian military leaders came from this group. He also participated actively in the defense of Palestine during the 1948 war. When al-Madani arrived in Kuwait in 1952 to work in its embryonic army, it had three lieutenants in it. One of them was another Palestinian earlycomer, Fathi Sidir, who, during World War II fought with the Allies and was captured by the Germans.

47

Wajih al-Madani participated in the establishment of many of the basic departments and units of the Kuwaiti Army. He offered his experience to his Kuwaiti colleagues to build a modern army. His career in the Army of Kuwait continued until 1984, with an interruption from 1965 to 1969, when he became the first commander-in-chief of the Palestine Liberation Army, the official army of the PLO.[40]

Many other Palestinians also provided essential services to the Kuwaiti Army. ʿUmar Zʿaytar, for example, founded and led the artillery and participated actively with Kuwait's troops in the 1973 war on the Syrian Golan front. In recognition of his achievements, Kuwait granted him citizenship. Furthermore, Khalil Shhaybar, a former Palestinian police officer, founded and lead the police force in 1951. His commanding role lasted until his retirement in the early 1980s. Talʿat al-ʿAlami, a Palestinian musician with other displaced musicians from Jerusalem, founded Kuwait's first military band in the early 1950s.

In the area of agriculture lie other contributions of great proportions. Yihya Ghannam of Tulkarim graduated from Khadduri agricultural school in Palestine just before the war of 1948.[41] After his arrival in Kuwait in 1954, he entered a creative and challenging battle with nature through a position as director of Kuwait's department of agricultural administration. Kuwait had little agriculture and few trees and little poultry and animal husbandry. Ghannam hired hundreds of displaced Palestinian farmers, who brought with them their centuries-old experience with agriculture. It was a challenge to discover what trees and crops were most suitable to Kuwait's hot weather, nonfertile soil, salty waters, and minimal rainfall. Yihya Ghannam was a decisive personality in the struggle that turned Kuwait into a blooming desert. By the late 1950s, trees started to surround the concrete that was eating the desert. A remarkable increase in poultry and animal husbandry took place. Cattle were imported, and chicken farms were established. In addition to a zoo and school gardens, a policy was instituted to provide free tree seeds and agricultural soil to private homes.

Ghannam stayed in his position until he became Kuwait's permanent representative to the Food and Agriculture Organization (FAO) in 1967. In 1969, the FAO asked the government of Kuwait to name him general director of the FAO regional office that covers the Middle East and North Africa. He is at present director of that office, which moved to Kuwait a few years ago.

The story of Palestinian participation in agricultural development in Kuwait, Qatar, the United Arab Emirates, Jordan, Egypt, and Syria, has been quite integral to the politics of Palestinian survival. For thousands of Palestinians it has meant a continued commitment to working in agriculture as their forbears had done for millennia.

In the area of finance is the example of Haydar al-Shahabi, a graduate of the American University of Beirut and one of five individuals who comprised the embryonic Ministry of Finance in early 1949 in Kuwait. He was first appointed as assistant to the director of the Finance Department; when he resigned in 1969 to enter the private sector he was deputy assistant secretary of state for financial affairs.[42]

This small sample illustrating the accomplishments of Palestinians in Kuwait is intended only to provide an insight into the fundamental role played by the Palestinian intelligentsia in Kuwait. Its contribution directly resulted from an obsession with professional standards, an obsession caused to a large extent by the need to find and maintain employment. This need for employment was, in turn, a basic response to the attempt to relieve the stateless conditions of the families of this group of refugees. In every area of the private and public sectors, the displaced Palestinian intelligentsia left its mark.

Furthermore, these examples demonstrate how every exiled population, in adapting to a new environment, follows strategies that reflect "the particular segment of the original society, and [its] prior acculturational experiences."[43] The majority of the earlycomer Palestinian intelligentsia were, in fact, urban; their experience was accumulated in cities such as Jaffa, Haifa, Lydda, Ramle, Gaza, Nablus, Tulkarim, and Jerusalem. Their education, knowledge of foreign languages, and experience with the British system of civil administration provided them with tools helpful to survival after the 1948 trauma.

The achievements of the earlycomer Palestinian intelligentsia were further influenced by the competitive and restrictive educational system in Palestine during the mandate era. Government secondary schools, in particular the Rashidiyah and al-Kuliyah al-ᶜArabiyah of Jerusalem, admitted only the students with the highest three scores from each city and district in Palestine. This made the high school and college graduates of pre-1948 Palestine a highly competitive group. The earlycomer Palestinian intelligentsia were part of a group of Palestinian achievers spread throughout most of the Arab world.

It seems, then, that diaspora peoples in the process of adapting to the circumstances of exile, have a proportionately higher investment in achievement than settled and more secure populations would normally have.

The Politics of Family Cohesion

This study rests on the hypothesis that without the politics of family cohesion there would have been no Palestinian group existence.

49

he family formed the cornerstone in the Palestinians' ability to regroup and reestablish their network.

The earlycomer intelligentsia provided the first patterns in the politics of family cohesion. Hard work opened the way for them, and they immediately provided both their effective and extended family networks with a more tolerable life. Their first priority was to rescue family members from suffering. Their decision to come to Kuwait had been a function of their responsibilities toward their families in the first place. They all had the task of providing their parents, their brothers and sisters, with the necessities of life. They also wanted to continue the education of their brothers and sisters, which had been disrupted by the war. Therefore, once they arrived in Kuwait, they regularly sent a large sum of their salaries to their families in Jordan, Syria, Lebanon, or Egypt.

Another trend associated with family was part of the early response to exile. Since the physical existence of the family was at stake, many of the predominantly conservative Palestinian families encouraged active participation of women in the work force. This involved young, middle-class, urban women, mostly graduates of Palestinian teaching colleges, who were willing to move away from their families. Many moved to Iraq, Saudi Arabia, Amman, or Damascus, but a number went to Kuwait. Such women played an essential part in the advancement of the education of females in Kuwait in both public and private schools.

In 1950, the first major wave of Palestinian working women independently recruited arrived in Kuwait. Among them were Myassar Shahin, 'Ulfa Qutayni, and Fayzah Kanafani.[44] When Myassar Shahin arrived in Kuwait, at the age of twenty-four, she was assigned as principal of one of the two secondary schools for women in Kuwait at the time. Shahin had been a high school teacher in Jerusalem. She was a graduate of Jerusalem's teaching college. Shahin worked as a high school principal for thirty-four years, making a positive impact on women's education in Kuwait until she retired in 1984.

Shahin, like many Palestinian women with university or high school degrees, found out that the family responsibilities she bore went far beyond being self-supporting women. Their role, like that of the male earlycomer intelligentsia, became that of supporting their exiled families. For them such responsibility was new; for the first time, young men and women were responsible for leading their families out of crisis.

In Palestine, women had been considered a burden and only temporarily, until marriage, part of their parents' household. Marriage at an early age was seen as a transfer of loyalty, commitment, and productivity to another family, that of the husband. After 1948, these traditional perceptions of women changed significantly. Women became symbols of sacrifice and courage. Their support of their families when

50

there were virtually no other means of survival created a new image of them. The women who came to Kuwait in the early 1950s began the tradition of female support of the Palestinian family. These women sent most of their salary to elderly parents who had no means of support after the exodus. They supported their younger brothers and sisters, helping to educate them through college. These women displayed independence and decisiveness. To accomplish their mission many of these women decided not to marry. In the course of my interviews with them, these women refused to talk about their contribution to the family. Friends and other family members helped me put the picture together. Though they had saved their families from imminent disaster, they were hesitant to claim credit. They took pride in the fact that their families were back on their feet. For this end, that is, the common good of the family, they were willing to sacrifice.

When the foundations of Palestinian society were shaken, deep-rooted values were undermined. The enhanced role of women is an example of how the uprooting and the crisis stemming from it became a force for change. It is quite evident that the need to confront the crisis subsumed many pre-1948 values that may have rejected the whole concept of a woman's becoming the center of a family's extended and effective network. In Kuwait, in every family, people repeat stories about the young women who suddenly became mothers and fathers to their brothers and sisters. The respect accorded to them and the sentiments surrounding their role have provided new perceptions of women in Palestinian society. The women who came to Kuwait in the 1950s were starting a new family tradition that went far beyond the experience of women in pre-1948 Palestine. This new reality laid the groundwork for a different, more active role for women in the affairs of their families, and hence in the society at large.

Another significant family trend appearing after the earlycomers arrived in Kuwait is the bridge they formed to facilitate the arrival of their family networks and their friends. This is a very decisive stage for the formation of family networks in Kuwait.[45] In fact, once in Kuwait, each earlycomer became a center for his or her family, distant relatives, friends, and fellow townspeople. Those who found jobs and opportunity wanted to provide that same opportunity to others in their personal networks. A displaced friend or a relative had only to hear that a cousin was in Kuwait to prompt references and requests for employment. Through the efforts of the earlycomers, thousands of other Palestinians came to Kuwait. Every family started with one or two individuals. After a decade or two, as a result of "chain migration," there were one hundred or two hundred members of that family in Kuwait. Whether from the intelligentsia, the peasantry, or the urban poor, the arrival of one individual from a particular

51

family established a foothold for that family. In a decade or two, as will be explained in chapter 5, the family became well represented and established in Kuwait's Palestinian community.

An example provided from the experience of Sa^cid Khuri of Consolidated Contractors Company (CCC) will demonstrate how powerful and motivating the force of the family can be. According to Khuri, his family's ordeal provided him with the motivation to withstand pressure and the hardships of working after 1948 in the Syrian desert in subhuman conditions.[46] He was particularly torn to see his father forced to cope with statelessness and poverty. The transformation of his father from a dignitary in Safad (Palestine) to a stateless refugee was the most emotionally devestating experiences Khuri has had.

In 1948, Sa^cid Khuri, Hassib Sabagh, and Kamil ^cAbd al-Rahman created what later became one of the most successful construction companies in the Arab world. The company, which started as a small subcontractor, operating through a U.S. company, Bechtel, in the 1950s, became a multinational corporation with a one-half billion dollar annual budget in the 1970s. The company's rise is a fascinating picture of individual effort and commitment by three displaced Palestinians. Through the company, Sa^cid and the cofounders helped family, relatives, friends, and fellow townspeople. They have also provided similar support to many Palestinians in the Middle East, through employment and philanthropic activity.

The response of the Palestinian family to the dilemma resulting from the war took different forms. Abdulmuhsin al-Qattan's experience serves as an example.[47] When Jaffa fell to the Zionists, al-Qattan was a freshman at the American University of Beirut. He was cut off from Jaffa and his family. For days he went to the port of Beirut to see if his family was on any of the arriving boats carrying thousands of refugees. He asked those who came from Jaffa about his mother and siblings. Finally, he got news of their safe arrival in Amman. Upon meeting them in Amman, he decided, as did many thousands of Palestinian students, to quit school and work to support his family. Al-Qattan's mother, however, insisted on carrying out the wish of his deceased father. His father, who had served as a soldier in the Ottoman Army had no formal education, and wished to educate his children. "How can the chain of poverty be broken if the chain of ignorance continues after every trauma?" his mother repeatedly insisted. Despite the difficulties, al-Qattan returned to the American University of Beirut.

The Preservation of a Political Identity

Despite the earlycomer intelligentsia's successful adaptation to the difficult physical conditions of displacement, psychological adaptation seemed impossible. Everyday was a reminder of the devastating loss of home. The daily prayers of the Muslim and the Christian Palestinians incorporated a prayer for a return to Palestine.

Unlike the Jewish diaspora experience, the Palestinian diaspora has not been definitively cut off from their homeland because over 40 percent of the Palestinians still live in Palestine. To the Palestinians of Kuwait, including the earlycomer intelligentsia, Palestine remains "home"; the diaspora in Kuwait has increasingly become a temporary and second home. To them the relationship with Palestine remains basic to their existence and continuity as a group. The diaspora culture revolves around Palestine as a state of mind, a concept, and a homeland.

Other, more particular, factors coincided with a continuing feeling of loss and victimization to form the post-1948 Palestinian political identity. By the mid-1960s, and because of political fragmentation and the continued occupation of their country, the Palestinians as a group were suffering from a lack of political, social, and cultural worth. No matter how successful an individual became, or how cohesive the family network was, national pride and dignity were constantly humiliated. Palestinians as a group became politically marginal and objects of Arab state manipulation. A form of abhorrent "dependency" developed in their relationship to the Arab world.

This political marginality, unknown before 1948, was a cause of great frustration. Before 1948 the Palestinians had political parties, a political life, and all the forms of social, cultural, and professional institutions then not in existence in many sectors of the Arab world. In the early 1960s, after more than a decade of waiting for Arab politics to find a solution to their problem, Palestinians started to develop their political assertiveness. More and more Palestinians began to lose confidence in Arab policy concerning the Palestine question. It became clear to them that, without active participation in shaping their own political destiny, they would remain worthless, rightless, and stateless.

By 1964, the Palestinians in Kuwait and other diaspora centers became convinced of the need to revive their political life and their social, cultural, and professional institutions. They started to dedicate themselves to the re-creation of an independent political life. This manifested itself in the support for the establishment of the Palestine Liberation Organization (the PLO). By so doing they hoped to recover the rights to their homeland.

Examples from the sample used in this study demonstrate how political identity was expressed by members of the intelligentsia. For instance, Abdulmuhsin al-Qattan, of al-Hani Corporation, has been a member of the Palestine National Council (the Palestinian parliament-in-exile) since the PLO's formation. He was elected chairman of the PNC during the 1969 session. He has also provided important financial support to the PLO and to Palestinian education and has participated actively in the establishment of some of the most important diaspora institutions.

Saᶜid Khuri of Consolidated Contractors is at present a member of the Palestine National Fund (PNF), which supervises the overall annual budget of the PLO. Through his company, valuable support has been provided to the PLO, and also to Palestinian educational and cultural activity. Hani al-Qaddumi, who currently owns a leading drug and medical equipment importing company, has been a member of the Palestine National Council since 1964. His contribution to Fatah in Kuwait during the early 1960s (the early days of its existence) was very important.

Khayriddin Abuljubayn, an earlycomer teacher, became the president of the Palestine Congress in Kuwait in March 1964. The second deputy was Yihya Ghannam, who was important in agricultural experimentation. This congress represented the community by holding public elections to present local Palestinian demands to Ahmad al-Shukayri, who was consulting the Palestinian communities concerning the formation of the PLO. Abuljubayn also became the first PLO representative to Kuwait (1965-1969) and is at present a member of the PNF and the PNC, representing the Palestinian community in Kuwait.

Three individuals in particular from this sample have made an enormous political contribution. The first is Khalid al-Hasan, cofounder of Fatah, member of its Central Committee, and a PLO leader. He is now head of the PNC's Foreign Relations Committee and director of the PLO's United Information (the department in charge of PLO information). The second is Wajih al-Madani, who joined Kuwait's army in 1953. Al-Madani was appointed by the PLO leader in September 1964, as commander-in-chief of the newly formed Palestinian Liberation Army. In fact, al-Madani's transfer from his post in the Kuwaiti army was done by prior agreement with the former Amir of Kuwait, Abdullah al-Salim al-Sabah. Al-Madani is credited with building the PLO's army from scratch. He is the founder of a guerrilla organization known as the Heroes of Return, which later joined with other organizations to form the Popular Front for the Liberation of Palestine.

The third is Salwa Abu-Khadra who had an important impact on women's participation in Palestinian nationalism. Abu-Khadra was one of the first women activists in the Palestinian community in Kuwait. It was quite a challenge in 1966-1967 to maintain her secret membership in

Fatah, which used to be an underground organization. During that period it was hard for women to even attend meetings much less return late after a meeting. After 1976 and the rise of Palestinian nationalism this changed in many respects. In this context Abu-Khadra was daring in her efforts to help establish the first PLO training camps for Palestinian women. In many cases she was quite convincing to conservative Palestinian families who objected to their daughters traveling to Syria, Algeria, or Lebanon to work in Palestinian summer training or scout camps.

With Myassar Shahin she cofounded the Kuwait chapter of the General Union of Palestinian Women. This union became the most effective of all PLO institutions and unions in Kuwait, a reflection of women's role in the new Palestinian society. Furthermore, Abu-Khadra created, out of her school, Dar al-Hanan, a center for Palestinian nationalism and education. That school had an impact on the nationalist consciousness of a whole generation of young women and men. In the early 1970s she became a member of the Palestine National Council. At present she is, in addition, the General Secretary of the worldwide General Union of Palestinian Women.

The rest of the sample has participated in a whole range of unions and associations, such as the doctors' union (1968), and the Palestinian Red Crescent Society (1969). Several members of this sample helped establish the Fund for Palestinian Higher Education in 1961. This fund has sent several hundred students through college and graduate school. Many similar institutions, both local and across the diaspora, have enjoyed either the active participation or financial support of members of this sample.

Furthermore, this sample formed the earliest bridge between the PLO and Kuwait. Several members of this group provided the PLO and the secret underground Fatah activists of the early 1960s their first contacts with Kuwaiti leaders.

The Incipient Patterns of Survival: A Comparative Context

The earlycomer members of the Palestinian intelligentsia who moved to Kuwait and other Gulf states in the aftermath of the 1948 war did not, by and large, belong to the financial, landed, and political elite. In fact, the former elite, which had dominated political and economic life, found itself after 1948 without its traditional sources of power. This sudden change and loss of supremacy affected its immediate choices.

Just after the 1948 war, during the most important stage of development of patterns of Palestinian survival and rebirth the leading families expressed unwarranted confidence in a quick solution that would allow for Palestinian return and self-determination. Many of them believed that the Israelis in a matter of months--or at most a year or two--would have to give in to U.N. resolutions and other international pressures and allow the Palestinians to return. Such overconfidence was shored up by the ability of the members of this elite to live on their investments without working in Beirut or Amman until such a solution were achieved.

This behavior proved harmful to this stratum as its investments shrank, hopes decreased, and responsibilities increased. Their need for employment became as urgent as other socioeconomic groups. Many chose to work in places close to Palestine so as to be able to return should circumstances allow. Some had Arab connections that opened up opportunities for them. Others had sizable investments that proved to be helpful in starting businesses. As Pamela Smith asserts, some of this stratum did quite well in those countries surrounding Palestine, particularly those who transferred their money before the war of 1948 into Lebanon and Jordan.[48]

But the question is one of proportion and comparison. By waiting in Arab capitals for a solution most of this stratum suffered a decline in influence and financial holdings. Some have reestablished positions of power, but the lead in the cultural, political, economic, and intellectual components of the politics of Palestinian survival was lost to a different social force.

The early pioneer intelligentsia who came to Kuwait, the nationalists who made up the Palestinian nationalist movement, or the writers, intellectuals, and the poets of lower- and middle-class origins came to the fore. The challenge to survive and the desire for equality, as well as the reaction against the failures of the former leading families, motivated the new forces.

The pioneers who came to Kuwait were participating in a broad social transformation. Most of those members of the intelligentsia who went to the Gulf early were of lower or middle-class origins. Almost all of them had either a high school or college degree, some working experience, and no investments outside of Palestine. They were penniless when the war ended. They needed to move quickly. Their work experience and education gave them the lead in finding employment and in building the diaspora structure. Through the will to achieve they "have in fact accumulated a society, but not in Palestine. . . .The most striking feature of this society-in-exile is its powerful bourgeoisie, which in the four decades since 1948 has traversed the historical stages lived through in a century and a half by the European bourgeoisie, from Enlightenment, to early industrialization, to capitalism, to late capitalism."[49]

Those who came to Kuwait and the Gulf in the late 1940s and early 1950s were self-made men and women with exceptional will and intelligence. They accepted and tolerated the harsh living conditions o Kuwait, something the former elite was not willing to do. As Husayn Qal°awi, who came to Kuwait in 1950, and opened the Orient Palace Hotel, the second modern hotel to be built in Kuwait, explained, "In Haifa I lost my work, chiefly a business founded by my great-grandfather, which expanded during my grandfather's and father's days. I lost everything, work, inheritance, and country. I had to start from scratch. My generation was a self-made working generation."[50]

However, this new brand of Palestinians, in responding to exile and establishing the foundations of diaspora structures, discovered that the traditional pre-1948 system, which depended on family and property to protect individual privilege, no longer existed. Education and hard work were the new tickets to survival. What they built in the diaspora was a new structure based on merit. But in no way can the new Palestinian diaspora structure be divorced from family. The earlycomer intelligentsia reestablished success in the social and family network.

NOTES

1. This number is an informal estimate based on research conducted in Kuwait.

2. Abba Eban, My People: The Story of the Jews (New York: Behrman House, Random House, 1968), p. 108.

3. On Kuwait's pre-1948 socioeconomic development, see Jacqueline S. Ismael, Kuwait: Social Change in Historical Perspective (New York: Syracuse University Press, 1982), pp. 17-36, 54-78; Najat °Abd al-Qadir al-Jasim, Al-Tatawwur al-Siyasi wa al-Iqtisadi Lil-Kuwayt Bayn al-Harbayn: 1914-1939 [The Political and Economic Evolution in Kuwait during the Interwar Period. 1914-1939] (Kuwait: Kuwait University, 1973).

4. A foreign population of Persians, Bahranis, and Omanis and Iraqis also existed, and may have added 10,000 to 15,000 to the 1936 population. According to the first census conducted by the Department of Social Affairs in 1957, there were 113,622 Kuwaitis.

5. On the rapid economic development and urbanization that took place in Palestine after 1850, see Alexander Scholch, "European Penetration and the Economic Development of Palestine, 1856-82," in Studies in the Economic and Social History of Palestine, ed. Roger Owen (Carbondale: Southern Illinois University Press, 1982), pp. 10-87; Sarah Graham-Brown, "The Political Economy of Jabal Nablus, 1920-1948," in Studies in the Economic and Social History of Palestine in the Nineteenth and Twentieth Century (Carbondale: Southern Illinois University Press,

1982), pp. 88-176; ^cAbd al-Qadir Yassin, "al-Tatawwur al-Sina^ci fi Fhilistin hita am 1948 ["The Evolution of Industry in Palestine until 1948"], <u>Shu'un Philistiniyah</u>, no. 80 (July 1978):81-98; Shimuel Avitsur, "The Influence of Western Technology on the Economy of Palestine during the Nineteenth Century", in <u>Studies on Palestine during the Ottoman Period</u>, ed. Moshe Ma^coz (Jerusalem: Magners Press, 1975), pp. 485-495; Sarah Graham-Brown, <u>Palestinians and Their Society: 1880-1946: A Photographic Essay</u> (London: Quartet Books, 1980), pp. 99-156.

6. Interview with Khayriddin Abuljubayn, Kuwait, summer 1985.

7. All of those I interviewed who were put in the concentration camps in Egypt provided a similar account.

8. The Kuwaiti house looked after Kuwaiti interests and was in charge of Kuwaiti students in Egypt. ^cAbd al-^cAziz Husayn became director of education in Kuwait, then minister of state, and is at present consultant to the Amir of Kuwait.

9. Salih Jasim Shhab, <u>Tarikh al-Ta^cLim Fi al-Kuwayt wa al-Khalij 'Ayam Zaman, [History of Eduction in Kuwait and the Gulf during the Old Days]</u>, Vol. I (Kuwait: 1984), pp. 59, 125.

10. Ibid., p. 170.

11. The Palestinian educational team played a very important role during those six critical years. When they arrived in Kuwait they were warmly received by all sectors of the Kuwaiti society (Shhab, <u>Tarikh</u>, p. 118). They came to Kuwait at the invitation of the Council of Education, directed by Shaykh Abdullah al-Jabir al-Sabah, and at the request of the Amir of Kuwait, who sent a letter to Hajj Amin al-Husayni, the leader of the Palestinian nationalist movement and the mufti of Jerusalem, asking him to nominate four Palestinian teachers for Kuwait. Out of fear that Kuwaiti anti-British sentiments would increase when the Palestinian teaching team informed the Kuwaitis about British policies in Palestine, the British did all they could to block the team's arrival (ibid., pp. 97-111). The first team arrived on September 5, 1936. They introduced history, geography, biology, physical education, scouts, geometry, English, and a course on civility and morality into the curriculum of the Mubarakiyah School (ibid., p. 125). Furthermore, the senior member of the Palestinian team and the director of the Mubarakiyah School, Ahmad Shahab al-Din, contacted, at the request of the Council of Education, two Palestinian women teachers and asked them to come to Kuwait to start the first modern girls' school in Kuwait (ibid., p. 162). Two sisters, Wasifah and Rifqah ^cUdah, arrived in Kuwait in 1936. After one year they were joined by the first Kuwaiti female teacher, Maryam Salih. Overall the Palestinian educational teams, which continued to arrive until 1942,

created an intellectual and educational atmosphere that went beyond their teaching mission (ibid., p. 159).

12. Interview with Khayriddin Abuljubayn and Husayn Najim (brother of Muhammad Najim and an earlycomer), Kuwait, summer 1985.

13. See D.M. Boswell, "Personal Crises and the Mobilization of the Social Network," in Social Networks in Urban Situations, ed. J. Clyde Mitchell, (Manchester: Manchester University Press, 1969), p. 245. See also A. L. Epstein, "The Network and Urban Social Organization," Rhodes-Livingstone Institute Journal 29 (1961):29-62.

14. Interview with Hani al-Qaddumi, Kuwait, summer 1985.

15. Ibid.

16. Interview with Khalid al-Hasan, Kuwait, summer 1985. For the same account and further details, see Alan Hart, Arafat: Terrorist or Peacemaker? (London: Sidgwick and Jackson, 1984), pp. 141-149.

17. This corresponds with Maslow's hierarchy of human needs. A. H. Maslow (1943) "A Theory of Human Motivation," in Classics of Public Administration, ed. Jay M. Shafritz and Albert C. Hyde (Oak Park, Ill.: Moore Publishing Company, 1978), pp. 80-95.

18. Interview with Salwa Abu-Khadra, Kuwait, summer 1985.

19. Boswell, "Personal Crises," p. 295.

20. The accounts of the trip to Kuwait that follow have been obtained from Khayriddin Abuljubayn, Hani al-Qaddumi, and Yusif Abuljubayn.

21. Interview with Myassar Shahin, Kuwait, summer 1985.

22. Based on interviews with the earlycomer intelligentsia, Kuwait, summer 1985.

23. Interview with ᶜAdil Jarrah, who was at that time director of the Office of the Foreign Minister and was present at this meeting. At the time of the interview, Jarrah was Kuwait's ambassador to the Soviet Union. He died in March 1986. Ahmad al-Shukayry often referred to this encounter in the years to come.

24. Bilal al-Hassan, "al-Filastiniyun fi al-Kuwayt" ["The Palestinians in Kuwait: Statistical Study"] (Beirut: Palestine Liberation Organization Research Center, 1974), pp. 30-31.

25. Interview with Khayriddin Abuljubayn, Kuwait, summer 1985.

26. Interview with Hani al-Qaddumi, Kuwait, summer 1985.

27. Interview with Ahmad ᶜAbd al-ᶜAl, Kuwait, summer 1985.

28. Interview with Hani al-Qaddumi and other earlycomers, Kuwait, summer 1985..

29. Interview with Abdulmuhsin al-Qattan, Kuwait, summer 1985.

30. Interview with Ibrahim Dabdub, Kuwait, summer 1985.

59

31.   The information on al-Miqdadi was provided by Abdulmuhsin al-Qattan, an earlycomer,and al-Miqdadi's son-in-law. Myassar Shahin and several other earlycomers provided similar accounts, Kuwait, summer 1985.

32.   The accounts in this section were provided by Dr. ^cAli al-^cAttawnah and Dr. Nazim Ghabra, Kuwait, summer 1985.

33.   Badriddine A. al-Khususi, <u>Dirasat fi Tarikh al-Kuwayt al-Ijtima^ci wa al-Iqtisadi fi al-^cAsr al-Hadith</u>. [<u>Studies in the Socioeconomic History of Kuwait in the Modern Age</u>] 2d ed. (Kuwait: That-al-Salasil, 1983), p. 167.

34.   Ibid., pp. 163-165.

35.   Interview with ^cAdil Jarrah, Kuwait, summer 1985.

36.   Interview with ^cAdil Rishiq, Kuwait, summer 1985.

37.   Interview with Bakri al-Taba^c, Kuwait, summer 1985.

38.   Interview with Khalid al-Hasan, Kuwait, summer 1985. For further information on al-Hasan's role in the Palestinian movement, see Hart, <u>Arafat.</u>

39.   The second is Hasan al-Dabagh, Kuwait's ambassador to Switzerland. A third ambassador, ^cAdil Jarrah, Kuwait's ambassador to the Soviet Union, died in 1986.

40.   Interview with Wajih al-Madani, Kuwait, summer 1985.

41.   Interview with Yihya Ghannam, Kuwait, summer 1985.

42.   Interview with Haydar al-Shihabi, Kuwait, summer 1985.

43.   James Hirabayashi, William Willard, and Luis Kemnitzer, "Pan Indianism in the Urban Setting," in <u>The Anthropology of Urban Environments</u>, ed. Thomas Weaver and Douglas White (Washington, D.C.: Society for Applied Anthropology, 1972), p. 86.

44.   Based on interview with Myassar Shahin and Fayzah Kanafani, who have taught in Kuwait since 1950, Kuwait, summer 1985. Also based on interview with Salwa Abu-Khadra, Kuwait, summer 1985. See also Yvonne Haddad, "Palestinian Women: Patterns of Legitimation and Domination," in <u>The Sociology of the Palestinians</u>, ed. Khalil Nakleh and Elia Zureik (New York: St. Martin's Press, 1980).

45.   Fuad Khuri has documented a similar process among Lebanese migrants to West Africa: "Kinship, Emigration, and Trade Partnership among the Lebanese of West Africa," <u>Africa</u> 35 (January 1965):389. For similar examples on Arab immigrants to the U.S. and chain migration, see Mary C. Sengstol, "Detroit's Iraqi-Chaldeans: A Conflicting Conception of Identity," in <u>Arabs in the New World: Studies on Arab-American Communities</u>, ed. Sameer Y. Abraham and Nabeel Abraham (Detroit, Mich.: Wayne State University Center for Urban Studies, 1983), p. 137; Sameer Y. Abraham, Nabeel Abraham, and

4680

Barbara Aswad, "The Southend: An Arab Muslim Working-Class Community," in Arabs in the New World, p. 167.

46. Interview with Sa^cid Khuri, Kuwait, summer 1985.

47. Interview with Abdulmuhsin al-Qattan, Kuwait, summer, 1985.

48. Pamela Ann Smith, Palestine and the Palestinians: 1876-1983 (New York: St. Martin's Press, 1984), pp. 112-143; idem, "The Palestinian Diaspora, 1948-1985," Journal of Palestine Studies 15, no. 3, issue 59 (Spring 1986): 90-108.

49. Edward W. Said, After the Last Sky: Palestine Lives (with photographs by Jean Mohr) (New York: Pantheon Books, 1986), p. 120.

50. Interview with Husayn Qal^cawi, Kuwait, summer 1985.

4

The Place of the Peasantry

The Palestinian peasantry constituted the second major group to arrive in Kuwait in the early 1950s. It had different, more difficult problems than the intelligentsia had. Peasants had to learn to adapt to city jobs. To survive in Kuwait, they had to become nonpeasants. They were transformed into an urban proletariat or an urban lower class. Though the emphasis here will be solely on the peasantry, many members of the urban poor pursued the same strategies, as many of them were of peasant origin.

Beginning in 1948, the displaced peasantry developed survival strategies and, as in the case of the intelligentsia, several patterns emerged. Each pattern was a response to post-1948 conditions. Focusing on these early responses permits a better understanding of later developments in the politics of Palestinian group survival. These responses indicate what foundations were laid and how family networks were employed in the beginning.

This chapter will explain how the need for income to provide basic needs for self and family forced the peasantry to take quite a risky route to find employment. The dangerous and long journey to Kuwait on the underground railroad was the first major risk. Once the peasants arrived in Kuwait, they immediately sought out relatives and members of their villages who had arrived before them. Thus, their first strategy for survival was based on personal village and family networks.

Although ties with peasant families from home were decisive in finding jobs for the arriving country folk, the Palestinian intelligentsia also participated actively in this process. How well did the peasants do in

63

adapting to city jobs and how did they survive in the new conditions of that early period?

The following is an account of the experiences and early survival responses of both the Palestinians who took refuge in the West Bank and the residents of the West Bank who chose to migrate to Kuwait. Those who arrived immediately after the intelligentsia were by and large from the West Bank (refugees and residents). They were the only Palestinians to arrive in Kuwait via the underground. Today, with family members who arrived legally in the 1960s and 1970s, they constitute about 60 percent of the community.

The Peasantry in the West Bank after 1948

No sector of Palestinian society has paid as heavy a price as the peasantry. The disruption the peasants experienced was more severe and the choices available to them were more limited than other Palestinian refugee groups. After 1948, the majority was thrown into makeshift refugee camps, and those who were not uprooted, that is, the residents of the West Bank, were severely hit economically. Most of them had few work skills beyond agriculture, although some had worked as laborers in Palestinian coastal industries.

The Palestinian peasantry was deeply connected to the land and community by centuries of settlement in the same village and on the same plot of land. Families lived together in the same house--father, mother, and married children--thus making the extended family the dominant social form among the peasantry until 1948. Every individual had a place in the family system; all had a strong need to preserve a community that revolved around families sharing one village.[1] Even when many of them left the village before 1948 to work in the coastal cities of Haifa and Jaffa, or on British installations on the coast, the majority became "commuters", spending all of their vacations and farming seasons in the village with their families.[2]

When the war ended, the West Bank entered a terrible economic crisis. It was flooded with refugees. The 363,689 refugees who sought refuge and protection in the West Bank took shelter in camps, villages, schools, and mosques.[3] They became a burden on the West Bank economy and on the 400,000 original inhabitants of the West Bank.

In addition to the problems created by the influx of refugees, thousands of West Bank residents who had been working away from home returned to their villages, causing further overcrowding.[4] Furthermore, the West Bank, for the first time, was cut off from access to the Mediterranean and from Haifa and Jaffa. The West Bank, a mountainous area, had always

64

depended on the coastal plains for agricultural land. Worst hit were the towns of Jinin, Tulkarim, Qalqilyah, and all the villages surrounding them, which were dependent on the lands located in the plains and valleys that had been taken by the Israelis. In 1949, with the conclusion of the Rhodes agreement with Jordan, Israel advanced its borders on the Jordanian side, which resulted in the loss of all the fertile lands and valleys that had belonged to the West Bank towns and villages.[5] Some of the villages were even cut in half, like Bayt Safafa; the Israelis occupied half, leaving the other half under Jordanian rule.

Furthermore, little rain fell from 1949 to 1951, which destroyed most of the remaining West Bank agriculture. Abd al-Ilah Qasim remembers how hard it was growing up in the village of Sinjil in the West Bank from 1948 to the early 1950s. His village was known for its grapes, but it suddenly lost everything when a disease destroyed all the grapevines. The villagers call these the years of the dates. Dates were sent to them as relief by the Iraqi government.[6]

Sizable numbers of refugees tried daily to return to their occupied homes and villages in Palestine.[7] But in all cases, they were caught and expelled. Some were even killed. The motives of those who tried to cross the border varied. Many wanted to return permanently while the fighting was still going on; others wanted to keep checking on the well-being of their property. Others went to bring food, and bedding to their families.[8]

Once return was totally blocked and the economic conditions of the West Bank became unbearable, both the refugees and the residents of the West Bank sought ways to survive outside the area. The destiny of whole families was in the hands of the young who were capable of travel and work. The patterns of population movement, as people tried to escape the economic, social, and psychological imbroglio, varied. In addition to movement to the city of Amman, two lines of migration developed: one in the villages of Jerusalem, Ramallah, and Bethlehem, where Palestinians predominantly continued their migration to the United States; and another in the Nablus mountain areas and the Jinin, Qalqilyah, Tulkarim areas, to the Gulf.

The Ramallah, Bethlehem, Jerusalem-area migration to the United States was led by numerous Christians. They had actually opened routes to the United States during the 1920s and 1930s. The Muslims who lived in the same towns and villages seized the opportunity of ties with friends and family to gain access to the U. S. route.[9] Some villages in that area, like Silwad, sent people solely to the Gulf, which was much more accessible and culturally manageable. But the majority of the unskilled laborers and peasants living in the West Bank and looking for a way out found it in the natural extension of geography, culture, and history which

Kuwait provided. They heard of Kuwait, of its oil, and the opportunities for survival.

The Underground Railroad

I have a cousin called Hasanain, who was smuggled across the border once. After more than seven hours' walking, darkness fell. Then the smuggler pointed to a cluster of far-off lights saying, "There's Kuwait. You'll reach it when you've walked for half an hour." Do you know what happened? That wasn't Kuwait, it was a remote Iraqi village. I can tell you thousands of stories like that. Stories of men who became like dogs as they looked for one drop of water to moisten their cracked tongues with. What do you think happened when they saw bedouin encampments? They bought a mouthful of water in exchange for all the money or wedding rings or watches they owned.[10]

Ghassan Kanafani

At first, the peasantry had no method of getting to Kuwait except the underground railroad. The majority did not have credentials to show the British Consulate in Jerusalem or Baghdad, which was responsible for issuing visas according to strict procedures during the years that Kuwait was a British Protectorate. The peasantry had nothing to offer except pride in its roots and the promise to adapt, learn quickly, and prove itself in the city as it had in the countryside. Most of the peasants and refugees had no contacts to help them; their relatives were generally as helpless as they were.

Therefore, the only route to survival open to them was the underground railroad. All through the 1950s, the peasants had to enter a humiliating world of suffering. As humiliating as it was, the peasants swallowed their pride and grabbed the opportunity to move to Kuwait. The majority were like the earlycomer intelligentsia, young males in their early twenties, many only fifteen or sixteen. They were the ones who ultimately saved many Palestinian peasants.[11] As in the case of the intelligentsia, the effective family network and, as a by-product of crisis, the extended family network, depended on those young men.

In all of this the power of the family and its role in controlling and motivating individual behavior is apparent. To the majority of those who came via the underground, the family was the central reason for their decision to move to Kuwait. No doubt, many with fewer family

66

responsibilities were motivated by the need to improve their economic lot, or joined the underground railroad because they saw everyone else doing so. But the desire to protect and support the family was the single strongest motivation.

The underground railroad, thus, is quite important to the Palestinian family and to network formation in Kuwait. It was a mechanism developed by the effective and extended family networks for bringing family members to Kuwait. Once they arrived, a bridge was formed between the sending and the receiving ends. Family members in Kuwait sent information about the trip to relatives in the village. They described the trip, its costs, and even gave names of individuals in villages and Bedouin settlements in Syria and Iraq from whom support could be sought.

A particular group making the trip was not composed only of kin, although frequently relatives banded together. Individuals from the same village or refugee camp or from nearby villages would also arrange trips together. In most areas there had to be someone at the other end to receive the arriving Palestinians. The first to leave were the most adventurous of all. Each village had its pioneers who left the homeland with no one at the receiving end to assist them.

Between 1951 and the mid-1950s, the underground railroad took thousands of peasants to northern Syria, on the Turkish border. From Qamishly, in northern Syria, they went to the village of Tel Kotchek on the Syrian-Iraqi border, where sympathetic villagers usually provided help to cross into Iraq. Under cover of night, groups of Palestinian peasants crossed the border. They walked through the agricultural lands of northwestern Iraq, where they traveled for fifteen to twenty hours before reaching a village or a Bedouin settlement where they could ask for help. After several days of hiding during the day and walking during the night, they reached al-Musil, a city in northern Iraq located eighty miles from Tel Kotchek. From there they went to Baghdad and then to Basra by train.

Once in Basra they had to find the connection that would take them across the desert to Kuwait. These guides were usually found in Basra's hotels. Hundreds of Palestinians arrived at these hotels every couple of months. Daily, men and boys who had made the proper arrangements with the dalil (the man hired for taking the group across the border) moved out of the hotel into the border area. They crossed the 80-mile desert strip on foot from Basra to Jahra (located 20 miles from Kuwait City). The trip was dangerous and the group had to evade Kuwaiti as well as Iraqi patrols, which meant they often walked up to 120 miles.

Scores of people from every village died in the desert. In many cases, the dalil abandoned the group or lied and told them that the lights they saw at night were from Kuwait City or Jahra. In one incident, nine

67

villagers from Silwad lost their way. Their relatives in Kuwait informed the Kuwaiti authorities, but when the army found them, they had died of exposure.[12]

Even those who went by sea suffered. The route was through the Fao area on the Iraqi side of Shatt al Arab, near the Kuwaiti border. Dalils could easily deceive the sea-borne Palestinians at night. They frequently provided incorrect information about the proximity of the shore and the shallowness of the water, so when the villagers went into the water, thinking it was a short swim or a short walk in shallow water, they discovered it was very distant and deep. Many of them drowned.

Hundreds of Palestinians were captured in Syria, Iraq, or Kuwait, after being smuggled in or while attempting to enter. After arrest and deportation, the desperate majority repeated the attempt; they had little alternative. By the mid-1950s, when Jordanian-Iraqi relations improved, the underground trail ceased to traverse Syria. The Palestinians could then travel directly to Baghdad and then to Basra.

The total number of those who came to Kuwait through the underground trail is not known, but it was at least several thousand. The trail continued in full operation until the late 1950s, after which travel between Kuwait and Jordan ceased to be regulated by visas or entry permits. Even when visas were reintroduced, the trail was not reactivated because of the improved conditions of the Palestinian people.

Muhammad Sa^{c}id Mansur, from the village of Bal^{c}a in the Tulkarim area, who was in the Kuwaiti army for twenty years, remembers the underground railroad. He could not go to Iraq directly from Jordan. His only route was to travel through Syria to Qamishly in northern Syria and then to the village of Mashrafiya on the Iraqi-Syrian border. In May 1953, after spending the night at the house of the shaykh of the town, he and two other Palestinians were helped to get to a place called the Rabi^c Center. However, on their way to the city of Musil, they were arrested by Iraqi police. In prison, they met many Palestinians who had been jailed for their participation in the underground railroad. One of them was Bakri al-Saddiq, who later became a successful entrepreneur in Kuwait. All eleven in the cell were deported to Tel Kotchek on the Iraqi-Syrian border, where they stayed in a Syrian prison for a few days.

After being deported to Syria, Mansur repeated the attempt from the Iraqi border with Jordan. When he arrived at the Iraqi border, he discovered, as he was trying to enter legally, that he was blacklisted because of his previous attempt. He pleaded with the officers in charge to allow him to go to Baghdad, in the company of the police, to clear his name, and they agreed. He failed to get a permit to stay in Iraq, but he escaped. From there he went to Basra, where all the Palestinians joined the underground railroad. In Basra, he stayed in the Dajlah Hotel, whose owner was helping Palestinians to get to Kuwait. In a month, a dalil was available. Mansur and several other Palestinians moved to the port of Fao. The dalil left them there in the open for two days without food or water before showing up again. Forty individuals from Iraq, Iran, and Palestine sailed for two days until they reached the shores of Salmiyah, six miles south of the inner city of Kuwait.[13]

Another account of the underground railroad was provided by Ahmad Msamih, who arrived in Kuwait at the age of sixteen in January 1954. Msamih was born in Shwaykih, near the town of Tulkarim. He had to leave school at the age of ten to support his family after the death of his father in 1948. For as little as 1.5 qirch per day, equivalent to no more than $3.00, he worked from sunrise to sunset in Tulkarim. He decided to go to Kuwait. He traveled by boat to Salmiyah. With him were twenty-five Palestinians from the villages of Dhinnabih, Shwaykih, and Dayr al-Ghussun, located near the city of Tulkarim. On arrival, the group managed to get help to get to Kuwait City. At the city's main gate, the authorities captured some of the Palestinians, but Msamih escaped.

In 1955, Msamih returned to the West Bank to see his mother and brothers and sisters. Since he could not find a job there, he decided to return to Kuwait. He had no visa or residence permit, and so had to again use the underground railroad. This time, he went by land. In al-Zubayr, near Basra, he met Bedouins who helped him cross the desert. He and a friend, Khalil Zaynah from Gaza, rode a camel for two nights. During the day, they hid in the desert from Iraqi and Kuwaiti border patrols. Msamih's thoughts kept turning to the irony of being pushed into the desert by forces beyond his control.[14]

Another account is that of Ibrahim Harb, originally from the village of Silwad in the West Bank. Harb was displaced in 1948 from Haifa, where he had moved to work. After returning to Silwad, like many others from his village who had worked in Haifa and Jaffa as laborers and craftsmen, he discovered that he had no chance of finding work. He had no choice but to go to Nazareth every week or two across the barbed wire, through the routes used by smugglers to ask money of his two brothers. Then he decided to travel via the underground railroad to Kuwait. He went to Qamishly, then to Tel Kotchek. But before he could cross the border, he was arrested, along with a whole group of Palestinians, by the Syrians. Local Syrian villagers exerted pressure on the local officials, so the group was set free. Then villagers from Tel Kotchek arranged a dalil to take the group across the border to Iraq. After thirteen hours of walking, they reached a small Bedouin settlement. The Bedouins took over from the dalil and arranged for the group's safe arrival in the city of Musil in northern Iraq. They continued by train to Baghdad and Basra.[15]

Jamil Dursiyah, a sixteen-year-old Palestinian Bedouin from the Hawarith Valley between Jaffa and Haifa, who was displaced in 1948, decided to join the trail after striking a Jordanian officer during a refugee mass protest in Tulkarim in 1953. The refugees were protesting the bad conditions in the camps. The only way to escape possible imprisonment and ill treatment was to run away. He joined a group of twenty-five men from Dhinnabih, ᶜAttil, and other villages around Tulkarim, who were on their way via the underground railroad to Kuwait.[16]

Separation and the End of a System

The Palestinian villagers who traveled to Kuwait on the underground railroad never forgot the sadness of their experience. Separation from their families weighed heavily on the thousands of villagers who moved to Kuwait. One of their saddest memories was of the day they left their home village, and in particular of the evening preceding their departure. During that evening, members of the village, many friends and relatives from surrounding villages, in addition to all the family came to the houses of those leaving to bid them farewell. Those who remained in the village saw the leaving of the young men as the beginning of a process which would slowly drain their village of its best people, yet everyone was aware of the necessity of their going.

It was hardest on the parents who stayed in the village. The extended family was the basic unit of economic and family survival.[17] The father had all his children, including the married men and their wives, living in his household. All obeyed him, respected him, and accorded him total and unquestioned obedience. To the father, a large family was a source of pride and self-fulfillment.[18]

The mother was also quite influential in the extended family. She ruled over her sons and arranged their marriages. She made sure they married good women who would obey her, respect her, and not turn her sons from her.[19] She was supreme among her sons and daughters. They, in return, were close to her, usually emotionally closer than to the father. Her best days were those when she was surrounded by her sons, who were rarely far from home.[20]

The breakdown of this family system and the sudden changes in the socioeconomic experiences of the Palestinian peasantry were painful. However, it is important to realize, as Lutfiyya's study of a West Bank village in 1966 demonstrates, that such a breakdown did not hit all villages equally, nor did it mean a total end to the extended family system.[21] The breakdown always depended on the degree and extent of migration in each village and area. For example, the Hebron villages experienced much

70

weaker migration tendencies, which may have contributed to the longer survival of the extended family as a system there. But for the refugees who were uprooted and the thousands of West Bank residents who were migrating, the physical collapse of the extended family was definite. Previously, every generation of peasants had passed through the life cycle of the extended family and had finally become heads of their own extended families. The middle generation of the 1950s, which was displaced, did not pass through this final phase. The older generation of the villages in the West Bank hit by migration watched as their sons left, never to return except for short visits. Married daughters had to stay alone while husbands went to the Gulf. Suddenly, the extended family was physically dislocated, leaving the mother and the father alone in the household. For the first time, the generational relationship was reversed. The older generation became dependent on the support of their children in Kuwait. They lost social and economic power, lost their family, a heavy price to pay for Palestinian displacement. Ahmad Msamih and many others who witnessed the disintegration of the extended family during the early 1950s recall how elderly parents walked the streets of the village with their eyes full of tears during the first few months after their sons' departure. Traveling just to nearby Nablus or Kafar Qaddum was considered by a Palestinian from Shwaykih a "ghurba" (estrangement), how could they consider traveling to the Gulf and Kuwait, which lay beyond the deserts?[22]

When the young men arrived in Kuwait and news of their safe arrival reached their village or refugee camp in the West Bank, the parents and family received visits and congratulations from the whole town. When news of loss or death in the desert reached the village, sadness overshadowed the whole village as family and parents passed through the sorrow and grief of bereavement.[23]

Arrival in Kuwait: The Early Experiences of the Peasantry

Joining the Village Network

The earlycomer peasants who arrived in Kuwait entered a most challenging struggle for survival. They were pioneers who opened up the routes to themselves and their families by literally walking to what they perceived as the "end of the world" in search of a decent life. They followed a set of basic strategies. Once they arrived at the inner city of Kuwait, these strategies laid the groundwork for their socioeconomic transformation.

The first thing every new peasant arrival did was to search for the family and townspeople who had arrived previously. On both the village and the family levels, this behavior strengthened ties and mutual support. Everyone who arrived had an address of a relative or someone from home who was in Kuwait.[24]

Once the villager found his family contact, the process of adaptation to Kuwait and to the new environment became easier. The new arrivals all remembered how sad they were to leave the family and the village, but how comforting it was to find friends and relatives from the village. To them, this constituted an element of security and proper introduction to Kuwait. Through such relationships, the arriving peasants learned how to manage their day-to-day affairs and how to take care of their basic needs. Through these village ties, the new arrival was introduced to the life of Kuwait and its people, culture, and habits.

The most important introductory arrangement was housing. Every new arrival found housing among his family and village network. Through shared housing, the first attempt at some form of collective security was created. Through housing, as well, the first step toward adapting to Kuwait was taken.

As new arrivals were coming to Kuwait from the villages of the West Bank or from its refugee camps, the population and density increased greatly. A whole village society of young bachelors developed in the "Arab houses" of the "mirqab" area located in the city of Kuwait. Each room in a house, or each house, resembled a village or a family, since villagers from the same family kin group or village lived together. Each room held as many people, as many beds, as could be stuffed into it. [25] For example, some villagers from the village of Bayt Safafa lived in a house called the House of the Forty during the 1950s, since it housed forty individuals from the same family. Another house, for the Husayn family of Bayt Safafa, was called by the arriving villagers al-Qattan House, since it resembled a two-story house built on a hill in the former village.[26]

Once the villagers' family network was formed following their arrival in Kuwait, they started looking for work. Again, relatives and home village ties were basic to the process of finding a job. They provided the peasant with the information needed to find a job. They led their arriving relatives to the inner city of Kuwait, where the unofficial labor market operated. In such places, hundreds of peasants who had come through the underground railroad assembled in order to be hired. Many new arrivals found jobs in the same departments or at the same construction sites where their townspeople and relatives worked.

During the early stages of adaptation, the concept of family started to take on a new meaning. Cousins who had feuded in the sending village decided to make peace. Distant cousins who had not interacted very often in the village shared the same room. Again, dormant relationships were activated by crisis and became effective relationships.

These incipient patterns of adaptation by means of the family network are another demonstration of the family's power to aid recovery from the 1948 war. Whereas other institutions were destroyed, the family survived the trauma and led the way in the immediate aftermath of the disaster. Just as in peasant migrations in Africa and Latin America, the family played an important role in bringing Palestinian migrants to the new environment and in facilitating their arrival and leading them through a process of adaptation to life in Kuwait.

Peasant-Intelligentsia Relations

A more significant source of employment for the bulk of the arriving peasantry, came primarily from the efforts of the Palestinian intelligentsia residing in Kuwait, and from Kuwaiti government officials and private investors, who were quite sympathetic to the displaced Palestinians. In all cases, the efforts of the intelligentsia were coordinated with those of the Kuwaiti officials. Kuwait's ambitious expansion was an important reason for the enhanced ability of the intelligentsia to help. In fact, the cooperation of the intelligentsia in helping to employ thousands of arriving peasants, marked the rise of a new Palestinian society in Kuwait cross-cutting peasant-urban relations.

To meet the developmental needs of the country, job interviews with these peasants were conducted on a mass scale, mostly by Palestinians who had been appointed because of their level of education. During the interview, the peasant was asked if he could read and write and if he had any previous work experience. Many were just sixteen years old or had no work experience outside of agriculture and were illiterate. Immediately after the interview, the applicant was assigned a job as an assistant cook, laborer on a construction site, driver, pipe fitter, or assistant foreman, depending on previous work experience and skill.[27]

The new job became a great learning and training experience, as it was intended to be by those employing the arriving peasants. In a few months, these new workers became skilled and capable of working without supervision. In a few years, they became foremen or electricians.

Jamil Dursiyah, a Palestinian of Bedouin origin from the Hawarith Valley who came to Kuwait at the age of sixteen in 1953, remembers that experience. After meeting his relatives, he went to the head of engineers in the Department of Public Works, Muhammad Khalaf, a Palestinian.[28] Dursiyah and many others were hired by Muhammad Khalaf. The Department of Public Works needed labor, and thousands of Palestinian laborers were pouring into the country.

73

Yusif Abuljubayn, the earlycomer from Jaffa, recalls how every day several young Palestinian men approached him at his work site asking for jobs.[29] He immediately hired them and was surprised at how hard they worked and how fast they learned. At one point, the Department of Public Works, where Abuljubayn had worked since 1953 as a superintendent, needed mechanics to meet the demands resulting from the increasing numbers of cars, trucks, and tractors in the department. Abuljubayn informed his superiors in the ministry that he would solve the problem in a couple of months. The second day he went to the site, there were hundreds of Palestinian peasants waiting to be hired. He immediately hired as many as he needed as assistant mechanics and, after two months of training on the site, he had an army of mechanics.

Through such experiences, the peasants were transformed into semiskilled and skilled laborers. And through support by the more fortunate earlycomer members of the intelligentsia, the peasants' chances of survival were enhanced. A mutual relation of support and dependence in the public and private sectors developed over time between the intelligentsia and the peasantry. It cut across city, village, and town lines and provided a much-needed link between the different Palestinian strata that were beginning to rebuild their structures. These people shared the same history, grievances, homeland, insecurities, refugee status, and dreams. They were motivated to ask about each other and look after each other. By so doing, they established a link with pre-1948 Palestinian society. During the 1950s, the embryonic form of a new Palestinian society in the diaspora was well-established.

The Work and Education Ethic: A Pass to Family Survival

The process of transformation implied quite a commitment to the hard conditions of labor in Kuwait. Many lived at the construction site. Conditions were quite difficult, particularly during the summer, when the temperature was between 110° F. to 120°F. Each one wanted to work as many hours as possible to satisfy family income needs in the refugee camp or village. Many even held two jobs, working fifteen to sixteen hours a day. Sa°id Khuri of Consolidated Contractors Company (CCC) was shocked by the amount of work to which these people committed themselves. In Yemen, where his company operated in the mid-1950s, he hired hundreds of Palestinian peasants who were coming to that country.

> When I gave them ten hours of daily work, they were not
> satisfied. They wanted more. When I raised it to fifteen,
> they still wanted more. They wanted to work and work,

day and night, to make up for the loss and suffering their families had to endure. Each one of them had a father, mother, grandparents, and seven to eight brothers and sisters to worry about.[30]

Yihya Ghannam, who headed the department responsible for agricultural development in Kuwait, was equally impressed by this phenomenon.[31] This motivated him to hire hundreds of Palestinian farmers to work on agricultural projects in Kuwait. Because he knew farmers and peasants from his days in Palestine, he could recruit those who could best do the job. Everyone was a hard worker; anyone who was not prepared to work hard did not come to Kuwait because its living conditions were enormously difficult. Kuwait became known as a country of hard, endless work, a country transformed into a construction site.

Hard work allowed the peasants to achieve two important tasks in addition to direct support of their families. First, they adapted to city jobs. They were transformed from unskilled to semiskilled and skilled laborers. This transformation took place in the overwhelming majority of Palestinian unskilled laborers in Kuwait, so now there are few Palestinian manual laborers. Many rose slowly in the hierarchy of the public sector. Many became junior or senior staff members in the oil companies. Others headed departments related to their acquired technical skills.

Many other former peasants became successful in the private sector. For instance, Ahmad Msamih of Shwaykih, who came through the underground railroad in 1954, became a wealthy entrepreneur.[32] During the 1950s, he started one of the earliest matahin in the country. Such stores roast, grind, and sell coffee, nuts, and spices. They are now spread all over the Middle East. In the beginning, he distributed nuts on a bicycle as an employee of another store. After learning the business, he bought equipment and started distributing nuts from his home. The business developed quickly. By 1955, he and his partner opened a store, al-Mathanah al-Duwaliyah, which is still one of the most successful of such businesses in Kuwait. The young boy who had to support his family at the age of twelve after the death of his father was, in the 1980s, able to make a major donation toward the construction of a school in his West Bank village.

Bakri al-Siddiq of Dhinnabih (near Tulkarim), who came through the underground railroad, had an experience similar to that of Msamih.[33] He became the owner of a construction company in Kuwait. All he started with was the will to succeed and an entrepreneurial mentality. While working as a foreman in the public sector, he contracted on his own to rebuild some of the old Arab houses that were destroyed in Kuwait during heavy rains in 1954. This project launched his career. Meanwhile, he

75

corresponded with an Egyptian institute and earned a degree qualifying him as assistant construction engineer. By the 1960s, he was able to provide financial support to the embryonic Palestinian nationalist movement. He also supported Palestinian education by cofounding and contributing to Mibarrat al-Siddiq (al-Siddiq Benevolent Society).

There is a widespread commitment among the Palestinians to support West Bank and Gaza institutions such as schools, hospitals, and universities. In Kuwait, as in other centers of the Palestinian diaspora, leading contributions have come from members of the rising Palestinian bourgeoisie. Many of the facilities of Palestinian universities, for example, have been built by means of such contributions. Such donations are not tax exempt. They are the result of a perception of group existence that realizes the link between the Palestinian future and the occupied Palestinian homeland.

The bulk of the achievement of this group consisted of the former peasants becoming skilled laborers, technicians, and owners of small businesses. The majority rose up the socioeconomic ladder, but within limits. Their main contribution lay in supporting the education of family members. In fact, the complexity of life in Kuwait and the diaspora created an obsession with education within the Palestinian peasantry also. When loss of land became a fact, investment in the mind, which cannot be confiscated by any power, became a way of survival. The obsession with education after 1948 was heightened as each family member told younger brothers and sisters, or sons and daughters, about their experiences and the experiences of their friends and relatives. These stories told of the helplessness that engulfed the nondegree holders among the Palestinians, compared to the greater opportunities of the better educated refugees.

The generation of peasants who went to Kuwait on the underground railroad sent their younger siblings to school and sent at least some of their brothers and sisters to college. By the early 1960s, a new generation of peasant Palestinians had graduated from college. Many of these new graduates were issued visas and came to Kuwait as pharmacists, doctors, engineers, draftsmen, technicians, and teachers. After a few years, they began to educate their older brothers' children, thus continuing the cycle.[34]

This trend among all Palestinians has made their level of education one of the highest in the world. In fact, the ratio of Palestinian students in college to the Palestinian population as a whole in 1976 was twenty per thousand.[35] In the same year the ratio for the Arab world as a whole was four per thousand. The ratio in 1975 for the United States was thirty per thousand, for the U.S.S.R., eighteen, France, nine, and England, eight.[36]

The older generation of peasants also sought ways to educate itself. Though the majority learned on the job, many acquired technical degrees and high school degrees while they were in their thirties. Yusif Abuljubayn was quite surprised to discover fifteen years later that some of the individuals whom he had hired as manual laborers and who had several years ahead of them to finish high school, had graduated from high school or earned a college degree. These were individuals who saved money and entered college after earning a high school degree through night study.[37]

A hypothesis advanced concerning the Jewish diaspora contends that "Jews, compared to the rest of the population, invested relatively more heavily in human than physical capital because human capital is more portable and difficult to confiscate than physical capital."[38] It seems that groups such as the Jews who are discriminated against and who have had "physical capital confiscated in the past might tend to take the probability of confiscation of an asset into consideration when making an investment."[39] According to Jamil al-Budayri, assistant general secretary of the Fund for Palestinian Higher Education, "Exiled populations who are constantly experiencing persecution learn to store their abilities in their minds."[40] In this context, Reuven Brenner and Nicholas Kiefer found the relative similarity between the Palestinians and the neighboring Arab states before 1948 in educational and occupational structures severely altered afterward.[41] Since 1948 Palestinians "in Arab countries seem to have developed an educational and occupational structure strikingly similar to that of Jews in the United States."[42]

According to Don Peretz, what explains the Palestinian "hunger for education" is that "most Palestinians, including the refugees, lived in or near to urban centers."[43] This resulted in their ability to rapidly adjust "to modern city life, developing aspirations for upward mobility and economic security found among all modern urban minorities."[44] "Like diaspora Jews and Armenians, Palestinians became a quasi-elite in many Arab countries such as Kuwait, Libya, and other oil states which were short of skilled labor."[45]

Conclusion

The peasants who came to Kuwait suffered even more from alienation than their urbanite countrymen. Whereas the urbanites had more education, a familiarity with city jobs and crafts, and a deeply entrenched entrepreneurial mentality, the peasants enjoyed few of these advantages. Their key to survival in the city of Kuwait was their physical strength, acquired from working the land, which they utilized in performing their manual jobs in Kuwait. But to succeed in Kuwait and meet the challenges confronting them, they had to change many of their old ways. They had to work much harder than any job in agriculture would require. They had to accept jobs (such as plumbing) that in Palestine were considered low in status. They subjected many of their notions about work and status to the test of survival.

The earlycomer peasants were the spearheads in the development of family networks. These pioneers brought their families to Kuwait and educated their younger brothers and sisters. With the passage of time, each family created its own network in Kuwait. The original decision to come to Kuwait, the underground railroad, and the early experiences of adaptation were all family oriented. In this subgroup of the Palestinian diaspora, the family network became central to the process of responding to the challenge of displacement.

NOTES

1. Rosemary Sayigh, <u>Palestinians: From Peasants to Revolutionaries</u> (London: Zed Press, 1979), pp. 13-14.

2. Ibid., p. 14.

3. "The Economic and Social Situation and Potential of the Palestine Arab People in the Region of Western Asia," study presented to the United Nations Economic Commission for West Asia by TEAM International (1983), p. 71.

4. Hani Hurani, "Mugaddimat Nushu' al-tabaqah al-ᶜamilah wa al-harakah al-naqabiyah fi al-'Urdun: 1950-1947" ["Introductions in the Rise of the Working Class and the Union Movement in Jordan: 1950-1957"], <u>Shu'un Filistiniyah</u> 85 (December 1978):80.

5. The people who used to live in this area provided the same account. See Avi Plascov, "The Palestinians of Jordan's Border," in <u>Studies in the Economic and Social History of Palestine in the 19th and 20th Centuries,</u> ed. Roger Owen (Carbondale: Southern Illinois University Press, 1982), pp. 203-206.

6. Interview with Abd al-Ilah Qasim, of Singil, and with villagers who lived in the West Bank during that time, Kuwait, summer 1985.

7. Simha Flapan, "Israelis and Palestinians: Can They Make Peace?" <u>Journal of Palestine Studies</u> 15, no. 1, 57 (Autumn 1985):58, 27.

8. For a well-documented study on the subject of preventing Palestinians from return, see Benny Morris, "The Harvest of 1948 and the Creation of the Palestinian Refugee Problem," <u>Middle East Journal</u> 40, no. 4, (Autumn 1986):671-685; see also Nafez Nazzal, <u>The Palestinian Exodus</u>

from Galilee, 1948 (Beirut: Institute of Palestine Studies, 1978), pp. 28-64; Sayigh, Palestinians.

9. During my research, I discovered that villagers from this area were not as numerous in Kuwait as in the rest of the West Bank. Abd al-Ilah Qasim provided me with many accounts of the migration trend to the United States. His previous work as investigator in the Mirqab police station, the area in Kuwait where most of the Palestinian peasantry came to reside, allowed him access to much useful information.

10. Ghassan Kanafani, Men in the Sun and Other Palestinian Stories, trans. Hilary Kilpatrick (Washington, D.C.: Three Continents Press, 1978), p. 39.

11. The information on use of the underground railroad is based on interviews with twenty Palestinian peasants who reported their experience and the experiences of others whom they knew.

12 Interview with Ibrahim Harb of Silwad, Kuwait, summer 1985.

13. Interview with Muhammad Mansur, Kuwait, summer 1985.

14. Interview with Ahmad Msamih, Kuwait, summer 1985.

15. Interview with Ibrahim Harb, Kuwait, summer 1985.

16. Interview with Jamil Dursiyah, Kuwait, summer 1985.

17. Sayigh, Palestinians, pp. 20-23.

18. For a description of the extended Middle Eastern family, see H. Ammar, "The Social Organization of the Community," Readings in Arab Middle Eastern Society and Cultures, ed. Abdulla M. Lutfiyya and Charles W. Churchill (The Hague: Mouton, 1970), pp. 109-134.

19. Yvonne Haddad, "Palestinian Women: Patterns of Legitimation and Domination," in The Sociology of the Palestinians, ed. Khalil Nakhleh and Elia Zuriek (New York: St. Martin's Press, 1980), p. 152.

20. Ibid.

21. See Abdulla M. Lutfiyya, Baytin, a Jordanian Village: A Study of Social Institutions and Social Change in a Folk Community (London: Mouton, 1966), pp. 142-167.

22. Interview with Ahmad Msamih and other Palestinians, Kuwait, summer 1985.

23. Ibid.

24 Based on interviews with twenty individuals who used the underground railroad.

25. Based on interviews with villagers and also with Abd al-Ilah Qasim, who was the investigator at the Mirqab police station during the 1960s, Kuwait, summer 1985.

26. Interview with Ahmad ᶜUthman, Kuwait, summer 1985.

27. Based on interviews with twenty peasant arrivals via the underground railroad. A similar account was provided by members of the intelligentsia who were active in interviewing or hiring Palestinians.

28. Interview with Jamil Dursiyah, Kuwait, summer 1985.

29. Interview with Yusif Abuljubayn, Kuwait, summer 1985.

30. Interview with Sa^cid Khuri, Kuwait, summer 1985.

31. Interview with Yihya Ghannam, Kuwait, summer 1985.

32. Interview with Ahmad Msamih, Kuwait, summer 1985.

33. Interview with Bakri al-Siddiq, Kuwait, summer 1985.

34. Based on interviews with the twenty persons in the sample who came via the underground railroad.

35. Muhammad Hallaj, "The Mission of Palestinian Higher Education," Journal of Palestine Studies 9, no. 4, issue 36 (Summer 1980):77. See also Nabeel Shaath, "High Level Palestinian Manpower," Journal of Palestine Studies 1, no. 2 (Winter 1972):80-95; Muhsin D. Yusuf, "The Potential Impact of Palestinian Education on a Palestinian State," Journal of Palestine Studies 8, no. 4 (Summer 1979):70-93.

36. Hallaj, "The Mission of Palestinian Higher Education," p. 76.

37. Interview with Yusif Abuljubayn, Kuwait, summer 1985.

38. Reuven Brenner and Nicholas Kiefer, "The Economics of the Diaspora: Discrimination and Occupational Structure," Economic Development and Cultural Change 29, 3 (April 1981):518.

39. Ibid.

40. Interview with Jamil al-Budayri, Kuwait, summer 1985.

41. Brenner and Kiefer, "The Economics of the Diaspora," p. 518.

42. Ibid.

43. D. Peretz, A. M. Wilson, and R. J. Ward, A Palestine Entity (Washington, D.C.: Middle East Institute, 1970), p. 32.

44. Ibid.

45. Ibid.

5

The Family as a Cross-National Entity

No understanding of the Palestinian family in Kuwait is possible without a good grasp of the most important aspect of every Palestinian family--its cross-national character. The unique events leading to Palestinian dispersion affected the family, settling it in clusters from one end of the diaspora to the other. Even though the original displacement was all to the West Bank, Lebanon, Syria, Gaza, or Egypt, after a decade or so, migration for the sake of physical survival made families in the West Bank or in Lebanon part of a wider network. Those who went to Kuwait helped bring part of their families also to Kuwait. The same practice was followed by those who went to Saudi Arabia, Qatar, Chile, or Detroit. In no case was there ever again a complete, permanent regrouping of the pre-1948 family.

The ongoing struggle for survival as a family in the diaspora has been further complicated by the extended family having become a cross-national entity, dispersed throughout the Middle East and even, for many, throughout Africa, Asia, and the Western World. It is quite a challenge to maintain solidarity as a family when each subunit is separated geographically, and holds different national citizenship. It is especially difficult for parents to be separated from their grown sons and daughters, who have sought opportunity in distant places, even sometimes residing on a different continent. Figure 3 illustrates the fragmented nature of each family network.

Figure 3: Local and Cross-national Networks

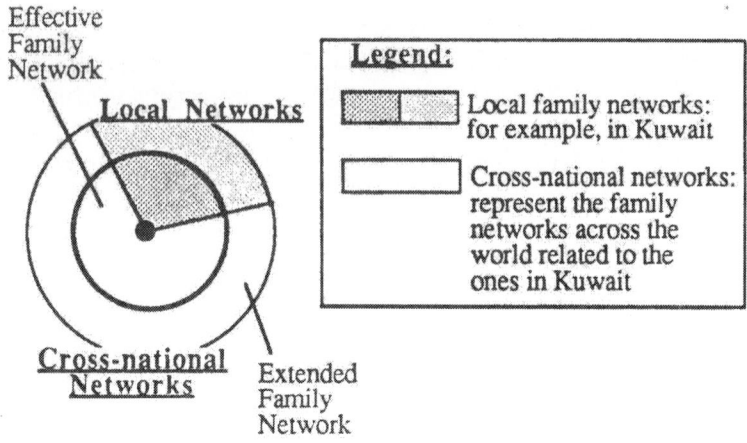

Effective Family Network

Local Networks

Cross-national Networks

Extended Family Network

Legend:

Local family networks: for example, in Kuwait

Cross-national networks: represent the family networks across the world related to the ones in Kuwait

The following three case studies demonstrate this overall demographic pattern. They show how the arrival of one individual to a country sets the stage for chain migration. They also show the extent of dispersion of each family and describe the citizenship and travel documents they carry.

The Qamar Family

The Qamar family is a Christian family from Jerusalem that was displaced in 1948. The grandfather, Banayut Qamar, was born in Jerusalem in 1850. The family knows little of Banayut's father and grandfathers. Banayut was a gunsmith in Jerusalem until his death in 1917. In 1884, he built a house in al-Misrarah, one of West Jerusalem's Arab neighborhoods, and started his own household.[1]

Banayut's son, Ibrahim, was born in 1888. In 1910, Ibrahim graduated from the CMS teaching college in Palestine. He immediately started teaching in Gaza. In 1914, he added a second floor to the house built by his father and married Nazirah Jahshan, a daughter of one of Gaza's Christian Arab families. That same year, he returned to Jerusalem, where he resided until 1938. In Jerusalem, he taught in several private and public schools.[2] Ibrahim's career as a successful math teacher during a time when only secondary education was available, brought him fame throughout Palestine. In 1938, he went to Gaza once again on a teaching assignment

82

for the CMS. His family remained in Jerusalem and he commuted until his death in 1942.

Ibrahim's eleven children were all born and reared in Jerusalem in the family house in al-Misrarah. They all held Palestinian citizenships and passports. In 1948, however, when Zionist military pressure on West Jerusalem increased immediately after the Dayr Yasin massacre, the family took shelter in East Jerusalem, living together in a room provided by the Lutheran Church. Two of Ibrahim's daughters, Mary and Fahimah, who were married and living in Bak^{c}ah al-Fawqah, another Arab neighborhood in West Jerusalem, also moved with their families and joined their mother, brothers, and sisters. During their stay, which lasted a month and a half, Fahimah gave birth to twins, Kamil and Kamilya, adding to the already crowded population of the room.

Part of the room was destroyed when East Jerusalem was shelled by the Zionists. At this point, both daughters moved with their husbands to Amman. The rest of the family moved to ^{c}Ayzariyah in the West Bank, where they sought shelter in the Russian Orthodox Church.

The family's survival choices had narrowed. The most accomplished member of the family and the one most capable of leading it through the first years after 1948 was the eldest daughter, Jawharah. By the end of 1948, she had moved to Damascus and found a teaching job. She was a graduate of a teaching college in Jerusalem and had previous experience. Jawharah, like many women in the post-1948 diaspora, took on the burden of the whole family. Her case is not one of a self-supporting, educated woman. Rather, she became responsible not only for herself but also for the rest of her family. Such responsibilities were not part of the woman's role before 1948. Jawharah's attitude is typical of the incipient patterns of survival adopted by all earlycomer Palestinians to Kuwait. The emphasis on family survival was so strong that it challenged many long established patterns. Jawharah's degree gave her the ability to lead the family from disaster to safety in a time of severe crisis. Like hundreds of Palestinian women who saved their families after the war, she never married and, in the mid-1960s, acquired an M.A. and an M.S. from two U. S. universities (Oklahoma and Columbia, respectively). She followed in her father's footsteps by having a successful career in math education, particularly after moving to Jordan in the late 1960s.

Jawharah's move to Damascus motivated her sisters, Jurjina, Salma, Afaf, Kawkab, Suhaylah, their brother ^{c}Isa, and their mother to follow. In Damascus they were all registered as refugees and their Palestinian passports were taken from them to be replaced by the stateless refugee travel document. (Syria, Lebanon, Egypt, and Iraq have issued such documents to Palestinian refugees in 1948.)

Soon after the family moved, Jurjina, who had married before leaving East Jerusalem, started the second independent family household in Syria. Afaf followed suit, and in a short period, Kawkab married a German national who worked in Beirut. They later moved to Germany and started a German chapter of the Qamar family. In two years, ᶜIsa completed high school in Damascus and went to the U.S. to Southern Methodist University in Dallas, Texas. He graduated as an engineer, stayed in the United States, and thereby formed a family chapter on another continent.

Two brothers (and the two married sisters who went to Amman) did not come to Damascus with Jawharah and the rest of the family in 1948. Banayut, the eldest son of Ibrahim, had been sent to college in the United States in 1937. He graduated in 1941 from the University of California at Berkeley as a civil engineer. He then married and stayed in the United States. He initiated another U. S. chapter of the family. The other brother, George, was studying in Great Britain during the events of 1948. When he graduated in 1950, he came to Damascus, where he worked and helped his family. In 1957, he traveled to Kuwait with his wife, a Palestinian from Haifa. He remained in Kuwait and thereby established a Qamar chapter there.

Fahimah and her husband, a member of the Farah family of Gaza, stayed in Amman. But Mary and her husband, who is also from Gaza's Farah family, went back to East Jerusalem in the West Bank in 1950. There they both worked with the United Nations Relief and Works Agency (UNRWA) until the mid-1970s. As their children grew and came to study in the United States, and as the pressure of Israeli occupation since 1967 became unbearable, they decided in 1980 to migrate to Canada. Their children faced another dilemma. Upon completion of their education, they could not find work in the occupied Palestinian territories and therefore had no alternative but to seek work elsewhere. One child was denied the right to return to his native city because he had not renewed his residency permit at the right time.

Thus, eleven brothers and sisters found themselves scattered across Syria, Jordan, Kuwait, Canada, the United States, and Germany. Their citizenship or travel documents ranged from stateless (all of those who stayed in Damascus and their children) to Jordanian, German, Canadian, and American. The family lost everything but themselves when the Israelis moved into West Jerusalem and confiscated their property. The Qamar family has not been allowed to return to al-Musrarah or to their house, which is still occupied by a Jewish family. Despite everything, though, the Qamar family has maintained a strong relationship. They have always kept their channels of communication open and have continually rallied to the support of each other, as they did in the aftermath of the 1948 displacement.

The Sammur Household

The Sammur family of Dayr Yasin is one of the village's major families. In 1948, the family comprised several extended households. In each household, parents lived with their married and unwed children. The average size of each household was thirty to forty members. The following account concerns one household.

This household, another example of a single patriarchal household, composed of four brothers with their wives and children in addition to their married children and their wives (totaling fifty-five), became another dispersed cross-national entity. Of the twenty-seven children of the four brothers, one was killed during the massacre of Dayr Yasin and the rest were dispersed as follows: four in the West Bank, ten in the East Bank of Jordan, five in Saudi Arabia, four in Kuwait, two in Qatar, and one in Paris.[3]

The family grew larger as those who were married had more children and others got married after 1948. There were 133 family members, descendants of the male line in the household, by 1985. If all descendants of men and women who lived in the household are included, the total rises to 170. Four of the original 27 brothers married first cousins who lived with them in the household. Most of the rest have married members of other Sammur households, or people from Dayr Yasin. The four brothers, and therefore, their descendants became Jordanian citizens, except for one, who later acquired U. S. citizenship.

The four brothers were sons of Sammur Musa Sammur, who originally built the house in Dayr Yasin this family lived in. Sammur was born in 1880 in the village of Dayr Yasin and died in 1925. The Sammurs owned quarries in Dayr Yasin and were quite prosperous in pre-1948 Palestine. This enabled them to educate their children. Of the twenty-seven children of the four brothers who owned the house, seventeen were sons. Of these, thirteen held college degrees or were able to complete such degrees immediately after 1948 (three physicians, one Ph.D., four M.A.s or M.A. equivalents, two engineers, and three with bachelor's degrees). None of the women who belonged to the pre-1948 household were formally educated beyond elementary school because of the state of women's education in Palestine before 1948, particularly in the villages. The first female born after 1948, Na^{c}mah, became a teacher in Qatar. She is the first degree holder of the household's female members.

The twenty-seven sons and daughers of the original founders had children who, in turn, moved to different diaspora centers seeking opportunity. As a result, the Sammur's diaspora became wider. They have been gathering almost every summer in Amman over the last three decades. All come to meet, to maintain the close relationship they dearly miss. The household survives through help, meetings, marriages, feasts, and financial support.

With such connectedness at the household level, the memory of Dayr Yasin has survived strongly. Although this household was luckier than many, the family has never forgotten the sadness of the event. The women have never forgotten how, after the massacre, they were captured, insulted, and robbed of all personal belongings. All their jewelry and money were taken before the Israelis put them in trucks that drove them through a nearby settlement where people threw garbage and insulted them until they were handed over to the Red Cross. Such memories run deep through the family and contribute to the family's solidarity and sense of a common heritage of suffering.[4]

The Abuljubayn Family

The Abuljubayn family's roots go back to Shaykh Ibrahim Ahmad al-Matbuli, a religious figure and a scientist, born in the Hijaz in 1660. Shaykh Ibrahim migrated first to Egypt, then to Gaza in 1700. In Gaza, he lived among its Arab population until his death in 1730. Shaykh Ibrahim had three sons. One of them returned to Egypt. Another, Hasan, apparently died early or had no children. The third was ᶜAbd al-wahid al-Matbuli, born in 1690. When his father went to Gaza, he was ten years old. In Gaza, ᶜAbd al-wahid became a religious figure, graduate of al-Azhar in Egypt, and a merchant. He married a Palestinian woman from Gaza and was totally assimilated into the city's Palestinian population, its network of relations and way of life.[5]

In 1715 in Gaza, ᶜAbd al-wahid had a son, Muhammad. Muhammad, like his father and grandfather, graduated from al-Azhar and became a religious figure (shaykh). He also became a successful merchant. He differed from both his grandfather and father in that he was born in Gaza and grew up as a native Gazan. He married a Gazan woman and was the first to be called "Abuljubayn," which means "the man with two pockets," a nickname denoting his generosity. This marked the beginning of the Palestinian Arab family of Abuljubayn.

It is interesting to note that Muhammad's uncle who returned to Egypt established a family there, known by the name of al-Matbuli, that has no contact with the one in Gaza.

Muhammad had four sons. Because of trade opportunities, three of the four migrated to other regions of Palestine, thus spreading the Abuljubayn family. Muhammad's first son, ᶜAbd al-wahid Abuljubayn, migrated to Jaffa. Upon his graduation from al-Azhar, he became a successful merchant and a respected religious figure. He died in 1820. Muhammad's second son, Abdullah, born in Gaza in 1763 and a graduate of al-Azhar and a shaykh moved to Dahriyah near Hebron. Muhammad's third son, born in 1766, moved in 1780 to the Palestinian town of Safad. He also was a graduate of al-Azhar, but became known as a merchant. Only one brother, Ahmad, stayed in Gaza. He was a shaykh and a graduate of al-Azhar.

The branches of the Abuljubayns struck roots. Each of the four sons intermarried with families of the towns to which they migrated, and joined the social network of the place. All of the branches of the Abuljubayn family assimilated so well in the Palestinian towns and cities to which they migrated that they became indistinguishable from the indigenous families. For example, ᶜAbd al-wahid Abuljubayn, Muhammad's first son, who migrated to Jaffa, had a son in 1800. His son, Muhammad, became chief merchant of the City of Jaffa and was one of the first people to build outside the city walls. The area where he built his house was later named Abuljubayn Street. His brother, Hasan, born in 1810, was an Ottoman government employee who had the keys to the gates of Jaffa.

Generally the power of the Palestinian native culture to assimilate foreigners is well documented. For example, though the Crusaders never intended to assimilate, many who stayed behind were absorbed into the Arab Palestinian culture. Many Europeans who migrated to Palestine, for instance, the Germans who established a colony near Haifa and other settlements near Jerusalem, were assimilated into the native culture of Palestine. The Zionists who came to Palestine, much like the Crusaders, never intended to become part of the indigenous culture. They displaced the indigenous Arab population to make room for their concept of Palestine.

The Abuljubayn family, all Palestinian citizens, was in Jaffa, Gaza, Dahriyah, or Safad on the eve of the 1948 trauma. Most of the displaced Safad branch ended up in either Lebanon's or Syria's refugee camps. The members of the Jaffa branch were displaced to Egypt or the West Bank and Jordan. The Gaza branch was provided with refugee travel documents, and many members of this chapter joined the diaspora in search of employment. But many remained in Gaza when it came under Egyptian rule and have been since 1967 under Israeli occupation. Since Dahriyah is located in the West Bank, the Dahriyah branch acquired Jordanian citizenships. But since 1967, this branch, too, has been under Israeli occupation.

After 1948, survival needs dictated that the Abuljubayns rearrange their existence in quite a wide diaspora. Many family members, particularly the young, moved in the 1950s and 1960s to Kuwait and other Gulf states. Some went to the United States and to Great Britain seeking work opportunity, but many stayed in Jordan, Lebanon, Syria, Gaza, or Egypt. The initial physical dispersion stemming from the 1948 displacement was followed, therefore, by a larger dispersal conditioned by the politics of survival.

At present, three chapters of the Abuljubayns (I lack data for the Dahriyah chapter) comprise 349 individuals holding many different citizenships and travel documents. There are 163 Abuljubayns who are citizens of 10 different nations and 186 stateless Abuljubayns with restricted travel documents from 4 different Arab states. (See Table 1.) Since carrying a travel document or being a citizen of a country does not necessarily, in the Palestinian case, coincide with residence, the family is distributed among an even wider range of states. (See Table 2.)

Examples of the educational levels and occupational distribution of this cross-national family may be helpful to the understanding of its various dimensions. Abuljubayn family members have achieved high educational levels. For example, of the Jaffa branch, which totals 242, 107 live at present in Kuwait. They make up the entire Abuljubayn family there except for 4 persons from the Safad branch. Among the Jaffa Abuljubayns in Kuwait who are over twenty-one, 45 percent are college graduates, 36 percent are high school graduates, and 19 percent have achieved intermediate-level education. To check changes occurring in education since 1948 among the Abuljubayns of Kuwait, educational levels were computed by generation. (See Table 3.)

Table 1. Citizenships and Travel Documents of the Abuljubayn Family

Citizenship/Travel Document	Numbers of Holders
Algeria	2
Egypt	3
Great Britain	5
Iraq	8
Jordan	82
Kuwait	4
Lebanon	6
Morocco	1
Syria	34
U.S.A.	18
Egyptian Travel Documents	89
Kuwaiti Travel Documents	3
Lebanese Travel Documents	66
Syrian Travel Documents	28
Total	349

Table 2.   Places of Residence for the Abuljubayn Family

Country	Number in Residence
Algeria	1
Egypt	7
Gaza	47
Great Britain	6
Iraq	7
Jordan	33
Kuwait	107
Lebanon	49
Qatar	10
Saudi Arabia	9
Syria	58
U.S.A.	14
West Bank	1
Total	349

Table 3.   Abuljubayn Educational Levels in Kuwait by Generation

| | % at Level of Education | | |
Date of Birth	Inter-mediate	High School	College
1920-1930	40%	60%	None
1931-1940	23%	54%	23%
1941-1950	9%	9%	82%*
1951-1965	5%	20%	75%
1951-1965 (but left Kuwait)	--	20%	80%

*No doubt, the events of 1948 had a direct effect on the sudden rise in educational achievement for this generation.

The occupations of the Jaffa branch worldwide vary. Of a total of 78 employed members, 12 percent are engineers, 22 percent are managers, and 17 percent own their own businesses. Three percent are doctors, 1

90

percent are actors, 33 percent are Government employees, 6 percent are teachers, 6 percent are technicians. (For the occupations and marriage patterns of the Abuljubayns in Kuwait, see Tables 4 and 5.)

Table 4. Occupations of the Abuljubayn Family in Kuwait

Occupation	Percentage
Managers	26%
Business Owners	21%
Doctors	3%
Engineers	2%
Teachers	10%
Government Employees	33%
Technicians	5%

Table 5. Marriage Patterns Among the Abuljubayns in Kuwait

Nationality of Spouse	Percentage
Palestinian from Jaffa	40%*
Palestinians from other than Jaffa	35%
Non-Palestinian	25%**

*This adds tremendously to their Jaffa network in and out of Kuwait.
**In comparison with other Palestinian families, the Abuljubayns have a high percentage of non-Palestinian marriages.

The participation of women of the Jaffa Abuljubayn family in the work force stands at 14 percent. They are employees, teachers, or secretaries. Despite the rise in educational levels among female family members, the overwhelming majority, particularly after marriage, continued to give up their jobs until the early 1980s when more women began to keep their jobs after marriage. Whether for economic reasons, or due to changes in values, or a little of each, this seems to be a slowly emerging trend among Palestinian women.

Each of the four chapters of the Abuljubayn family has maintained relationships with the others. Although almost all of the Abuljubayns in Kuwait belong to the Jaffa branch, communication exists with the Gaza and Safad branches. A family tree was drawn in 1978 as a result of interchapter communication. Recently the Dahriyah chapter, which had lost contact, initiated contact with the Jaffa chapter.

NOTES

1. Interview with George Qamar, Kuwait, summer 1985; interview with ᶜIsa Qamar and Mary Qamar-Farah, Austin, Texas, fall 1985.

2. Ibrahim Qamar appears in a photograph of the staff of the College des Freres in Jerusalem in 1934 (second from the left, first row) in Before Their Diaspora: A Photographic History of the Palestinians 1876-1948, ed. Walid Khalidi (Washington, D.C.: Institute of Palestine Studies, 1984), No. 230, p. 175.

3. Interview with Dr. Zuhdi Sammur, Kuwait, summer 1985.

4. For information about the events in Dayr Yasin, see David Hirst, The Gun and the Olive Branch: The Roots of Violence in the Middle East (London: Futura Macdonald, 1978), pp. 123-129; Jacques de Reyner, "Dair Yassin: April 10, 1948," in From Heaven to Conquest: Readings in Zionism and the Palestine Problem until 1948, ed. Walid Khalidi (Beirut: Institute for Palestine Studies, 1971), pp. 761-766.

5. Most of the material in this section is based on data provided me by Nadir Abuljubayn, who has collected, over the last eight years, an enormous amount of data on his family. Nadir is the first Palestinian born in Kuwait (1950). He is the eldest son of Khayriddin Abuljubayn, an earlycomer Palestinian (see chapter 3). This section is also based on interviews with Khayriddin Abuljubayn and Yusif Abuljubayn, Kuwait, summer 1985.

6

Family Networks:
Social Dynamics and Survival

To the earlycomer intelligentsia and peasant Palestinians who went to Kuwait, family and physical survival in the aftermath of the 1948 war were motivating forces that led them to Kuwait. Their first priority was to ameliorate the suffering of their families. All had to provide their parents, brothers, and sisters with the necessities of life. They also wanted to continue the education of their brothers and sisters, which had been disrupted by the war. Those pioneers became the bridgehead of the Palestinian community in Kuwait. Their presence facilitated the migration of many other members of their scattered families and friends. They helped their families reknit tangled social and physical threads. In other words, the Palestinians who came to Kuwait after the exodus and during the 1950s provided the foundation for a new and different superstructure in the diaspora.

The new structure was based on the development of every Palestinian family in Kuwait. New family networks were formed, which, in essence, held together the informal personal and familial relationships that could have been totally destroyed in the wake of the dispersion. The Palestinian social and family network facilitated the group's survival by providing a support system and an operating base.

This chapter is about these networks, and the post-1948 Palestinian family. It attempts to explain the functions and behavioral patterns evident in Palestinian family networks in Kuwait and to analyze the relationship between these local networks and their extensions in other countries and in the occupied territories.

The post-1948 Palestinian family came to be a complex world of relationships and networks. Each family followed strategies that employed all possible relationships to enhance its capacity to survive dispersion. By so doing, the Palestinian family ensured a central role for itself in the survival of the Palestinians as a group.

The family network that evolved in each diaspora center had particular functions in the community. Networks evolved and family relationships were maintained through a system of duties, obligations, services, and commitments. The fulfilling of regular and traditional family obligations (wajib) makes family a continuing, evolving relationship on both the local and the cross-national levels. In death and in marriage, family is present to support, comfort or celebrate. In visiting and weekly social relationships, as on religious occasions, family is a priority and a source of social and emotional fulfillment. In housing patterns and economic enterprise, family provides connections and encouragement. In facing the challenge of educating the children, dealing with old age, or confronting economic or emotional crisis, family steps in as a support system.

The family has also had an important role in political socialization. This guarantees it a central role in maintaining an ongoing relationship with the homeland. In other words, the family in Kuwait has become much more than an agency of individual survival; it has become the agency that protects and reknits the Palestinian social fabric in the diaspora, thus making it possible for the Palestinians to exist cohesively at the group level.

Death

Death is an event of solidarity for every family network in Kuwait, following age-old Palestinian traditions. Every member of the Palestinian family in Kuwait, in addition to the members of the social network of friends, comes to the house of the deceased to take part in a three-day-long mourning period.[1] Both the effective and extended family networks provide support to the next-of-kin during the mourning period. By bringing food to the immediate family and by being present during mourning, the family demonstrates its solidarity. During the mourning period, the immediate family is never left alone. This company is committed to the family obligation to help heal the wounds of the bereaved and to show respect to the dead.

Mourning means many things to the Palestinian family. Chief among them is the atmosphere of solidarity created by the event. Both the extended and the effective family networks merge into one support network by means of which relationships are strengthened and recharged. In other words, during the mourning period the network's cohesiveness and solidarity are enhanced. The gatherings and communications provide an occasion for renewing ties, discussing new issues affecting the group, and resolving family disputes.

The importance of a death is felt not only locally, but also by the total family network in Kuwait and across the diaspora. During mourning, members of the effective family networks come from the occupied territories and from across the diaspora to the ceremony. Those who cannot come, telephone and speak individually with every member of the family who happens to be present. Family members from the diaspora who cannot attend, observe the mourning period wherever they are. The closest family house in terms of blood ties in each country starts a period of mourning which continues for three days. Family, friends, town and village members show their respect and committment to the family by their presence.

A special aspect of the diaspora form of mourning is the daily ads (several appear every day) that are run in Gulf, Jordanian, and other Arab newspapers. Such ads announce that the family members are mourning the loss of a member in the occupied territories and all over the diaspora.

Marriage

Arranging marriages is a highly serious matter, like waging war or making big business deals.[2]

Regardless of whether couples marry by choice or by arrangement, every marriage among the Palestinians of Kuwait is preceded by negotiations between the two families or, in many marriages, between members of the same family. Marriages in both city and country in the Middle East are similar in their ability to bring together two families. The process leading up to marriage contributes to the realignment of networks.

In the Middle East the traditional preference is for endogamous (intrafamily) marriage. Whereas in the past, first cousin (Ibn al-ᶜAm or Bint al-ᶜAm) marriages were preferred, now kin marriges, however distant the relationship, are preferred. Therefore, many of the marriages between Palestinians from the same village or city, at one level or another, reinforce blood ties. Relationships that are loosely connected by marriages of two or three generations ago are tightened by a new marriage. This constant retying of threads from the same fabric, reinforces the family cohesion.

95

The mechanisms of the merger between two related or unrelated families involve traditional duties performed by the family members of the prospective bride and groom. The first formal step is taken by the men of the groom's family, who go to meet the men of the bride's family. During the meeting, the father of the groom proposes a marriage. Usually, this meeting involves locally residing grandfathers, uncles, and other close male relatives from the maternal and paternal sides of each family. This meeting is a test. If the two families like each other and discover commonalities and even blood ties, it bodes well for the steps to follow; if not, then more complex negotiations take place. If the bride and groom already know each other, there is more pressure on the two families to find a common ground. The meeting is a form of guarantee by means of which the relatives of the groom are assuring that he is a responsible young man who is ready for marriage and has the consent and backing of his family.[3]

After the meeting, family consultations follow that include the effective family network living in the West Bank, Gaza, Lebanon, and Amman. These consultations are important because marriage involves more than the two persons getting married, more even than the immediate families. A Palestinian marriage is in effect a merger of two families.

Even with the changes that have taken place in modern Palestinian relationships, most families still feel the importance of family consultation. According to a survey conducted in 1976 by Basim Sarhan, a sociologist at Kuwait University, 39 percent of one hundred family heads interviewed said they always consult their families in important matters such as marriage and divorce, 35 percent said sometimes, 4 percent rarely, and 17 percent said they do not consult their families. Five percent did not respond. Of the total sample, 64 percent said that consultation was a serious process by which they were able to evaluate what they were about to do in a more enlightened way. Thirteen percent said that consultations are informative and required by kinship ties. Six percent said they do not seek their kin's approval, and 17 percent gave no answer. In the case of conflict between the individual and the rest of the family on a particular course of action, 63 percent said they would not be obligated by family opinion; 16 percent said they would abide by family views; 15 percent said they would look for a compromise; 6 percent did not answer.[4]

Palestinians attempt to keep their collective social existence intact by insisting that, in most cases, the two parties to the marriage be Palestinian. Through a survey that was part of an M.A. thesis at the University of Kuwait (1978), Wajih Yasin Muhammad found that of a sample of three hundred family heads, 92 percent said they preferred a Palestinian husband for their daughters; only 8 percent said it did not matter. For their sons, 80 percent said they preferred a Palestinian wife;

5.3 percent chose an Arab; 1 percent a foreigner; and 13.7 percent said it made no difference.[5]

Other important issues are considered during the pre-marriage consultations. The status and reputation of the groom's family are important factors in the decision of the bride's family to accept the marriage. In this context, class, village or city origin, professional and educational level and other issues of status are important.

Once the bride's family accepts the marriage proposal things usually go smoothly. Before 1948, the mahr (an agreed-upon sum of money or goods transferred from the groom's family to that of the bride similar to a dowry) was very important.[6] Now, many Palestinian families in Kuwait have stopped taking money as mahr (dowry). Instead, since mahr is required by Islamic law, some families make the transfer symbolic. Other families expect jewelry for the bride and a jihaz (trousseau). Part of the mahr is required as alimony to the wife in case of divorce.

Education seems to have become dominant in family discussions of marriage proposals. Surprisingly, it has become more important than family background and status, although, before 1948, the latter was the most decisive element. In Kuwait, education has become the bridge between families of dissimilar background, status, and values. City families have married into peasant families; former aristocratic families intermarried with former poor, unknown families. Marriage has, for the first time in Palestinian society, cut across village-city, class, and family strata.[7]

Negotiations leading to marriage between families of differing backgrounds are usually more difficult. The families may have different concepts of what is proper during a marriage ceremony or an engagement period. The conflict of values is usually mediated by the bride and groom themselves taking a more active than usual role in the negotiations.

After the bride's family notifies the groom's family of its acceptance, a date is usually announced for a Khutbah (engagement). As the engagement, which is a trial period for everyone involved, progresses and the marriage date approaches, both families become more involved. But it is only at the actual marriage ceremony that everyone in the extended and effective family networks gathers.

The wedding ceremony marks the change in the relationship between two family networks. After the marriage, the merger is strengthened by the network established by the new husband and wife. The level of interaction between the family networks of both remains a function of the background, status, and values of the two families. Yet, what matters in the process of forming new family networks is that the bride and groom create around themselves new sets of relationships.

iages involving families that have intermarried before and marriages .in the same family end up creating an even tighter network.[8]

Marriages among Palestinians today always contain a cross-national aspect. Non-local aunts, uncles, grandparents, and close cousins from the matrilineal and patrilineal sides of both families usually arrive in Kuwait a week or two before the marriage. They participate in the preparations and meet members of the other family. The local family network in Kuwait and important segments of the effective family network living in other countries, particuarly from the West Bank, Gaza, Jordan, the United States, and Spain strengthen their ties and solidarity through these reunions at marriage celebrations. Relatives are usually meeting in person for the first time in years. For days they relive memories of pre-1948 Palestine and share all the news from family chapters who reside in different places.

Marriage is one of the most inclusive family events in post-1948 Palestinian families. The power of both death and marriage stems from the capacity of each to bring family from all branches of each network together. Such reunions strengthen already-existing ties and establish new ties and networks.

Visiting

Visiting is another activity that recharges the Palestinian family network in Kuwait. Visiting among relatives in Kuwait is a weekly or a daily practice for many. According to Sarhan's survey, when the Palestinian family heads of his sample were asked how often they visit their relatives in Kuwait, 4 percent said they visited on a daily basis, 17 percent said they visited two or three times weekly, 37 percent said they visited once a week, 26 percent said once a month, and 14 percent said occasionally (death, marriage, and the feast).[9] In the sample of three hundred family heads interviewed by Wajih Muhammad, 74 percent said they visited their relatives constantly, 24.3 percent visit sometimes, and 1.7 percent did not have relatives in Kuwait.[10] Even when it came to spending leisure time, 72.7 percent spent it with relatives, 20 percent with other Palestinians, and 7.3 percent with friends.[11]

Visiting is the cement and the building block of every family network.[12] Individuals and families substantiate ties by spending long hours together. The visiting might be prompted by special occasions, such as the birth of a child or the graduation of a son or daughter from high school or college. When people leave Kuwait for a vacation, family members are expected to visit and bid farewell. When they return, the

98

family gathers to congratulate them on a safe return. But visiting also occurs without special reason, perhaps simply as a daily habit.

Visiting is for the most part enjoyed and encouraged in most sectors of Palestinian society in Kuwait, even though it consumes much time and effort. But with the obsession for attaining better educational standards for their children, many Palestinian parents have regularized the family interactions in ways which do not interfere with the ability of their children to study.

The holy month of Ramadan, when all Muslims fast from sunrise to sunset, is an example of how holidays, particularly religious holidays, provide regular occasions for families to visit. During the twenty-eight to thirty-day fasting period, the family gathers at least once in the house of each family member. They either come after sunset, when all have had their meals, or at evening mealtime, and stay until midnight. Some families organize their meetings so that one member of the family plays host every other night. These nights become parties with conversation, political discussions, chess playing, and riddle solving being frequent activities.

Visiting also extends to members of the effective family network living in the diaspora or in the occupied territories. It is hard to find a Palestinian family in Kuwait, in fact, that does not have relatives from distant places visit every two or three years,[13] and despite the expense involved, families in Kuwait consider it a family obligation to visit relatives in other locations. Every father and mother want their children to be strongly linked to family in and out of Kuwait. Basim Sarhan's survey demonstrated how often such visits occur. In response to questions on traveling outside Kuwait to meet relatives, of Sarhan's sample of one hundred, 6 percent said they did it more than once a year, 29 percent said once a year, 18 percent said once every two years (since they were entitled to one vacation every two years), 17 percent said they visited their relatives outside Kuwait every three years. Only 27 percent said they had not visited in two years.[14]

The visiting may get even more complicated. Since every Palestinian family is widely dispersed and individuals hold refugee cards or citizenship from many different places, there are always people who cannot come to Kuwait or other Middle Eastern areas. Brothers and sisters who emigrated to far distant countries after the 1948 war have been unable to see each other for two or three decades. Restrictions on holders of the stateless refugee travel documents in the Arab states have also prevented visits.

Therefore, Palestinian families dispersed across many countries have devised ways to compensate for their inability to see each other as often as they want. The reunion of the Kanafani family held in the summer of 1983 in Cyprus provides an example.[15] The Kanafani family is from Jaffa and was displaced in 1948. Most of its members ended up in Syria and Lebanon; a few remained in what became Israel in 1948. As the need for work affected every member of the family, many moved to other countries, including the Gulf states, Cuba, and Denmark.

My interviewee, Fayzah Kanafani came to Kuwait as a teacher in 1950. In 1953, Fayzah married Husayn Najim, another Palestinian teacher who came to Kuwait in 1948.[16] The family, like all Palestinian families, has ended up with a number of different travel documents and citizenships. Thus their physical separation has been maintained by the borders separating enemy states. When the Kanafani family of brothers and sisters and close cousins decides to meet, it simply has no place to congregate. Over 50 percent of the family probably will not be able to get visas to any one particular Arab state.

Because of crisis events and geographical considerations, a reunion of the Kanafani family was postponed several times. The situation was so frustrating they, and other families, even considered meeting their close relatives on a ship in the Mediterranean. Finally, the family established a center for its reunion in Cyprus, in a residence that later became a Kanafani family house. In 1983, they all traveled to Cyprus, for different periods of time. Fayzah's aunt, accompanied by her married daughters' and sons' families, came from Beirut. Their travel documents varied from Lebanese citizenship to stateless. From Acre (Israel), two of Fayzah's first cousins and the brothers of those coming from Lebanon came with their wives and children. They carried Israeli passports. The young people, cousins of Fayzah, working in Kuwait, came on Lebanese documents and passports to meet their parents coming from Beirut. One of Fayzah's brothers, who works and lives in Copenhagen, was able to make it to Cyprus. He carries a Danish passport. Another family member who works in Cuba and is a Cuban national also attended. Every week, several would leave, to be replaced by others for a week or two. Throughout that memorable summer, at one time or another, all thirty-seven family members from the effective network of both sides of the family gathered in Cyprus to visit.

The visiting patterns of the Palestinian network mirror the visiting patterns of the Middle Eastern family in general, though in the Palestinian case visiting in the family is conducted under more difficult conditions. These visiting patterns, including those associated with death and marriage, have reinforced and strengthened the ties that make up the diaspora Palestinian family networks. Hence, as Hildred Geertz suggests in the Moroccan context, such visits amplify "public comment on these ties. Discussion of personal affairs continues uninterrupted by spatial scatter. Relationships are not permitted to weaken through disuse, as more

100

distant outposts are continually drawn back into the effective web of obligations, expectations, aid, and criticism."[17] Be it occasioned by death or sickness, marriage or divorce, happiness or sadness, Muslim or Christian holidays, this tradition of visiting strengthens the network of relationships that contribute to family unity, solidarity, and cohesiveness.

Housing

The family network as an integrating agent can also be seen in housing patterns in Kuwait. Through housing, the Palestinians sought collective family security. In Kuwait, each newcomer found housing among members of the immediate effective family network for as long as needed. In the bachelor neighborhoods of Kuwait's old city, in particular the Mirqab neighborhood, every newcomer from among the peasantry and urban poor also found housing through the effective family network (see chapter 4). When Kuwait City extended beyond the city gates, Palestinian families moved as well. In fact, during the 1960s, particularly after 1967, the bachelor society of Kuwait's Palestinians became a family settlement outside the original gates of the city. For example, members of the Safi family of the village of Malhah came to live in the Nuqrah area in Kuwait in proximity to each other.[18] In many cases, clusters of families from a larger family group came to live near each other in a particular neighborhood. Raja Sumrayn of Qalonya, for example, finds living with his wife and children in the same block as his brother, two cousins, and their families to be most helpful in establishing family security through daily interaction.[19]

Housing arrangements are no longer necessarily patrilineal. Closeness to the wife's immediate family is also common. In many ways, the atmosphere resembles that of the traditional Palestinian village. This is even truer as the children of the effective, closely related family grow accustomed to seeing each other on a daily basis.

In most cases, when a nuclear family moves to a new apartment, it watches other vacancies in the block or building. When a vacancy occurs, the first family reserves it for a related family: c.g. a brother and his family, a sister and her family. The neighborhood gradually fills with members of the same family. In the neighborhoods of Hawalli, Nuqrah, Salmiyah, Khitan, and Farwaniyah, where the majority of Palestinians live, some buildings are 30 to 60 percent occupied by members of one family. In many cases, a narrow street leads to a set of small buildings in which many apartments are occupied by relatives. These neighborhoods are currently suburban extensions of Kuwait City. (See Map 2.)

101

What is important here is how housing arrangements strengthen the effective and extended family network in Kuwait. It is clear from the data that people living close to each other (same building, street, or neighborhood) usually interact more often than people living some distance apart. They even share meals if living in the same building or adjacent apartments. The women working at home frequently help each other with day-to-day responsibilities.

Not all members of an effective family network live close together, however, for a number of reasons including rent costs, children's schools, and workplace. According to Sarhan's 1976 data, 19 percent of the one hundred conjugal household heads interviewed said their relatives lived in the same neighborhood; 4 percent said in the same street; and the rest said their relatives were distributed in different localities in Kuwait.[20] Yet, these data about housing must be viewed in context. Had the same families been asked the same question in 1968, the percentage of those living in the same street or neighborhood would have been higher. Because of the influx of new refugees in 1967, many families shared an apartment for a year or two. And if the same question were asked in 1986, the data might show that a higher percentage of Palestinian families in Kuwait are living together again, due to the economic crisis and the doubling and tripling of rent prices since 1978. Changes in lifestyle, salary, or place of work may have caused separation within some families because of the move of some members to other sections of Kuwait city. But many families, especially in lower-income groups have chosen the solution of living in the same house or apartment. Such families cook together, eat together, and share utilities, bills, and rent. This is a form of network strengthening and continuity through housing patterns. Rather than the network's being weakened and further disrupted as a result of economic crisis, it becomes more effective and cohesive.

Map 2 Neighborhoods With Predominant Palestinian Population

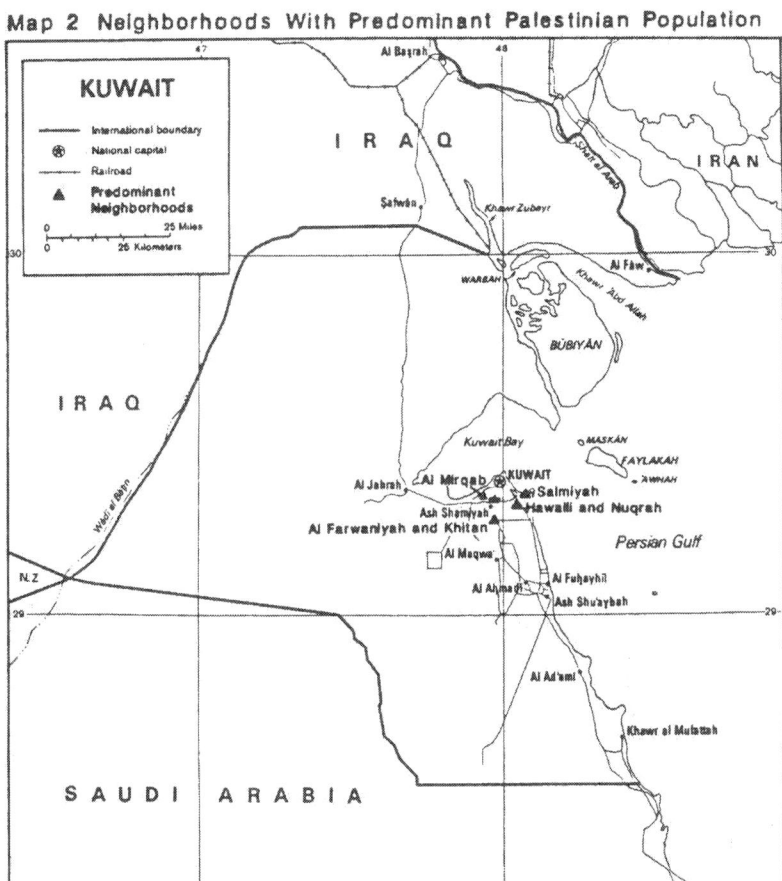

Economic Enterprise

As in pre-1948 Palestine, family and economic enterprise were interrelated and mutually reinforcing in Kuwait. For instance, enterprise owners prefer to extend employment opportunities to family members.

The example chosen demonstrates how family and economic enterprise overlap.

Rabah al-Natshih was born in 1937 in Jerusalem. His father, the son of a construction worker, was a merchant who, like many Hebronites seeking opportunity, migrated to Jerusalem in the early 1930s. There, he started a mathanih (single of matahin). Such stores roast, grind, and sell coffee, nuts, and spices. In 1941, he moved to Bethlehem, where he started a similar store. Meanwhile, Rabah went to school; on completion of the seventh grade in 1954 he joined his father in the shop.

During this time, the economic pressures were great in the West Bank. In 1956, Rabah decided to join a brother who had gone to Kuwait three years earlier. In Kuwait, he was employed in the Department of Education at a modest salary. After a short period, Rabah and his brother, who worked as a driver, started a mathanih in Kuwait. In many ways, this store, Matahin al-Khalili (the Mills of the Hebronite), was an extension of their father's store in Bethlehem.

Matahin al-Khalili flourished with the Kuwaiti economy. More workers were needed, as were more managers, accountants, and storekeepers. The Natshih brothers immediately thought of members of their family. They sent visas to their cousins in the West Bank and offered to employ some of the Natshih relatives already in Kuwait. Soon almost everyone working in the stores owned by the family was a Natshih. Six of those who had worked with the Natshih brothers for eight years started similar stores of their own. Rabah himself had three additional stores in different parts of Kuwait. By the 1970s, ten Natshih-owned stores were operating in Kuwait City. In 1981, Rabah's brother moved to Amman, where he started a wholesale store for coffee, spices, and nuts named the Khalili (Hebronite) Company for General Trade. This made Amman, in addition to Kuwait and Bethlehem, a new center for the economic enterprise of the Natshih family.[21]

The Natshihs hope the tradition of their stores will be maintained by allowing the younger generation to take over. Rabah plans to follow a tradition started by his father in the 1930s by having his son, also employed as an engineer, work in the family's stores. The family is also trying to ensure that future generations continue in the family business. Starting a factory related to the business that the family has been in for fifty years is a possibility they are studying.

104

The Natshih example demonstrates how an economic family network (that is, overlap of the effective network and economic production) evolves and spreads through an effective family relationship.

Family Funds: The Role of Modern Organizational Style

In response to economic crisis and added family responsibilities, since 1976, both effective and extended family networks in Kuwait have united to create funds (sanadiq) for particular purposes or for emergencies. The fund (a foundation or association) is, in fact, the highest expression of family cohesiveness and strength. It brings the least-important relationships in the network to the center. Its operations force family members to meet as often as the fund requires. Through this obligation, all become more involved, and all members of the family network are held responsible to the collective will of the family.

By the mid-1970s, in response to new challenges affecting the Palestinian community in Kuwait, Palestinian families formed funds aimed at meeting the crisis. The added family challenges stemmed from the rise in Kuwait, after 1967, of fully developed family structures with very few investments or resources. The Palestinian family, like all foreign manpower families in Kuwait, confronted problems of housing, rent, retirement, public schooling, disability, and widowhood.[22] See Ch. 9.

But the main challenge was college education. Higher education, which became a family obsession immediately after the displacement experience, became more difficult to manage in the 1970s as a result of the tightening of educational opportunities for Palestinians in the Arab world. Palestinians in Kuwait and the diaspora increasingly looked to Europe, the United States, and other countries for higher education. This strained the resources of the family and made higher education a difficult mission. Each student sent to the United States for college costs the family at least $12,000 per year. Families have gone bankrupt or have lived on the bare minimum in order to educate their children. In Kuwait, for instance, of four thousand Palestinian high school graduates each year, and despite outstanding grade point averages, only 7 to 10 percent may enter the University of Kuwait.[23] This is a function of the 10 percent quota Kuwait University has allocated for on its non-Kuwaiti, non-Gulf high school graduates.[24] At least one thousand of the four thousand pursue a college education in the United States.[25] Many of them belong to limited-income families.

The hardships that low-income Palestinian families endure to finance the education of their children can only be admired. Some families have gone as far as advertising in the daily newspaper their need for money to continue the education of their children. During my interviews in response to a question on how these families manage, one family head said, "We have moved to a smaller apartment and simply reduced the amount of food and some other necessities we consume." As foreign expatriates, these families, particularly the families who came to Kuwait after 1961, are not entitled to free public schooling. Since foreign expatriots cannot own property, or enjoy retirement benefits, the economic burden of low-income Palestinian families, approximately one-third of the community, becomes devastating. The statelessness of Palestinians, once again, is at the root of of an almost insurmountable problem.

But the family has developed new tactics to battle this difficulty. During the 1950s and 1960s, the family met educational and other challenges informally, but since the mid-1970s, a more formal family association has developed.

During the last eleven years, hundreds of family funds (sanadiq) have been established in Kuwait. Their sole purpose is to help the family cope with the crisis of the diaspora. In the face of fewer opportunities and mounting crisis, the family network can provide through these funds a temporary, yet important cushioning factor.

Family funds are predominantly subsidized by the working male members of the family; some are mixed or have women participating in them through a separate committee structure. The background of the family, past acculturation experiences, levels of education, and the number of its working women are all factors that influence women's participation.

In addition to the formal functions of family funds (having to do with education, housing, disability, retirement, death, and widowhood), they informally provide for the continued linkage of all members, strengthened bonds, and the survival of the family system. For example, the thirty-six conjugal families that make up the Tahah family of the West Bank village of Bidya in Kuwait established a fund for the sole purpose of support, education, and care of the sick and disabled in the family. In 1981, for instance, the fund sent money for a surgical operation to a family member in Bidya. In their monthly meeting, local family issues such as residency permits, retirement, sickness, education, and economic problems are discussed. Even issues concerning family members in the village and in other diaspora areas are discussed.[26] Such meetings are politically relevant as well, because the problems that brought them to meet in a family fund are very much a result of political problems stemming from their continued displacement.

The Abuljubayns of Jaffa also have a family fund. The firstcomers, Khayriddin and Yusif have stayed in close contact since their arrival in Kuwait in 1948. During the late 1960s, both led the project that invited thirty family heads from the family branch in Kuwait to a meeting to establish the Abuljubayn family fund. Each month, every member pays in ten Kuwaiti dinars. After three months, one of the members receives the funds collected as a loan. Within two years of establishment, the family fund had provided loans for marriages, education, and other needs in the amount of ten thousand dinars (approximately $30,000). In 1982, the fund was able to invest money in the stock exchange and make a profit for each member. In 1983, a parallel fund was formed for the younger generation, which had not joined the original fund. Seventy family members participated, all working members of the family and their spouses.[27]

These funds, of which hundreds have been established in Kuwait, can be understood in the context of an expanding family role in the Palestinian diaspora. In addition to the efforts of the working father, sister, or brother, education also became a responsibility of the more well-to-do members of each family. Although such efforts became an established family tradition, family funds gave them a more institutionalized form. Those in deep economic trouble now found more available solutions to their problems through this formalization of the expanded family role. The family fund brings to the fore the extent of support included in the Palestinian family relationship. Though we have discussed important aspects of emotional support (death, marriage, and visiting), the economics of the relationship is no less significant.

Sarhan's survey again demonstrates how economic support is proferred, both by individial family members and by funds. The survey shows that financial support is not considered the responsibility of only the well-off members in each family. In fact, individuals with very limited incomes are willing to go to some lengths to help a cousin or a brother. According to Sarhan's survey, 27 percent of those asked about their willingness to help a relative in need said they would assist their relatives even if it meant economic difficulty for themselves. Another 69 percent said they would help if they were financially capable. Only 2 percent said they would help only if that relative had helped them. In response to a question on actual incidents of support, 60 percent said they exchanged support with their relatives or they had supported a relative in need several times. Twenty-five percent said they had supported relatives a few times, 9 percent said rarely, and 4 percent said they had never done it before. Two percent did not respond. When asked how spontaneous the support was, 19 percent said the support to their relatives came as a result of a request from the relative in need; 16 percent said it was given when one of the family elders asked for it; 39 percent said the support was spontaneous following their realization that the relative was in need; 22 percent said that their support was through the family fund; and 3 percent did not respond.

107

When asked about the type of support they provided, 62 percent said it was "financial," and that they gave it to their relatives and did not want it back. Twenty-two percent said it was a commitment to the family fund, and 7 percent said it was a loan. Three percent said it was a financial-sponsorship type of help, and 6 percent did not respond.[28] In response to a question on what motivates financial assistance of other family members, 32 percent said death of the family head, 19 percent said illness, 14 percent said unemployment, 10 percent said low income, and 25 percent said all of the above.[29]

These funds are not only local funds for the family network in Kuwait. There are usually chapters or similar funds of the same family in Jordan, Gaza, or the West Bank. In many cases family funds established in Kuwait motivate those in Jordan or the West Bank to follow. In other cases, the reverse happens. The point is that what goes on in the family network in one place has implications for family in other places. The Khatib family of the West Bank Village of Sawyah, for example, has a fund combining the efforts of the four working brothers and their working adult children in Kuwait. Through the fund, not only have they sent several family members to college, but they have also paid for the education of their brother's children still living in the West Bank.

By every account, these funds are a vehicle for a continued recycling of relationships from extended to effective, and from loose to cohesive. Furthermore, although Khuri, in his profile of family associations in two suburbs of Beirut, states that such family funds are temporary, the Palestinians case suggests otherwise.[30] Although many Palestinian family funds formed in the 1960s and early 1970s did not last long, those formed since are of a more permanent nature. It seems that the immediate needs, complex problems, and length and uncertainty of the diaspora have all forced the family to respond with more formal, permanent solutions since the late 1970s. Many of those family members who opposed the fund idea in the early seventies were calling for their formation in the 1980s. Crisis reappears as a major motivating force in family behavior.

Family Centers

Many families have found that to maintain family cohesiveness and transmit that cohesiveness to the young, they need a family center (markaz or diwan). The establishment of such centers has been solely the function of the family networks in Jordan. They buy a house, build, or rent one, and then transform it into a family center which is a modern form of the traditional diwan (guest house and family gathering place). Such centers in Jordan become centers for the entire family across the diaspora. Some centers send out newsletters about the family. Many of the family's wakes, marriages, and parties take place there. The significance of the centers stems partly from their location. Since many visitors come to Jordan or pass through it on their way to or out of the West Bank, the centers have facilitated cross-national communication. In many cases, these centers are extensions of formal family associations with chapters in Kuwait and other diaspora countries.

The Natshih family, for example, which settled in Hebron and became one of its major families eight hundred years ago, was not satisfied with the informal attempts to keep the family together, so it decided to formalize its efforts. Members wanted to maintain links and transmit interest in the family to the younger generation. They opened a diwan in Amman in addition to the one in Hebron. In this center, wakes are conducted and meetings of all the men in the family take place every Wednesday and Thursday. Similar meetings of the women take place every Friday. A biweekly dinner and lunch bring together all the family in Jordan and family members who are in Jordan visiting or on their way to the West Bank. Many friends come to these gatherings. Ties are renewed and the young are introduced to the rest of the family. Interestingly, many marriages--such as between Natshihs in the United States or the West Bank and other Natshihs in Qatar or in Kuwait--develop out of such meetings.

The Gaushih family (of Jerusalem) has also found that maintaining extended family communication can best be achieved by establishing a family center.[31] The center itself is the property of the Gaushih league. The league, usually through meetings at the center in Amman, performs many important functions such as providing scholarships for family members or providing financial support to those in need all across the diaspora. In the center, family members (particularly the young) also engage in sports and recreational activities. Like the Natshih family center, it is a meeting place for the Gaushihs coming from the diaspora and from Jerusalem. It is also a place for marriages, parties, and wakes.

The Gaushih league performs an additional function. It publishes a newsletter, which is distributed among family members in the West Bank in addition to family members in Latin America, the United States, the Gulf, and Europe. The newsletter provides information on death, birth, educational attainment, success, social events, and many other family issues. It also includes addresses of family members. Furthermore, the league once a year honors those students from the different family chapters who graduate from high school with honors. If the honorees cannot attend the ceremony at the center, the award is sent to them. The flow of communication and information about the situation in every part of the diaspora, as well as in the village or city of origin, is natural in such centers. In many cases, they are a place for political debate and nationalist activities. During crisis, fund raising is instituted and transmitted through the centers to those in need in the diaspora or the West Bank.[32]

Although functions of family centers appear to be similar, there are certain differences. Some family centers are heavily used and dominated by the young; others are dominated by family elders and have more formal rules and regulations. Some are totally segregated by sex and others are not. This is a function of the previous acculturation experience and depends on the sector of Palestinian society from which the family comes.

Through these centers, a fulcrum for a stronger, more close-knit effective and extended family network is provided. The centers include in their membership both the patrilineal and the matrilineal sides of the family. They represent the practical effective and extended family relationships as defined in this study.

The Ancestral Homeland

In addition to the functions already discussed, the Palestinian family has a political role to play. In the absence of self-determination and statehood, under which national agencies could educate children about their history, political education becomes the responsibility of the family. Parents, relatives, aunts, older brothers and sisters, and family friends provide vivid and detailed information about Palestine to the young people. Village history, the history of Palestine, and the encounter with Zionist colonization are presented informally in response to questions from the children. In many cases, folktales and children's stories that have been passed down from one generation to another transmit information about the homeland, its geography, agriculture, landscape, towns, and cities.

One of the most important aspects of family life in Kuwait is the way family gatherings start and end, particularly among those of peasant origin. Such family meetings are usually held weekly or biweekly. Among the well-connected, highly sociable peasantry, they are often held daily. They meet with the children around, listening interestedly to what those who know Palestine and the village have to say about what has befallen the Palestinians and their country.

At the outset of the gathering, the participants talk about work problems, the economic crisis, the weather, political events, Arab politics, and problems of day-to-day life in the diaspora. They cover every topic from human rights to rent, residence permits to the future. But the central theme of the discussion usually shifts into long recollections of the past. The mood becomes optimistic, joyful, and full of hope. Life in the old village--marriages and week-long festivals, the harvest, and the social atmosphere--is discussed. The land is vividly described, the zaᶜtar (thyme) covering the ground, the orchards and the olive trees that enhance its beauty. There is no end to the stories about every aspect of life in pre- 1948 Palestine.[33]

Such gatherings and the endless talk about who the Palestinians are and why they have no country of their own have become a tradition. Most important, the pre-1948 picture is presented to the children against the reality of the present. The security of the past is always compared with the insecurity of the present. The importance and significance of this informal education increases when the children encounter non-Palestinian children who may have their own concept of what a Palestinian is.

Tawfiq Farah has documented the Palestinian family's role in educating children about Palestine through a survey conducted among Palestinian school children ages eleven to sixteen in Qatar. He found that 55 percent perceived the father's role as determinative, whereas 23 percent said that both parents had a determining role, and 9 percent that they had learned national loyalty from their mothers. Another 3 percent learned about Palestine from siblings, or friends, or the radio. Only 9 percent said they had learned national loyalty from their teachers. In response to a question on the amount of political discussion concerning Palestinians and Palestine, 37 percent stated that they discussed the Palestinian issue with their parents all the time, 16 percent said most of the time, 40 percent said sometimes, 5 percent said rarely and 2 percent said never. Of the one hundred children, of which the majority were born either in Jordan or Qatar, and most of whom have been living in Qatar since age ten, 97 percent answered "Palestine", or their former villages and towns, in response to the question "Where are you from?"[34]

These factors have helped shape a Palestinian identity well connected to the ancestral homeland. Memory, like ᶜAshura to the Shiites, or the Jews' memories about life in Palestine while in Babylonian captivity, or the Nubians' memory of Nubia,[35] is a constant re-creation of the past. In many ways, memory becomes the Palestinians' only condolence during their statelessness.

An equally important linking event is a summer visit by children living in Kuwait to their grandparents' house in the West Bank or Gaza. This is also common among the West Bankers and the Gazans, as well as among the refugees who have families living in refugee camps. In a survey I conducted in summer 1985 among 102 Palestinian children aged nine to seventeen, of whom the overwhelming majority were born in Kuwait and were members of the Palestinian scouts movement and the General Union of Palestinian students in Kuwait, 75 said they had visited

111

Palestine. Of these, 33 stated that they had visited their hometowns several times, some as many as eight or ten.

The entire Palestinian population visits the West Bank or Gaza at one time or another, since the majority still have relatives there. Although visits are short (they are not allowed by the military authorities to stay more than a month or two), they have far-reaching effects on the family. The children develop familiarity with the village. Their roots take on a material form. What they have heard about the land, events, the Israelis, and occupation becomes a closer reality. Not only the land, or the village, or the camp becomes real, but also the traditional activities such as planting and harvesting become concrete.[36] The experience of visiting an uncle or a cousin in an Israeli jail, or witnessing collective punishment in a village, or night searches and arrests, only increases their sense of solidarity with their family and the wider cause. When a youngster hears later on a Kuwaiti news report that a curfew is imposed in the village of Burqah or the city of Nablus or Gaza and that mass arrests have taken place, his or her level of identification with those involved and with the unfolding event is very real and very high.[37]

These types of visit give the children the deeper, richer meaning of "home" that ancestral connections substantiate. After the summer season ends, the children return to their schools in Kuwait with firsthand knowledge of Palestine. The need to return to their ancestral homeland is strengthened and is transmitted to other youngsters in school and in the neighborhood.

This type of visit--much like a pilgrimage to the majority of the 350,000 Palestinians living in Kuwait--are very special events for the parents as well. Many adults and families are able to visit their own former houses in Haifa, Tiberias, Ramle, or Jerusalem, at present occupied by Jewish families. These visits, unlike the nurturing visits of the children to their grandparents, are more likely to be traumatic as the disturbing reality of displacement is brought closer. Many Palestinian exiles, seeing their former houses for the first time after thirty years or more, suffer heart attacks or physical collapse. The Abd al-Fatah family, for example, composed of father, mother, and five children, came to Kuwait in the 1950s. They decided to visit their Haifa house in the summer of 1972. After being allowed a brief visit, the father, Khalil, experienced tremendous stress at the steps of his occupied house. That same day he had a heart attack and died.[38]

Since the beginning of the diaspora, the family has provided the means by which Palestinian nationalism is protected and preserved. In the minds of the Palestinians, the worth of the family emanates from its place of origin, its founder, and its history. The actual piece of land is intertwined with the ongoing attachment to the Palestinian heritage. It is

112

meaningless, therefore, to identify a Palestinian family in isolation from its village or city of origin. There are no Abuljubayns without Jaffa, Gaza, Dahriyah, and Safad; Samurs without Dayr Yasin; Qamars without Jerusalem; or Sumrayns without Qalonia. Palestinian families trace their existence back hundreds of years, in some cases to Roman times. The scholarly literature traces the Palestinian Arabs to the original Philistines and Cananites who settled the land. For example, the Ramahah family of Salamah, a village near pre-1948 Jaffa, belongs to a larger hamulah, which traces its origins to Roman times. In the village, the family was called "the Romans" by other families. Such families naturally value roots in the villages and towns of Galilee and the West Bank, or the cities of Jaffa, Lydda, and Ramle.[39]

The culture of the family in a Middle Eastern milieu that gives precedence to origin and to the ancestral homeland over birthplace, citizenship, or residence makes the family the strongest link to the piece of land on which the family resided before 1948. The manner in which the Palestinians lost their homeland has contributed to this attachment and the resistance to assimilation. Whereas in the Jewish experience, the synagogue and the family became the two institutions that transmitted Jewishness, in the Palestinian experience, the family has been the most central in transmitting Palestinianism and a strong attachment to Palestine.[40]

Dispute Mediation

Social change, by necessity, gives rise to tension. It breeds insecurity, fear, and conflict. The type of social change Palestinians have experienced since 1948 has been quite intense. Different branches of families separated before 1948 by differences in status and wealth experienced major changes in their relationship after 1948. When a poorer branch rises in educational and financial status, it causes a major readjustment in the family, sometimes resulting in conflict. Disputes may result from financial disagreements or over uneven honoring of family obligations; they can be over issues of marriage, divorce, respect, or authority. Older brothers who still believe they are the second in command after their fathers in relation to their younger brothers and sisters may run into conflict with a more independent generation. Cultural lag makes it normal for many to continue to believe that outdated rules unadapted to the new conditions may still function. This becomes a source of conflict and dispute in the family. People normally try to assert the older models of behavior first. Only after continued failure do they try to change and find new ways. In the meanwhile, there is tension over the unresolved issues.

These sorts of disputes do interfere in family relationships at some level. Disputes may involve brothers and sisters, parents, children, or anyone in the family network. There are also cases in which the same large family may end up applying its system of solidarity to some of its branches while ignoring others because of conflict.

Despite all of this, however, the family as a system is seldom destroyed. What is important to our discussion is the ability of the family to resolve tension and provide new solutions to existing problems. This kind of flexibility, allowing accomodation and compromise, has been at the heart of survival of the family in the diaspora. It is in a constant dialogue and interchange with the surrounding dynamic environment. The Palestinian family cannot be as rigid, inflexible, and tradition-bound as it was before 1948.

Danger and crisis have contributed to the strengthening of bonds in each family. In many cases, and despite disagreements between family members, the working relationship has continued because of the uniting role played by other family members. A certain amount of tension is always present in human relations, but this does not interfere with the basic family system and the functions it has performed for displaced Palestinians since 1948.

When tension and, in many cases, personal dislike, arises among members of a Palestinian family, the people involved seem to realize that they are in one way or another obligated to each other and, therefore, ought to be able to cope with their differences. With the continuing crisis, the obligation is deeper, and family members are forced into a greater dependence that stems from a common plight. Through family mechanisms related to marriage, death, visiting, and economic support, the family retains its ability to relieve many of its inner tensions.

Once family members become aware of a dispute, it is only a matter of time before mediation starts. It seems that all are threatened when a quarrel develops. Out of fear of being drawn into a conflict that may tear the family apart, family members, and particularly the elders, have an immediate interest in mediation. Mediation in the Middle East is held in high esteem and is seen as an honorable task. It has always fallen to family elders and leaders, who see the family as their legacy. They have a paternalistic attitude toward it and will do whatever they deem necessray to ensure its survival.

Reconciliation may take place during a death, marriage, a religious holiday, or at the birth of a new child. The family tries to settle the conflict as fairly as it can and without offending either party. Compromise is involved on both sides. According to Sarhan's survey, to a question on family disputes over financial matters, inheritance, marriage, or any other reason, 78 percent said they would solve the dispute within the confines of the family. Eighteen percent said only if family mediation failed would they think of going to court. One percent said they would seek a village leader to solve a problem, and only 2 percent said they would immediately go to court. One percent did not respond.[41] But, as Rugh asserts with regard to the Egyptian family experience, "people avoid leaving unresolved tensions within their circle of intimate connections. One reason is that when tensions exist the person loses the full potential support relationships provide; the person is unable to face the world with a cohesive group at his or her back".[42]

Independent, nonfamily mediators have a role to play too. There have been cases in which such individuals have resolved disputes between family members or between individuals belonging to different Palestinian villages or towns. In Kuwait, Hajj Khalil Musa al-Zir has been involved in mediation efforts.[43] Al-Zir, who was born in 1917 and came to Kuwait in the 1960s, is one of five thousand Ta[c]amrah--one of the most numerous Palestinian Bedouin tribes. (Most of the Ta[c]amrahs still reside in the West Bank in the Bethlehem area.) He often hears cases referred to him by the PLO in his home. These may involve car accidents, financial disputes, family conflicts, or other matters. When he receives a case, usually involving two or more Palestinians, he explains to them how traditional (tribal) mediation functions and asks for an [c]atwah (a truce) between the two disputants. He starts collecting facts, interviewing people, and investigating until he has all the relevant information. He then begins a set of discussions with the individuals involved and their families and friends in an attempt to discover common ground. He finally provides a solution that all parties recognize for its fairness.

Conclusion

For a dispersed, uprooted Palestinian people, the family has proved to be a decisive institution involved in the preservation of their society. If it were not for the family, particularly in the years following the 1948 war, no Palestinian society of any significance would have survived the dispersion experience. Although the physical dislocation and the gravity of the loss were extremely intense (massacres, refugees, loss of homeland, and statelessness), the family and the primordial relationships remained intact. When all formal Palestinian institutions were totally destroyed, the social, personal, and primordial relationships were not. Although families suffered personal loss, were scattered and deprived, bloodlines could not be erased. The sinews of the social system held it together even though they were scattered and stretched. This enabled the family to activate, to adapt to the new circumstances, and to enter a process whereby it literally wove a new Palestinian social fabric. The Kuwait case seems to prove that the Palestinian family networks gave order and meaning to post-1948 Palestinian society.

By becoming practical and less rigid, and by gaining a contextual meaning, the family succeeded in creating new networks for its survival both in Kuwait and across the diaspora. It often found the means to maintain its cross-national body, as it did its local one. It also maintained a strong relationship with the family still in Palestine. Through patterns associated with death, marriage, visiting, housing, economic enterprise, family funds, clubs, and centers, an elaborate network of relationships came to promote family cohesiveness and continuity. Hence, family mechanisms became a framework for group action among people who consider themselves family. The Palestinian family is a network of relationships based on blood and marriage that demands from the individual certain responsibilities and commitments that go beyond the conjugal family.

In this study, crisis and challenges stemming from an unpredictable environment have been claimed to be basic to the cohesion of Palestinian family networks. Whether a crisis takes the form of physical harm, war, statelessness, or economic stress, it remains a basic factor in the dialectical internal balance of solidarity in Palestinian family networks. Therefore, one tends to find a correlation between crisis and the effectiveness of family networks.

Each of the basic expressions of family solidarity and cohesiveness is part of the total family system. While meeting important economic, psychological, or personal needs of individuals, each output of the system increases family cohesiveness and solidarity. Therefore, while the family has preserved the social bonds of the older generation, which Palestinians call Jil al-Nakbah (the generation of the catastrophe), and saved them from total collapse, it has also provided solidarity and a sense of social cohesion for the young generations, who continue to call on the family to deal with an ongoing crisis. The family, through contemporary adaptations of age-old traditions, exists in a continual process of reaffirmation.

NOTES

1. This section is based on analysis of the data collected through the interviews.

116

2. Hildred Geertz, "The Meaning of Family Ties," in Meaning and order in Moroccan society: Three essays in Cultural Analysis, ed. Clifford Geertz, Hildred Geertz, Lawrence Rosen (Cambridge: At the University Press, 1979) p. 363; quoted in James Bill and Carl Leiden, Politics in the Middle East 2d ed. (Boston: Little, Brown and Co., 1984), p. 92.

3. For different context, see Hildred Geertz, "The Meaning of Family Ties" (Morocco), pp. 363-377; Dale Eickelman The Middle East: An Anthropological Approach (Princeton, N.J.: Prentice-Hall, 1981), pp. 124-128; and Daniel Bates and Amal Rassam, Peoples and Cultures of the Middle East (Englewood Cliffs, N.J.: Prentice-Hall, 1983), pp. 201-204.

4. Basim Sarhan, "al-^{c}A'ilah Wa-al Qarabah ^{c}Ind al-filistiniyin fi al-Kuwayt: Nata'ij 'awwaliyah Li-bahth ijtma^{c}i" ["Family and Kinship among the Palestinians in Kuwait: Preliminary Results of Sociological Research"] (Paper presented to al Ma^{c}had al-A^{c}rabi lil-Takhtit al-'Iqtisadi wa-al-Ijtima^c, Kuwait, 1976), pp. 70-71. The survey included one hundred Palestinians, seventy-one men and twenty-nine women. Ninety-two were Muslims, eight were Christians, and all were married. Fifty-three were of peasant origin and forty-seven of urban origin.

5. Wajih Yasin Muhammad, "al-Takayuf al-ijtima^{c}i Lil-Usrah al-filistiniyah al-muhajirah ila al-Kuwayt" ["Social Adaptation of the Palestinian Migrant Family to Kuwait] (MA thesis, Kuwait University, 1978), p. 219.

6. Bates and Rassam, Peoples and Cultures, pp. 202-203.

7. Fieldwork interviews.

8. Robert Springsborg, Family, Power, and Politics in Egypt (Philadelphia: University of Pennsylvania Press, 1982), p. 73; Bill and Leiden, Politics in the Middle East, p. 92.

9. Sarhan, "Family and Kinship", pp. 61-62.

10. I had to change Muhammad's 7.3 percent for those who do not have relatives in Kuwait to 1.7. Adding up Muhammad's original percentages gave a total of 105.6 percent, probably because of a typographic error. Wajih Muhammad, "Social Adaptation of the Palestinian Migrant Family in Kuwait," ``p. 217.

11. Ibid., pp. 217-218.

12. See the special issue of the Anthropological Quarterly 12, no. 1 (January 1974), entitled "Visiting Patterns and Social Dynamics in Eastern Mediterranean Communities."

13. Sarhan, "Family and Kinship," p. 62.

14. Ibid., pp. 62-63.

15. Interview with Fayzah Kanafani and her husband, Husayn Najim, Kuwait, summer 1985.

117

16. In July 1972, as this family was on a visit to Lebanon, a car bomb meant for Fayzah's brother, Ghassan Kanafani, reknowned novelist, writer, and spokesman of the Popular Front for the Liberation of Palestine, killed both Ghassan and the seventeen-year-old daughter of Husayn and Fayzah.

17. Hildred Geertz, "The Meaning of Family Ties," p. 335.

18. Interview with Ibrahim Safi, Kuwait, summer 1985.

19. Interview with Dr. Raja Sumrayn, Kuwait, summer 1985.

20. Sarhan, "Family and Kinship," pp. 61-62.

21. Interview with Rabah al-Natshih, Kuwait, summer 1985. For an interesting article on the overlap between family and economic enterprise, see Fuad I. Khuri, "Kinship, Emigration and Trade Partnership among the Lebanese of West Africa," Africa 35, no. 1 (January 1974):385-395. See also Samir Khalaf and Emilie Shwayri, "Family Firms and Industrial Development: The Lebanese Case," Economic Development and Cultural Change 15, no. 1 (October 1966):59-69.

22. See "Fhilistiniyin fi sin al-sittin wa kabus 'usmuh al-taqaᶜud" ["Palestinians at the Age of Sixty and the Nightmare of Retirement"], in al-Anba' (Kuwaiti daily) (June 27, 1985); "Jawlah fi ihtimamat al-filistinyin fi al-Kuwayt" ["A Journey into Palestinian Concerns in Kuwait"], in al-'Anba' (August 1, 1984). Also see al-Anba' for August 2, 1984; and Ibn al-balad, "al-Philistinyin fi al-Kuwayt" ["The Palestinians in Kuwait"], al-Raʹi al-ᶜAm (March 30, 1985); for an interesting article that sums up the dilemmas faced by expatriots, see T. Farah, F. al-Salem, and M. K. al-Salem, "Arab Labour Migration: Arab Migrants in Kuwait," in Sociology of Developing Societies: The Middle East, ed. Talal Asad and Roger Owen (New York: Monthly Review Press, 1983), pp. 42-53.

23. In 1983, 3,974 Palestinians graduated from high school in Kuwait. In 1984-85, the number was 4,264: Ministry of Education, Statistics Department.

24. Asᶜad Abd al-Rahman, "Educational Attainment among the Palestinian Community in Kuwait" (Paper presented to TEAM International, part of a study on the "Economic and Social Situation and Potential of the Palestinian Arab People," presented in March 1983 to the United Nations Economic Commission for West Asia) (Beirut, November 1981), p. 20; see also Sarah Graham-Brown, Education, Repression, and Liberation: Palestinians (London: World University Press, 1984), p. 136.

25. According to Assistant Consul Gene Sweeney of the U. S. Embassy in Kuwait, from October 1982 to October 1983, 1,150 Palestinian students from Kuwait alone were granted visas to study in the

United States. The yearly average has been 1,000 during the 1980s. Phone interview, Kuwait, summer 1985.

26. Interview with ᶜImad Tahah, Kuwait, summer 1985.

27. Interview with Yusif Abuljubayn, Kuwait, summer 1985.

28. Sarhan, "Family and Kinship," pp. 63-65.

29. Ibid., p. 65.

30. See Fuad I. Khuri, "A Profile of Family Associations in Two Suburbs of Beirut," in Mediterranean Family Structures, ed. J. G. Peristiany (Cambridge: Cambridge University Press, 1976), p. 81-100.

31. Interview with Dr. Subhi Gaushih, Kuwait, summer 1985.

32. Interview with individuals who have participated actively in such centers, Kuwait, summer 1985.

33. Based on interviews conducted among Palestinian families, Kuwait, summer 1985. The characteristics of family gatherings were often brought up during the interviews. I am indebted to Ibrahim Abu-Hijlih for his in-depth comments on this subject. Abu-Hijlih has been, over the last few years, collecting data on pre-1948 peasant culture and folklore. He has acquired many stories, themes, proverbs, and family histories by listening and recording carefully what is said during gatherings.

34. Tawfiq Farah, "al-Tanshi'ah al-wataniyah lil-'atfal al-filistiniyin fi Qatar"["National Socialization of Palestinian Children in Qatar"], Majalat Dirasat al-Khalij wa al-Jazirah al-ᶜArabiyah (July 19, 1979):44-45. See also a similar study: Tawfiq E. Farah, "Political Socialization of Palestinian Children in Kuwait," Journal of Palestine Studies 6, no. 4 (Summer 1977):90-102.

35. For an interesting study on the Nubians and their relationship to their homeland, see Hussein M. Fahim, Egyptian Nubians: Resettlement and Years of Coping (Salt Lake City: University of Utah Press, 1983).

36. Based on discussions with twenty parents and children.

37. Ibid.

38. Telephone interview with Suhayr Abd al-Fatah (daughter), Los Angeles, spring 1987.

39. See Ilene Beatty, "The Land of Canaan," From Heaven to Conquest: Readings in Zionism and the Palestine Problem until 1948, ed. Walid Khalidi (Beirut: Institute for Palestine Studies 1971), p. 3-23.

40. Chaim I. Waxman, America's Jews in Transition (Philadelphia: Temple University Press, 1983), p. 160, 181.; see also Calvin Goldscheider and Alan S. Zuckerman, The Transformation of the Jews (Chicago: University of Chicago Press, 1984), p. 170.

41. Sarhan, "Family and Kinship," p. 66.

42. Andrea Rugh, <u>Family in Contemporary Egypt</u> (Syracuse, N.Y.: Syracuse University Press, 1984), p. 105.

43. Interview with Hajj Khali al-Zir, Kuwait, summer 1985.

7

The Social Foundations of
Village and Town Survival in Kuwait

In the villages, the men meet every night in their
clubs. The women meet on their way to and from
the well, or the spring, where they go to draw
water or to wash their clothes.

In a little village, everybody knows all about each
other. Life is rich when shared with others. The
closer the fellowship between people, the more are
they concerned with each other. This is true,
particularly in an Arab village where strong ties of
kinship exist and the sense of fellowship is keen;
within the family, within the clan, and also within
the village. This may lead to solidarity but easily
also to the conviction that there is no happiness
except within their own circle.

Hilma Granqvist,
Palestine, 1925-1927[1]

The family is at the root of village survival in Kuwait. Through
its day-to-day relations and commitments it has been basic to the existence
of a Palestinian society in Kuwait. As shown in chapter 6, social
relationships, which were conditioned by culture, traditional practice, and
day-to-day needs in pre-1948 Palesine, have forcefully influenced the post-
1948 role of family networks. By the same token, another network based
on old friendships and on village and town ties (that is, ties not determined

by blood) came to be part of the effective and extended social network. An overlap occurred between family and nonfamily relationships. As the exodus took place, village and town relationships suffered from dispersion. As each person sought to help family, however, many nonfamily ties were also strengthened. With time, as every family brought parts of its network to Kuwait, the former village and neighborhood structures came into existence again.

The villagers' and townspeople's strong sense of community allowed them to draw on such ties in the diaspora. According to Lutfiyya, who studied a Palestinian West Bank village in the mid-1960s, villagers "tend to relate themselves to one another. 'We are all cousins,' is a remark often made to a stranger who may ask a villager if he were related to someone in the village who is not a close relative. The villagers refer to themselves as 'we,' as against all others, who are 'they'. This community feeling stems from the biological as well as cultural resemblance that the villagers bear to one another."[2] Hence, as Stirling asserts in the Turkish context, "people belong to their village in a way they belong to no other social group. On any definition of community, the village is a community--a social group with many functions, not all of them explicit, and to which people are committed by birth or marriage, and bound by many ties."[3]

Therefore, when villagers and townspeople are dispersed and exiled, a clustering of social networks around village, place of origin, and kinship produces a predictability of the relationships. This predictability is a function not only of "past association, but is also based on the implications of future interaction."[4] According to Jacobson, "One strategy, therefore, for coping with the uncertainty of urban life is to limit interaction to those with whom association at a future time is expected."[5] Expectations lead migrant villagers and townspeople to seek first family, then village relationships. According to Josef Gugler and William Flanagan, migrants first seek "the extended family, [then] home village, village group to which it belongs, 'subtribe,' 'tribe,' 'supertribe,' nation, race."[6] As a result of these strategies, the city becomes a reflection of rural towns and villages, as if each had been uprooted and replanted in a section of the city or in a sector of the economy. The network of the village in the city becomes an extended form of the closer, face-to-face daily village relations.

This chapter addresses the question of how the families that made up a village or town in Palestine survived as a unit in Kuwait. What mechanism revived the exiled populations of villages and towns destroyed in 1948? The same question applies to the exiles from still-surviving towns and villages located in the West Bank and Gaza and to the very few who escaped destruction in what became Israel proper in 1948.

This chapter focuses on three informal social occasions that extend from the family to the village or town community: marriage, death, and the feast.[7] Without these three social bases, the Palestinians of Kuwait would not have evolved their village networks. These ceremonial occasions provide an ongoing mechanism for the continued reproduction of village and town social relations in the prolonged and increasingly complex diaspora.

The extent to which customary social obligations and ceremonial practices surrounded the life cycle in each village and town in Palestine is impressive. Marriage, the feast, death, and birth were full of ritual, symbolism, and integrative process,[8] which provided them with the capacity to become the social foundations of village survival in exile. In fact, Egyptian and Middle Eastern villages in general share the same level of involvement in ceremonial practices. According to Ammar, "Village life, on the whole, whether in religious or social spheres, is very ritually and ceremonially conscious, and almost invulnerable on this level. Greeting, hospitality, eating, praying, exchange of social obligations, circumcision, marriage, and dozens of items of life are shrouded with ritual and traditional prescriptions."[9]

Consequently, the Palestinian community in Kuwait has become much more than the sum of its families. Each village or town network in Kuwait has become almost a clone of the older village. As Abu-Lughod has observed in the case of Egyptian migrants to Cairo, "With a lower capacity for assimilation, they tend to build for themselves within the city a replica of the culture they left behind."[10] However, such re-creations are not literal. Rather, it is through the social networks and bonds that the villages and towns of Palestine can be found in Kuwait.

Marriage

Dancing is the main thing on these evenings [marriage]. Directly after the moon rises, one hears trilling and singing of women in the village; that is the signal that the festival has begun....After this preliminary grouping, the inhabitants of the village collect; the women go into the house where they dance the whole evening; the men stand outside and make big fires to boil the coffee and for illumination....Meantime, the dance of the men has begun.[11]

H. Granqvist, Palestine, 1933

In the fifty-three years since Granqvist wrote the above, Palestinian marriage festivities have continued, despite displacement, to involve the whole village in Kuwait. Whenever marriage involves a member of, for example, the village of Malhah or of Shwaykah, almost all members of the Malhah or Shwaykah network in Kuwait attend.[12] All ages and both sexes, regardless of whether the marriage is segregated (women in one hall, men in another) or mixed, attend. Rather than celebrate in the village square, like in the old days, marriages in Kuwait take place in rented halls.[13]

Marriage ceremonies in particular furnish village members with a unique opportunity to refresh village ties. The crowds are usually large. The population of most Palestinian villages in Kuwait ranges from a couple of hundred to six or seven thousand. During the event, however, villagers break into small groups to converse and exchange information about work, daily life, and children.

Palestinian parents, out of a strong desire to belong and to discover their roots, find in marriage an occasion to introduce their children to the village network. When they have integrated their children into the network, they experience great pride. According to Ahmad ⁽Uthman of Bayt Safafa,

> When I attend those ceremonies, I am always introduced to the young by their fathers. Though I may not have a constant relationship with many of the families present, the marriage ceremony keeps our ties alive and, in particular, creates new ties based on the participation of the young. In fact, the young are more enthusiastic about village marriage ceremonies than the old. To them the ceremonies have a mystique about them, and they are curious to meet their fellow villagers.[14]

More interestingly, the marriage festival revives the folkloric atmosphere of the village. The participants sing folk songs and dance traditional dances. Many marriages are a replica in every detail of the festival that took place in the village traditionally, but whereas the village festival continued for a week, this one lasts usually for only three to five hours.[15] The families of the bride and groom intentionally choose to re-create the festive atmosphere of the village in Kuwait. To them, it is a source of identity and pride in their heritage.[16] It is part of their continued existence.

The young learn and internalize the dancing and singing. Those who have good voices become good folk singers.[17] In fact, the majority of village youngsters learn their folklore through the marriage festival. It is rare to find a youngster, though born and reared in Kuwait, who does not know at least some of the songs and dances of his or her village.

The families attending the marriage festival are related by centuries of living in the same village and by intermarriage. To one degree or another, everyone in the village is a relative. This adds strength and cohesion to village survival. The village overlaps their concept of family. In other words, the village is the extended network of the family network. It is the social unit that mediates between the family and the wider society. Hence, marriage and marriage festivals provide the opportunity to reproduce and maintain the village in the diaspora.

The marriage festival also provides an occasion for introductions that may result in additional intravillage marriages. Either the young take the initiative in seeking marriage partners, or their mothers investigate the possibility.[18] Every new intravillage marriage reinforces the historical marriage ties already in existence among the different families.[19]

Above all other relationships, marriage in Middle Eastern societies is a powerful linking factor, since it brings two families and their networks into an alliance. Its effect goes far beyond the groom and bride. In fact, it is important enough that families may resist having the groom and bride make the decision themselves. Although since 1948 the Palestinian family has been increasingly less influential in such decisions, it is still quite assertive about its right to veto or agree to a particular marriage.

Marriage and the Community's Developmental Process

After 1967, the Palestinian diaspora social structure, in Kuwait and the Gulf, ceased to be predominantly composed of bachelors. Prior to that time, and particularly among the Palestinians of peasant origin (the majority of Palestinians living in Kuwait), the women and children remained in the village or the refugee camp while their husbands worked in Kuwait. Palestinian men living in Kuwait used to go to the West Bank and Gaza or to Jordan and Lebanon to marry Palestinian women.[20] After marriage, they would return to Kuwait and visit their brides only once every year or two. After the occupation of the West Bank and Gaza in June of 1967, this phenomenon ceased. The war and the new waves of refugees prompted every husband working in Kuwait to bring his immediate family with him.

For the first time, the Palestinians in Kuwait established a natural husband-wife, male-female ratio. This establishment of nuclear families in the same location had an effect on the pattern of marriage introductions.[21] Rather than going to the West Bank, Gaza, or Jordan to marry a relative or

125

village member, Palestinian men started to look for brides who were part of their family or village already living in Kuwait. This resulted in an increase of inter-Palestinian marriages taking place in Kuwait. Since the majority of Palestinians are younger than eighteen, such marriages can be expected to increase rapidly. In other words, in the foreseeable future, there will be more marriage festivals in Kuwait, which will further strengthen community cohesiveness and reinforce the village as a unit of survival in exile.

The Feast

Now the men are going from house to house in the village to greet their neighbors. On this day they all make friends. Sitt Louisa calls it the great Feast of Atonement. The men embrace and make peace with one another. Outside the houses the women greet the approaching male relatives, take their hand which they kiss and lift up to their forehead. This takes place after the prayer in the mosque.

H. Granqvist, Palestine,
1930-1931[22]

Several important religious occasions perform integrative functions in Palestinian society: Christmas and similar religious holidays for Christians; the ʿId for Muslims. The first ʿId is a three-day feast during which Muslims celebrate the end of the month of fasting. The second ʿId takes place when Muslims celebrate the beginning of the Hajj season. The following examples will focus on the functions of the ʿId.

During the first day of the ʿId in Kuwait, after the morning prayer in the mosque, the village men start a day-long tour of village homes. Married and unmarried brothers, with their father and children, move by car from one house to another. In each apartment, they spend fifteen to thirty minutes drinking coffee and wishing family members a happy feast. Dr. Khalil al-Khatib, a physician working in Kuwait from the village of Sawyah, near Nablus, spends the entire first day of every feast visiting members of his village, for example. He and his four married brothers and their children cover at least fifteen village houses.[23]

Today, most families, rather than visiting every house in Kuwait, choose a set of houses to visit. Visiting the older brother or the most respected individual in a particular family, for instance, symbolizes respect and fulfillment of duty to that family.[24] According to Ibrahim Safi, member of the administrative council of the Malhah village fund in

126

Kuwait (Malhah was incorporated into Israel proper in 1948, and all its people became refugees at that time), "During the feast village members visit each other selectively. First, they visit all their relatives, then they visit the village elders and the most respected individuals from the different families in Kuwait. By doing so, they reach quite a proportion of the village in Kuwait."[25] By the end of the first or second day, both the effective and extended family networks have, for the most part, been visited.

As each family conducts its feast tour, it runs into many other villagers who are conducting their own traditional ceremonial tours. They express happiness at meeting, renew ties, converse, and hope to see each other again.

The feast, like marriage, then, performs a linking function at the village level. Its significance lies in its ability to re-establish traditional ties of a Palestinian village or town displaced to Kuwait, by reinforcing the sense of belonging, unity, and cohesion.

Death

Treatment of death and burial customs is not completed by the statement that the body has been interred. Even after the burial there are many ceremonies and duties to be performed.
There are the series of meals and demonstrations of grief, visits of condolence by relatives, the arrival of men and women comforters from other parts of the country, from other villages.

H. Granqvist, Palestine,
1925-1927[26]

Just as they have learned to share their joy through diaspora networks, the Palestinians in Kuwait have also learned to share their grief. They meet as a group to demonstrate their grief over the death of a member of their community. Through the continuation of traditional customs associated with death, they demonstrate who they are and the continuity of past ties. Since the ties themselves are part of their definition of the self, the reinforcement of these ties strengthens cultural unity and social cohesion.

All day long during the three-day mourning sessions that follow the death of a village member, the entire village in Kuwait surrounds the immediate family of the deceased with emotional and social support.[27] In fact, on learning through the village network of a death, people

127

immediately start to assemble in the house announced for the mourning. If the deceased was living in Kuwait, it is usually his or her house; if not, it is the house of the closest relative. If a close relative does not live in the country, then a more distant relative will start the mourning.[28]

According to Jamil Durssiyah, cofounder of the Hawarith fund, an association serving the sixty-five hundred Palestinian Hawarith tribes (who are of Bedouin origin) in Kuwait, "When a death occurs, many of the Hawariths do not go to work that day. And we all meet each other during the period of mourning. Even if the dead person and his family were not on good terms with other Hawarith families, they still go. In death, all differences are put aside."[29]

The presence of mourners during the three-day period of mourning has several connotations. The different families show respect to the deceased person and his or her family. Their participation eases grief. Just by being surrounded by others, Palestinians, like all Middle Easterners and other gregarious societies, experience a sense of shared grief, and therefore relief. Those who die in places where there are no family and village members to mourn are pitied.

The most important aspect of mourning is its impact on the social network. During mourning, the village network, which is an integral part of the extended social network, gathers. Ties are renewed, and the village's existence as a concrete entity is reasserted. Death, as sad as it is, like the feast and marriage, brings old and young together, thereby recharging relationships.

In addition, mourning is a form of intensified village interaction that has politically oriented functions. People make an effort to talk about politics, economics, and social issues, as well as about the dead person and his or her good deeds.[30] They exchange information about each other's concerns, especially the challenges facing them in exile or in the occupied West Bank or Gaza.

As the village members in Kuwait mourn their loss, other members in Jordan, the West Bank, the Gulf, and the rest of the world, also participate, each in their respective localities. In many cases, ads placed by the village appear simultaneously in newspapers throughout the world. This is quite common if the deceased is a particularly distinguished individual or was killed during combat, an air raid, or a demonstration in Gaza or the West Bank. Such ads appear almost daily in Kuwaiti newspapers. For example, several ads were placed in several newspapers in Kuwait and Jordan in September 1982 by former members of the village of Qalonya (Qalonya's population of one thousand was displaced in 1948) to mourn a university student killed in combat in Lebanon during the invasion of 1982.[31] The ads that appeared in Kuwait's al-Qabas and al-Ra'i al-A^{c}m stated,

The people of the village of Qalonya, Jerusalem, in Kuwait, the West Bank, Jordan, and the diaspora mourn the martyr of righteousness and duty: Muhammad Raja Sumrayn, who died in combat in the field of sacrifice in Bahamdun Lebanon. We approach the family of the deceased with our sincerest condolences. We hope that God will provide his family with patience. We all belong to God and to God we shall all return.

Jordan's al-Ra'i had six similar ads for Sumrayn of which one was placed by members of the village of Qalonya in Jordan, and the rest by members of other families from the same village.

In Kuwait, each village mourns several members annually. This provides the village with a recurring mechanism by which ties can be reproduced in the midst of grief.

Additional Integrative Effects

Other social events contribute to the strengthening of the village network. For instance, after the birth of a child in Kuwait, many former village members come to congratulate the family. In many cases, the father invites village men to a luncheon, and the mother receives visitors for quite an extended period after the birth. In pre-1948 Palestine, women were congratulated at their homes after delivery,[32] and men were expected to distribute sweets, if it was a boy, in the men's club.[33]

The arrival in Kuwait of family members from the West Bank, Amman, or Gaza on temporary visits provides another link. In Kuwait the entire village meets them and inquires about relatives in the West Bank or in Gaza, many of whom send letters and presents to their families with the visitor. The house where the guest is staying becomes a village house or even a club during the period of the stay. People come to meet the guest and invite him or her to lunch at their houses. This intensifies communication at the local level. Even villagers formerly from nearby villages in Palestine come to ask about the person and in the process renew intervillage ties.

"Visions of the Return"

The survival of village social ties experienced through ceremonial occasions is just one expression of Palestinian commitment to the lost

129

homeland. An added integrative force derives from people's emotional attachment to the original village. The Palestinian yearning to return to the same villages and towns from which they were expelled in 1948 is strongly integrated into the mechanism of village solidarity and existence in the diaspora. The compelling force of such human emotions reinforces village ties among the Palestinians in Kuwait.[34]

The village and the town of origin are by themselves a unifying factor, so compelling that members seek against great odds to protect their memory, their past, their history, their songs, their distinct dialect, traditions, and ties. Through creating a powerful mystique about the old village, they develop a compelling rationale for return. The Palestinian becomes as "Zionist" as those old Zionists who translated "aspirations and emotions into achievement and action."[35] To the Palestinian, the re-establishment of the settlement of Qalonya, Malhah, or Dayr Yasin is as possible as the establishment over a span of one hundred years of the present Israeli colonies and settlements in Palestine. The Palestinian emotion concerning the village or town of origin is as intense as the sentiments expressed by the psalmist:

> If I forget thee, O Jerusalem, let my right hand forget her cunning. If I do not remember thee, let my tongue cleave to the roof of my mouth; if I prefer not Jerusalem above my chief joy.[36]

Ibrahim Safi, an elderly Palestinian from the village of Malha who had been living in Kuwait since 1954, decided in 1978 to take his wife and children to his occupied village, inhabited since 1948 by Jewish settlers. While in the village, showing his children his house, now occupied by Moroccan Jews, and while pointing to the property of his family and other families in the village, several settlers expressed unhappiness about the visit. An Iraqi Jew was among them, and engaged in the following discussion, which demonstrates the emotional attachment Palestinians have for their lost villages and towns:

> **Settler:** Why have you come to show your children your house? Is your house any dearer to you than my house, which I left behind in Baghdad? I surrendered twelve keys for my twelve-room house to the Iraqi police. When I gave my keys to the Iraqi corporal, he told me, "You son of a dog, get out of here." They rudely took the keys and I left for Israel. Your house here is not any dearer to you than mine in Baghdad.

130

Safi: Remember, although you went to the police station to give up your house keys, mine are still in my pocket. I never gave up anything: not my home, my land, my village, or my rights. You don't consider Iraq home, but I have always considered Palestine and this village as my only home. Yes, I have come here to show my children their lands, the land of our grandfathers who tilled and planted olives in it for hundreds of years. I have told them, "When I die, show this land, your roots, to your children." My home is definitely dearer to me than yours is to you. Since you left Baghdad, you have been happy and satisfied in our homes and in our homeland. Since we Palestinians were forced out, we have never settled, have not experienced happiness, and our thoughts have continuously been fixed on what you have taken from us.[37]

The Palestine that existed before 1948 still lives in the minds of villagers and townspeople in Kuwait.[38] The map of pre-1948 Palestine is firmly embedded in young Palestinians born in Kuwait, among whom the mystique of return is strongest. If Palestinians were permitted to return, every village destroyed in 1948 would have the potential for regeneration along the same family and village lines around which its life revolved before 1948. In other words, among the Palestinians of Kuwait, a superstructure is built along the lines of the villages and towns of the homeland, Palestine. The desire to return and actuate this structure is probably the most invincible emotional strength of the Palestinian diaspora.

Reciprocity of Relations

Alya quoted: "Joy is a debt, and death is a debt."
Sitt Louisa: "This means, the meal of joy is a debt, and the meal of death is a debt."
Alya added: "What they have been given must be returned. All is a loan, *qurda*. Everything is a loan, *den*, even the footsteps, even the tear in the eye. If thou weepest with me I weep with thee.
H. Granqvist, Palestine,
1925-1927[39]

Visiting during the feast, participating in marriage and death and other village occasions, provides the participant with a sense of deep relief in the fulfillment of obligations. Participation in each of the major events of the village, be they joyous or sad, elicits a reciprocal response. Each person feels secure in the understanding that the fulfillment of such obligations will result in reciprocal support from others in his or her time of death, marriage, or other occasion requiring respect.

Interfamily and intervillage relations are governed by the same reciprocal principle. If this principle is not observed, relations crumble and a crisis develops. In fact, those who do not honor the values and ways of the village are isolated from the village and are accused of arrogance and indifference. They drop out of the village entity, though their families remain solidly a part of it. This informal banishment is limited to a particular household or individial.[40]

Urbanites

The fact that these examples have come from villages does not lessen the importance of marriage, the feast, and death for Palestinians of urban origin. Although the peasantry has set an example with its close-knit relations and ability to survive, Palestinians of urban origin have a similar record. Indeed, marriage, death, and the feast also serve an integrative purpose for them. Certainly, those of urban origin visit, socialize, and fulfill the responsibilities the culture encourages. Yet, in comparison to peasants, urbanites have more complex, relatively less-personal networks, which relate to the social framework of the city of origin. The village is an interrelated unit of families that have intermarried and coexisted for centuries; urban populations have been more open, and involve a larger, more complex network of ancestral origins. Hence, not all Gazans or Jaffans can be part of every social activity involving death, marriage, and the feast, but a sizable percentage does participate in such occasions. Thus each former city may be broken into sections that resemble neighborhoods (mostly based on intermarriages with families from the former city) established in exile.

Conclusion

The preceding sociological realities together form the bases of village survival in Kuwait. None of the factors can be separated. All form part of a process that provides the village with its informal system of existence. Without these social foundations, many of the four hundred

132

villages and towns destroyed in 1948 would not have been able to re-establish ties.

Before the diaspora, the village composed what amounted to a social and economic unit. In the diaspora, it has become a set of informal relations that are often strengthened by marriage, death, the feast, and similar events. Such events, in conditions present in Kuwait, have functionally compensated for the lack of geographic proximity.

Village networks in Kuwait and the rest of the diaspora are a result of a multiplicity of factors. On the one hand, they have to do with natural informal ties that existed in pre-1948 Palestine. Such ties, based on friendship or marriage or similarity in values and attitudes, provided the channels for the rise of diaspora village structures. But this was not enough. The need for collective security in the face of a painful, prolonged diaspora caused the family network to treat village ties as an extended social network with the potential of becoming effective in times of crisis. In fact, the whole process of revival is an act of self-defense at the individual, family, and village levels. Without this continuing need to defend the social, psychological, cultural, economic, and political units, many of the ties embodied in village and town would have been less strong. This urgent need to be present at every village funeral and marriage to identify oneself with the village or to look after fellow villagers and townspeople would have been much weaker, and might have died among the younger generations. Instead such ties have strengthened. Empathy resulting from common suffering and destiny is a driving force in the increased need of the Palestinians to strengthen their village and town ties.

Most Palestinian village or town gatherings have a strong political aspect to them. Events in the Palestinian camps in Lebanon as well as in the occupied homeland are talked about in every group gathering. All discussion is dominated by the uncertainties of the future. The young tend to be more hopeful and militant, whereas the old, who have witnessed the disappointments, are more pessimistic.

In sum, the village, like Palestine, has become for the exiled Palestinians a state of mind. It is always remembered in a positive way. None of the problems they faced in the original village are recollected. The poverty of some, the class distinctions, the bad harvests, and family feuds have all assumed a secondary status in memory. The suffering since 1948 and the nature of the Palestinians' exile and dispossession have converted the village and town of origin into an ideal.

NOTES

1. Hilma Granqvist, <u>Muslim Death and Burial: Arab Customs and Traditions Studied in a Village in Jordan</u> (Helsinki: Societas Scientiarum Fennica. Commentations Humanarum Lifterarum, 34.1, 1965), pp. 19-20. Dr. Hilma Granqvist (1890-1972), a Finn of Swedish extraction, was the first scholar ever to conduct an ethnographic study of a Palestinian Village (Art'as). She lived in the village for three years between 1925 and 1931. See <u>Portrait of a Palestinian Village: The Photographs of Hilma Granqvist</u>, ed. Karen Seger (London: Third World Center for Research and Publications, 1981), pp. 9-11.

2. Abdullam Lutfiyya, <u>Baytin: A Jordanian Village</u> (London: Mouton and Company, 1966), p. 175.

3. Paul Stirling, <u>Turkish Village</u> (New York: John Wiley and Sons, 1965), p. 29.

4. David Jacobson, "Mobility, Continuity, and Urban Social Organization," <u>Man</u> 6 (December 1971):633.

5. Ibid.

6. Josef Gugler and William G. Flanagan, <u>Urbanization and Social Change in West Africa</u> (Cambridge: At the University Press, 1978), p. 75.

7. In almost every case, my interviewees brought to my attention the importance of marriage, feasts, and death to village survival in the diaspora. My own attendance at such social events has helped me appreciate this fact.

8. See Granqvist, <u>Muslim Death and Burial</u>; idem, <u>Birth and Childhood among the Arabs: Studies in a Muhammadan Village in Palestine</u> (Helsingfors: Soderstrom and Co. Forlagsaktiebolag, 1947); idem, <u>Marriage Conditions in a Palestinian Village</u> Vol. 1, (Helsingfors: Societas Scientiarum Fennica. Commentations Humanarum Litterarum 3.8, 1931); idem, <u>Marriage Conditions in a Palestinian Village</u> Vol. 2, (Helsingfors: Societas Scientiarum Fennica. Commentations Humanarum Litterarum 6.8, 1935). See also Lutfiyya, <u>Baytin</u>; Hamed Ammar, <u>Growing Up in an Egyptian Village: Silwa, Province of Aswan</u> (New York: Octagon Books, 1900), p. 78; Stirling, <u>Turkish Village</u>.

9. Ammar, <u>Growing Up</u>, p. 78.

10. Janet Abu-Lughod, "Migrant Adjustment to City Life: The Egyptian Case," <u>American Journal of Sociology</u> 67, no. 1 (July 1961):23.

11. Granqvist, <u>Marriage Conditions in a Palestinian Village</u> Vol. 2, pp. 35-36.

12. Interview with Ahmad Msamih of Shwaykah, and Ibrahim Safi of Malhah, Kuwait, summer 1985.

13. See Lutfiyya, <u>Baytin</u>, p. 135.

14. Interview with Ahmad ᶜUthman, Kuwait, summer 1985.

15. See Lutfiyya, Baytin, p. 135; see also Granqvist, Marriage Conditions in a Palestinian Village Vol. 2, pp. 30-138.

16. Fieldwork interviews, Kuwait, summer 1985.

17. Ibid.

18. Taghreed Alqudsi-Ghabra, "City and Village in a Palestinian Wedding Song" (unpublished, Austin, Texas, fall 1984).

19. See Robert Springborg, Family, Power, and Politics in Egypt (Philadelphia: University of Pennsylvania Press, 1982), p. 73; James Bill and Carl Leiden, Politics in the Middle East 2d ed. (Boston: Little, Brown and Company, 1984), p. 92.

20. Asᶜad Abd al-Rahman, al-'Awdaᶜ al-taᶜlimiyah lil-jaliyah al-filistinyah fi al-Kuwayt. [Educational Attainment among the Palestinian Community in Kuwait] (Paper presented to TEAM International, part of a study on the "Economic and Social Situation and Potential of the Palestinian Arab People," presented in March 1983 to the United Nations Economic Commission for West Asia) (Beirut, November 1981), p. 8. All field interviews have confirmed this observation.

21. Ibid.

22. Granqvist, Muslim Death and Burial, p. 184.

23. Interview with Khalil al-Khatib, Kuwait, summer 1984 and summer 1985.

24. This stems from the extensive symbolism and protocol involved in Middle Eastern interfamily relations.

25. Interview with Ibrahim Safi, Kuwait, summer 1985.

26. Granqvist, Muslim Death and Burial, p. 87.

27. My observation and fieldwork interviews support this statement.

28. See chapter 6.

29. Interview with Jamil Dursiyah, Kuwait, summer 1985.

30. Field interviews.

31. al-Rai' (Jordan), September 1982; al-Rai' al-ᶜAm (Kuwait), September 12, 1982; Al-Qabas (Kuwait) September 12, 1982. See al-Rai' al-ᶜAm and al-Qabas, Kuwait, September 12, 1982.

32. Granqvist, Birth and Childhood, pp. 89-92.

33. Ibid., pp. 79-80.

34. A. L. Tibawi, "Visions of Return: The Palestine Arab Refugees in Arabic Poetry and Art," Middle East Journal 7, no. 5 (Autumn 1976):507-526.

35. Ibid, p. 509.

36. Quoted in ibid, p. 508.

37. Interview with Ibrahim Safi, Kuwait, summer 1985.

38. On the existence of two maps for Palestine--one Israeli and another Palestinian--see Meron Benevisti, Conflicts and Contradictions (New York: Villard Books, 1986), pp. 197-202.

39. Granqvist, Muslim Death and Burial, pp. 87-88.

40. On social boycott and its relation to social control, see Richard T. Antoun, "Pertinent Variables in the Environment of Middle Eastern Village Politics: A Comparative Analysis," in Rural Politics and Social Change in the Middle East, ed. Richard Antoun and Iliya Harik (Bloomington: Indiana University Press, 1972), p. 133.

8

Village and Town Funds and Associations

The re-created and strengthened family, village, and town ties resulting from the informal mechanisms at work in Kuwait laid the groundwork for an additional survival mechanism, the village and town fund. Since the mid-1970s, hundreds of such funds have sprung up. Their impact on the cohesion of the former villages or towns is impressive. In fact, a friendly form of competition has taken root among Palestinian villages and towns in Kuwait for the establishment of such funds.

Although the effective and extended family networks meet many needs and perform basic functions in Kuwait, other needs call for higher forms of organization. As the network is enlarged and as increasing economic pressures create more needs, the family is forced to expand its functions. These expanded functions give rise to the village funds. Such associations are based on informal ties and networks and they exist to strengthen these ties and to support needy members. The informal, voluntary associations may be funeral benefit societies or savings associations for a particular village or town. They may help those who cannot send their children to school, or they may support others who cannot pay their rent.

According to Janet Abu-Lughod, the migrant's adjustment in the new urban environment "is further facilitated by the formal and informal institutions he develops within his small community, one of which . . . . [is] the village benevolent society."[1] In Cairo, "the Directory of Social Agencies . . . . lists more than 100 village benevolent associations." These societies "extend aid to members" and "provide burial facilities."[2] To the migrant family, the village fund becomes an important additional mechanism of support stemming from former village ties. It represents a meeting ground on which several families merge into a wider unit, that is, the village association. These associations and funds contribute to the stability of village and town social relationships. For a people who are experiencing intense geographical mobility and its resulting disruptions, such associations give them "a place and an identity in urban society regardless of their movement into and out of various urban centers."[3]

This chapter portrays the village and town funds in the context of background and occupations of Palestinian village and town populations. Representative cases of funds including populations from different geographic areas, from village and town, and from Bedouin communities have been chosen. Gaza, a city (district) and Tarshiha, a village, do not have associations, but they have been included because of their importance in the survival of town and village in Kuwait.

The Hebronites

The Hebronites, a model of solidarity, are by far the most organized and formally integrated group among the diaspora Palestinians. Unlike many villages and towns destroyed in 1948, Hebron was occupied alongside the West Bank, East Jerusalem, and Gaza in 1967. Like the rest of the towns and villages of the West Bank and Gaza, its population suffered from partial displacement. More than half of the Hebronites still live in their city, Hebron. They make up, except for a few Israeli settlers, the entire population of the city.

In Kuwait, Jordan, Saudi Arabia, and the rest of the diaspora, the Hebronites have managed to set up an extremely efficient support system. Indeed, the Hebronites set an example in diaspora solidarity as early as 1952. As their diaspora became larger, they carried with them their family and town loyalties. Among the Palestinians, they earned a reputation for closeness, dedication to each other, and stubbornness when confronting the complex challenges of the diaspora. Much more than any other Palestinian community in exile, they have acquired a special group consciousness. According to Rabah al-Natshih, president of the Hebronite Fund in Kuwait, "this has been a great asset in the diaspora. There is nothing wrong with it. On the contrary, if all members of the Palestinian towns in exile followed the Hebronite example, their ability to survive would be enhanced."[4]

The cohesiveness and organization of the Hebronites is, to a large extent, a function of the transitional nature of Palestinian society, which embodies a mixture of modernity and tradition. They have, more than any other group of Palestinians, achieved an even balance of these two forces.

138

For instance, among the Palestinians of peasant origin, the relationship between traditional values, occupations, and family allegiance, on the one hand and modern values, occupations, and education, on the other, was, particularly in the 1950s, strongly skewed toward tradition. Among Palestinians from other cities, such as Haifa or Jerusalem, the mix was relatively skewed toward modern skills, occupations, and education.

The Hebronites, known for their traditional trading skills and craftsmanship, are in essence a product of an ancient city that preserved its strong hamula (combining several families who share the same patriarchal ancestor) and family system. The closeness of the Naqav desert, where most Palestinian Bedouins lived, and their strong trading links to Hebron, helped strengthen the hamula system in Hebron.[5] No doubt the slower pace of economic change, before 1948, in Hebron as compared to Jerusalem, Jaffa, and Haifa is another factor. But, since 1948, they have supplemented their traditional family system and their traditional trading mentality with modern educational skills. Indeed, since 1948, the Hebronites have been molded by this unique set of opposites. This balance of the hamula tradition with modern education has made them exceptionally capable in the task of survival in the diaspora.

The first Hebronites in Kuwait after 1948 began the process of informal support and dedication to one another. In addition, their trading skills found an outlet in Kuwait's private sector. The rest found enployment in commercial, government, or professional jobs. By supporting one another and by creating opportunities for one another, they have come to be concentrated in particular economic sectors. By the 1970s, a sizable percent of the Hebronite work force in Kuwait (the total number of Hebronites in Kuwait is now estimated at eight thousand[6]) was working in trade and freight-related occupations. Consequently, some of the best and largest companies involved in transporting goods between Kuwait, Saudi Arabia, Iraq, Jordan, and Lebanon, such as Yalli and CAlayyan, are owned by Hebronites. Hebronites are very important in trucking in Kuwait. They have matched this with a similar performance in Jordan's transportation system, thus making them special traders from one end of the Middle East to the other.

The Hebronites' strong sense of solidarity made them leaders in the effort to utilize their informal town relations to create an association for themselves. Such efforts in Jordan and the West Bank go back to the 1950s. In Kuwait, the movement started in 1976.[7] Prior to 1976, the informal interfamily solidarity network worked to the satisfaction of all Hebronites. They were committed to the support of one another whenever they informally met. But in 1976, the socioeconomic pressures stemming from a prolonged diaspora created a need for a formal support structure. According to CAbd al-Majid al-Natshih, a lawyer from Hebron and cofounder of the Hebron Charitable Fund and the University Graduate Union of the Hebron district in Kuwait,

> Before the 1967 war, the Hebronites sought temporary work in Kuwait. After the war, the Israelis blocked their return. This marked the beginning of a difficult diaspora for all Hebronites in exile. In 1967, the social and economic pressures resulting from such exile started to have a deep effect on the Hebronites, thus making formal solidarity among them a natural outcome to the post-1967 reality in Kuwait.[8]

The idea of a Hebronite fund in Kuwait came to a head when, in 1976, a Hebronite who enjoyed a fairly good standard of living died. During the three-day mourning period, to the surprise of friends and relatives, it was discovered that the man had left nothing substantial to take care of his immediate family.[9] Like the majority of Palestinians in Kuwait, the family depended for its living on the husband's salary. Since expatriates cannot own property and are not entitled to retirement benefits, once the supporter of the family dies, the family becomes totally helpless.[10] Suddenly, it is difficult to pay for the children's college education, to cover the rent, or even to pay precollege expenses. The fact that expatriates who arrived after 1961 and who are not engineers and physicians, or who do not work for the Ministries of Health and Education have not since 1979 been able to put their children in free public schools only complicates the matter. A 1978 rent law that permits the "landlord to increase the rent by no more than 100 percent after five years" has created a serious crisis as well.[11]

Several leading Hebronites known for their community commitment called a meeting immediately after that death in 1976. Sixty concerned Hebronite community leaders attended. The sixty were able to form a Kuwait chapter of the Hebronite Charitable Fund. Since 1976, the fund's council has been able to draw on overwhelming support from the majority of Hebronites in Kuwait.[12] In fact, fieldwork in Kuwait turned up few Hebronites who had not renewed their fund membership. In two adjacent buildings in Hawali housing fifteen families from Hebron, for instance, only two did not pay their twelve-dinar annual membership fee.

The fund supports its members in case of death, economic crisis, or total disability.[13] In case of death or disability, the immediate family receives financial support. If the deceased or disabled was unmarried, the immediate family receives one thousand dinars (Approximately $3000); if married, thirteen hundred dinars are immediately given to the spouse and children. The spouse receives an additional three hundred dinars.[14] In all cases involving the disability or death of a working parent, the fund finances the higher education of the children already enrolled in college who are willing to repay this no-interest loan upon graduation.[15]

The fund has strengthened informal Hebronite solidarity in other ways. For instance, when one of Hebron's dignitaries visits Kuwait, the fund's council can mobilize several hundred Hebronites to welcome him at the airport. The fund also conducts an annual ceremony for Kuwait's Hebronite high school graduates. Likewise, member parents looking for brides for their sons are allowed to look at the membership lists, which provide data on the age and the education of every family member.[16]

The success of the fund encouraged its members and founders to establish in Kuwait in 1980 a chapter of the Hebron University Graduate Union. This union, which restricts its membership to Hebron's university graduates, is dedicated to the encouragement of education among the members of the Hebron community in Kuwait. The union provides "financial and moral support to students" and "pursues any effort aimed at improving the social, scientific, and educational standards in the district of Hebron."[17] From its establishment to 1985, the union had financed the higher education of thirty students from the community in Kuwait.[18]

The Hebronite Fund in Kuwait, like all Palestinian family and village relationships, has an ongoing cross-national aspect. It would seem that, by nature, a dispersed people cannot but reflect, through its ties and associations, its essential cohesiveness. Therefore, every Palestinian activity in one country has a counterpart in another. While local needs and the structure of every community are basic to the process that makes Palestinians in Kuwait or elsewhere create a fund, the spread of ideas and methods of combating the problem is very much influenced by the constant interchange between the scattered Palestinian communities. Once a village or family fund begins to operate in Kuwait or Amman, for example, it is concerned with its local and cross-national constituencies. The dispersed whole is very important because all members consider themselves part of a wider network of family and village ties.

Each fund, then, has national headquarters in addition to the local chapters. A fund may start in Kuwait or Amman or the West Bank, but as needs and ideas spread, it slowly establishes chapters in other countries. Hebron's University Graduate Union in Kuwait, for example, was initiated after a visit from the president and founder of the union in Jordan. In this context, both encouragement from the leadership of the union and the Kuwait Hebronites' awareness of the need for such a fund made the foundation of a local chapter possible.

To clarify the broader context of many of the village and town funds in Kuwait, an example from the Hebron University Graduate Union will be helpful. This union, though established only in 1980 in Kuwait, has been operating in the town of Hebron and among Hebronites as a successful educational institution since September 1953. Its founder, a renowned philanthropist and lawyer, ^cAbd al-Khaliq Yaghmur, started the league as a voluntary association aimed at combating the prevailing low educational standards in Hebron during the early 1950s.[19] Yaghmur's efforts were directed at starting a secondary school that included senior high school. This school has awarded four thousand Hebronites the Egyptian high school (Tawjihi) degree between 1955 and 1967.[20] More significantly, Yaghmur's efforts and financial support from the league made it possible for many of those high school graduates to pursue higher education in Egypt.[21]

In addition to making high school education available, the league's record during the last three decades has been quite impressive. In 1955, it founded the first public library in Hebron.[22] In 1966, the league started a fully-equipped secondary and intermediate school in Hebron. In 1978, it established in Hebron a two-year polytechnic college. This college has graduated hundreds of qualified individuals.[23] Through the polytechnic, and to improve its standards, eight students are sent annually to the United States and Great Britain to earn an M.A. or a Ph.D.[24] In 1973, the league's chapter in Amman established a student housing center on land bought by the league. This center at present houses 120 Palestinian students who come from the West Bank to study in Amman. The project envisions the creation of an additional building, which will house up to 200 more students.[25] The center also provides other services, such as locating apartments for Palestinian students arriving from the West Bank.[26] Furthermore, since 1980, the league has financed printing of several important out-of-print books on Palestine.[27] It has also conducted cultural activities and social gatherings and has sponsored speakers on a variety of subjects.[28]

In addition to the strength of the Hebronites' informal network and the efficency of their formal association, another, more important factor, has enhanced the influence of the Hebronite funds in Hebron, Amman, and Kuwait. The ability of the institution to establish democratic structures has been basic to its strength and growth. In the words of Muhammad ^cAyach Milhim, cofounder of the league's Kuwait chapter,

> the league's success is attributable to the commitment and
> impartiality of its president, ^cAbd al-Khaliq Yaghmur, the

well-founded supremacy of the spirit of democratic dialogue, and a fair voting process. These factors attracted the largest possible number of league members to active participation in its three chapters. In this the league became an example for many funds, associations, and institutions in the diaspora.[29]

Spread of the Funds

The Hebron Charitable Fund in Kuwait resulted from a deeply felt need. Its initiation, however, was directly influenced by the death of a Hebronite in 1976. It is remarkable how a small incident can, if conditions are ripe, produce a significant amount of activity in response. Many such funds created between 1970 and 1975 did not survive for more than a year or two in the absence of appropriate conditions.[30] The case of the Hebronites, which involved a death and coincided with deeply felt social and economic pressures, led directly to the formation of hundreds of formal Palestinian village and town associations throughout Kuwait. The Palestinian villages and towns in Kuwait looked to the Hebronite Charitable Fund and to Hebron's long record in diaspora organization as a model.

The Jerusalem Fund exemplifies a fund influenced by the Hebron experience but based on looser, more informal ties. This fund, established in 1980, is designed to continue the support of the Palestinians in Jerusalem and the Jerusalemite community in Kuwait. To create this fund, the founders had to call on the informal Jerusalemite network in Kuwait. Its formation was influenced by the special attachment Jerusalemites have to their city. When the fund was formed, families such as the Dajanis, Husaynis, Khalidis, Nashashibis, Budayris, Daqaqs, Abdos, and Gaushihs sent representatives to the meeting.[31]

The Jerusalem Fund emphasizes support to Jerusalem, primarily through several fund-raising parties supported by the fifteen thousand Jerusalemites living in Kuwait.[32] The first fund-raising party was dedicated to the support of a Jerusalem-based association responsible for the Aqsa schools. A new school was established, others were expanded, and transportation for students in Jerusalem was provided. In 1984, eighty thousand dinars (Approximately $240,000) were raised for the expansion of a Jerusalem hospital, and needy Jerusalemite families were also provided support through local Palestinian charitable organizations.

Through the fund, a children's band was established to perform traditional songs of the Jerusalem area, in line with the fund's policy of strengthening the commitment to Jerusalem. The fund also asked children of members to write essays about their house and neighborhood in

Jerusalem; through this assignment many have learned who they are and where they came from.

Nablus followed Jerusalem by forming a fund in Kuwait in 1982. The Nablus Fund basically dedicated its efforts to the support of widows and of students in need of funding to continue their schooling. At least two hundred families have received support from the fund since 1982. Support has taken the form of paying the family's rent, electricity bill, or the tuition of a child in elementary school.[33]

Competition as Motivation

The tendency of villages and towns to compete with each other points up the magnitude of intertown and village competition in the Palestinian diaspora. In Middle Eastern society, families see themselves in reference to other families. The same is true of villages, towns, and neighborhoods. Families, towns, and villages observe the behavior of other families and towns. It is important to them that they not be left behind.

If one studies the development of education or migration to Kuwait from this particular angle, ample evidence is found to support this thesis. If a town or family in Palestine, for instance, sends its young to school in a particular city, other villages and families follow suit. If a family in a village starts a new business, interfamily competition is initiated by other similar businesses springing up. After a few years, other villages follow the new trend. During the 1920s, it took only one individual in a village to send a child to school to prompt even the most hesitant, in the family and the village, to do the same after a few years. "His son will become a government employee and will make as much as all our family combined," people say. This competitiveness has been exported to Kuwait.

Such competition may have both positive and negative results. Families, villages, and towns keep committing themselves to each other through such competition. Immediate need is not the only motivating factor. Some of those who came to Kuwait in the early 1950s from the West Bank were motivated by this same interfamily and village competition. In some instances, family and village members who were not hit as hard as others by the economic crisis collectively decided to go to Kuwait anyway after seeing that other families and villages had already gone. They realized that those who went first might, after returning, change the power structure of the village. They were drawn to the competition in order not to be left behind. Long-term needs and interests were at stake.

The influence of this type of competition manifests itself in free enterprise, in political activity, in almost every sphere of life. Underlying

144

all of these areas of endeavor are interfamily and intervillage power relations. This aspect definitely has a motivating force with tremendous impact on Palestinians and on all family-oriented societies. Whereas in the West individual competition is supreme, in the East, it seems, family and village add to and overlap individual competition.

Therefore, the survival of a particular village or town is seen by villagers and townspeople in reference to other villages and towns. It troubles members of a village to realize that another town is forming an association and they are not. Once Hebron, a major city, started its fund in Kuwait, Jerusalem and Nablus immediately followed. When Raja Sumrayn was convincing representatives of Qalonya's different families in Kuwait of the need for a fund, he told them that Qalonya must demonstrate a solidarity of spirit similar to that of the other Palestinian village networks in Kuwait City. He, like his fellow village members, felt they needed the fund not only to meet important and pressing economic challenges, but also to prevent their lagging behind in village solidarity.

The Gazans in Kuwait

Unlike the Hebronites, those who came to Kuwait from Gaza had no history of establishing formal associations. But, like the Hebronites, they had a close family network. Almost every important family from the district of Gaza, including the towns of Khan-Unis and Rafah, have members in Kuwait.[34] Such families include, among others, the al-Za^cnun, al-Shawwas, al-Rayyises, al-^cAlamis, Abu-Ghazalahs, al-Farras, al-'Agahs, Zu^crubs, al-'Astals, al-Khazindars, and Abu-Nahyahs.

Among the fifty thousand to sixty thousand Gazans in Kuwait, a system of continued family relations, support, and help has survived.[35] Although the Gazans have not yet developed a formal association in Kuwait, they have been successful, through intrafamily and interfamily communication at marriage, the feast, death, and other social events, in reinforcing their relationships at every level.[36] Furthermore, like the Hebronites and, for that matter most Palestinians, their support of each other in employment and times of need has also reinforced their solidarity in exile.

Their high level of education has also strengthened their solidarity in Kuwait. When the Egyptian universities opened their doors to all Gaza residents immediately after the war of 1948, thousands were able to obtain a college education. This allowed them to close the huge gap between them and most of Palestine's other cities. The majority of Gazans in Kuwait and in the Gulf are graduates of universities and teaching colleges, employed as teachers, physicians, and engineers. The sole reason for the low percentage

145

of laborers, technicians, and similar occupations from the district of Gaza in Kuwait and the Gulf is lack of opportunity. Because all Gazans carry stateless travel documents, which restrict their movements in and out of Egypt, and due to geographic reasons, this strata did not make it to the Gulf. Instead, the majority of those who came were professionals who arrived in Kuwait on a contract basis during the 1950s and 1960s for the Ministries of Education or Health and other interested employing agencies.[37] Fifty percent or more of them are employed in the public or private schools as teachers.[38] The majority of Gazan women work in teaching jobs as well, which has an impact on family structure and size.[39]

During the summer of 1985, the idea of a formal fund started to attract a following among the Gazans in Kuwait. During 1985, members of the town of Khan-Unis of the district of Gaza met several times to start a fund. The charter was voted on and meetings were scheduled. The cities of Gaza and Khan-Unis will probably soon be part of the trend toward community groups maintaining funds and fund organizations.

The Peasantry and Village Associations

The Village of Qalonya

Like the towns, villages were also motivated to establish funds. In fact, the majority of villages in Kuwait have such funds. The village of Qalonya, located to the west of Jerusalem, was destroyed by the Israeli army in 1948. All of its people became refugees, and the village and its lands were incorporated into Israel proper.[40] Its members regrouped in Amman, the West Bank, the Gulf, and the United States. At present, the exiled population of the village comprises almost 7,000.[41] The majority reside in the West Bank and in Jordan. Four hundred and fifty Qalonians live in Kuwait, and almost 350 live in the United States, mostly in Chicago. Many reside in the Gulf, and some in Great Britain.

In 1976, Dr. Raja Sumrayn of Qalonya consulted with village elders and working members in Kuwait about the need to address the problems facing their diaspora.[42] The village's informal social bonds were clearly not sufficient to solve problems of retirement, illness, accident, death, and education, although many of these problems were being addressed through family or family funds. Therefore, forty working members met several times in what they called the General Assembly of the Village of Qalonya in Kuwait. This resulted in the establishment of the Qalonya Association for Social Development. An executive committee of seven was elected.

146

In 1980, news of the association reached village members in Chicago and Amman. Immediately, they formed similar associations. The association's temporary headquarters is at present in Amman. This expansion of activity is the norm for such funds. The Singil Association of the West Bank village of Singil is another example of a fund that began in Kuwait and collected large sums of money from village members, and then transferred it all to Amman to establish the Singil Association in Amman.[43]

The villagers of Qalonya in the diaspora are still grouped in three interrelated large hamulas. The first one, Khattab, comprises four major family units: the ᶜAskars, Dirbas, Makhlufs, and Hamdans. The second hamula is al-Ghalith. It comprises the Mishᶜal and Ghalith families. The third is Abu-Saᶜd, which is made up of the Khatib and ᶜAbbud families.[44] Each of these hamulas is divided into several smaller families, which are named after their particular founder, usually the fifth grandfather of the hamula line. The ᶜAskar family is further divided in the same manner into the Sumrayns and Matars.[45]

Qalonya, as before 1948, still has three mukhtars (the highest official position in a village).[46] They reside in Jordan and are recognized by the Jordanian authorities.[47] These mukhtars are agreed upon by all the village families. Their authority is to a large extent symbolic, yet they perform some essential functions on the village level. The particular mukhtar assigned to each family signs death and birth certificates. In fact, these mukhtars are the only individuals who can legitimately verify all birth certificates of the generation born before 1948.

The Village of al-Malhah

The case of Qalonya is quite similar to that of hundreds of Palestinian village networks in Kuwait. Al-Malhah is another village that fell to the Israelis in 1948.[48] At present, it has a population of five thousand distributed between the West Bank, the Kingdom of Jordan, the Gulf, and the United States. In Kuwait, there are twelve hundred individuals who hail from al-Malhah. In 1982, al-Malha fund was established in Kuwait. It immediately drew the support of the majority of the village members. The fund was actually a chapter of a parent organization for al-Malhah located and registered in Amman.

In addition to its financial commitments, the fund in Kuwait promotes village integration. For instance, every month the elected village council of al-Malhah's fund conducts a meeting with members of one of the village's families in Kuwait. During the meeting, the council ar ᵗʰᵃ family discuss their concerns and views. Such meetings guarantᵉ

147

council members become known to every village member and that the council acquires a special knowledge mixed with a deeper appreciation of the dilemmas facing individuals and families in Kuwait.

When a village elder or dignitary comes from the United States or Amman or the West Bank, the council meets him at the airport and encourages village members to visit him after arrival. In summary, the al-Malhah Council, like the other councils that have sprung up since 1976, has added to its financial functions a commitment to promote traditional village values and cohesiveness.

The Village of Tarshiha

Tarshiha has not established an association, but it has established another mechanism for strengthening village ties. The villagers have quite a fair standard of living, which, as in the case of Gaza, has motivated them less to provide social welfare functions through a village association. When a villager needs help, others informally generate immediate aid.[49]

Tarshiha is in northern Palestine. In 1948 most of its inhabitants were transferred to Lebanon's Burj al-Barajnah refugee camp. Over the years, much of Tarshiha's refugee population has been able to acquire a college education and move to the Gulf or to Jordan, where they have worked as government employees, engineers, or doctors.

At present, there are between eleven thousand and thirteen thousand village members worldwide, of which the majority carry stateless travel documents issued after 1948 by the Lebanese government. The Tarshihans' will to educate themselves has set an example among the diaspora Palestinians. Of the forty-one heads of Tarshihan families in Kuwait, twenty-two have college degrees, mostly acquired after 1948. The rest, who have high school degrees, have demonstrated outstanding ability in their work. This has provided them with a most needed mobility. Furthermore, of eighty-eight of their children who are over eighteen, sixty-two, or 70 percent, have now earned college degrees.

The members of the village of Tarshiha in Kuwait total approximately 252. There were 41 original nuclear families, which belong to four larger ones. But as the young men and women married, the number of Tarshiha households in Kuwait increased to 84. Instead of a village fund, the Tarshihan community in Kuwait decided to invest in the maintenance of their cohesiveness by other means. As their community in Kuwait grew, they established a habit of meeting every Thursday evening in the house of one of the villagers. During these meetings, many members of the community gather to play chess and discuss social, cultural, or political issues. Those who cannot make it to the gathering one week are usually

148

present the next. These evenings spent together promote solidarity and reinforce social ties for the Tarshihan diaspora.

Tarshiha has a remarkable record of attendance in marriage, death, feast, and many other occasions. The night before Muhammad Samarah was interviewed for this study, he was at a gathering for many village members and village friends in Kuwait. The gathering was to celebrate the fact that a young woman from the village had made a remarkable score on her high school exam. Even at such informal occasions the majority of the Tarshihan community is in attendance.

Such gatherings are not unique for Tarshihans. Every year, families, villagers, and friends from village and town networks in Kuwait meet together when a family or village member achieves an outstanding high school score. This particular success establishes a model to be emulated by younger villagers. The family and the village community reinforce this model to encourage students to be diligent in their studies. Without such competitiveness, few Palestinians could make it into Arab universities, which set high entrance requirements and impose strict quotas. It is not surprising, therefore, that, for almost a decade, 75 to 95 percent of the fifty highest scorers in the yearly high school exit examination in Kuwait are Palestinians.[50]

The Hawarith Bedouin Tribes

The Palestinian Bedouins are known for their intense, but informal, ties. The Hawariths were a leading force in establishing a solid, more formal structure among the former Bedouins now living in Kuwait. In fact, the sixty-five hundred Hawariths in Kuwait, like all of Palestine's former Bedouins, have one of the most closely knit networks of all Palestinians. Their responsibility to one another surpasses that of the peasants and the urbanites. Their loyalty to family and willingness to commit resources, time, and effort in support of one another are unquestioned. Pride in being able to deliver aid to one's kin is an integral part of the group consciousness.

Before 1948, the Hawariths inhabited the area between Haifa and Jaffa to the west of Tulkarim. For hundreds of years, they resided in the valley that became known as the Hawarith Valley living in Buyut sha°r (homes made of camelskin). All of the Bedouins who inhabited the valley, including those who migrated to it over the years, became known as Hawariths. Therefore, although the original Hawariths gave the valley its name, other tribes who inhabited the valley adopted its name.[51] The Hawariths were quite settled in the valley and very proud of their independent lifestyle. Some of them did leave during certain seasons of the

149

year to take their cattle to the West Bank hills near the villages of A^cttil and Shwaykah,[52] but they always returned.

Under the British mandate (1920-1948), the Hawariths continued to farm the valley, engage in animal husbandry, and fish. They also worked in manual jobs in British army camps. When tensions eased with Jewish settlers, they worked in the coastal settlements.[53] By the 1920s , many were working for Palestinian grove owners in the coastal areas.

In 1948, the Hawarith lands fell to the Israelis and all of the Hawariths were displaced. The majority were displaced into makeshift refugee camps established in the West Bank, in particular, the Tulkarim camp. There are no accurate estimates of the number of the Hawariths at the time of their displacement, but, according to Hawarith council members in Kuwait, the figure was not less than eight thousand.[54]

The loss of land, home, way of life, cattle, and all property was not easy to endure. The Bedouins, who were proud of being free and were adherents of tribal codes that fulfilled their needs, were suddenly confined to camps. Having to live in a refugee camp was particularly humiliating to them.

In 1952, three young Hawariths came to Kuwait on the underground railroad.[55] Many followed. One after another, they came to Kuwait to seek a decent living. Because of their former life-style, which depended on animal husbandry and crop agriculture, they had no real skills that equipped them to handle urban occupations. Unlike urban Palestinians and the majority of the peasantry, modern education was not available to them prior to 1948. This put them at a gross disadvantage. On arrival, they found employment in manual labor in hundreds of projects in Kuwait.

The Hawariths were able in a few years to acquire the necessary skills to improve their socioeconomic status. At present, most of the younger generation is employed in jobs that reflect their having acquired a high school or college education. The majority now graduate from high school, and most of those who graduate either acquire a college degree or technical training in a two-year college.

In Kuwait, the emotional closeness of the Bedouins, as well as their ability to direct informal systems of support has enabled them to be a leading force in several initiatives that have had an important impact on the Palestinian community. In this respect, the role of the Hawariths is as significant as that of the Hebronites. Furthermore the overall influence of the Bedouin group in matters of culture is as powerful as the influence of the intelligentsia in matters of business and finance.

For example, in 1962, two years before the formation of the P.L.O., Hawariths started the ^cAwdah (Return) Club, the first Palestinian athletic club in Kuwait. In Kuwait the trend toward athletic clubs among Palestinians took root only after 1967. Thus the early formation of a

Hawarith-sponsored club was a pioneering initiative. Through this club they maintained their togetherness while at the same time encouraging sports among the Palestinians in Kuwait. As a result, similar Hawarith clubs were formed in Jordan and the West Bank. In the 1960s, the Hawarith ᶜAwdah Club was officially incorporated into the PLO-run athletic clubs. The club continues to be led and directed by the Hawariths. They continue, as well, to make up the majority of its members.

In addition to the athletic club initiative, in 1974 the Hawariths started the "Band of Popular Palestinian Art," the first politically oriented folklore band for the Palestinians in Kuwait. Later, they established the "Artistic Return Band." Both bands were composed of Hawarith volunteers committed to the revival and popularization of Palestinian political folklore. The folklore they promoted was peasant folklore unknown to them before 1948. In many ways, their initiative amounted to a commitment to the wider Palestinian national identity. As a result of this commitment to the revival and maintenance of Palestinian folklore, seven competing Palestinian folklore bands were created in Kuwait.

In 1981, after consultation between the members in Kuwait and Hawarith leaders in Jordan, the Hawariths decided, in order to confront problems in education and social security, to form a league called the Fund of the Members of the Hawarith Valley. For example, in 1982 a Hawarith delegation representing the fund met President Saddam Hussayn of Iraq and requested scholarship seats in Baghdad University. Iraq now provides ten scholarship seats to the Hawariths. The fund also strongly encourages intra-Hawarith marriages by providing money and a valuable gift to any Hawarith man who marries a Hawarith woman.

The fund has a General Assembly composed of the majority of the Hawariths in Kuwait. It also has an elected Board of Directors. The board decides on all day-to-day matters related to allocation of resources and commitments. The most important committee in the fund is the Founding Committee. It is composed of the six major Hawarith figures in Kuwait.

Interestingly, the Board of Directors and the Founding Committee are both composed of middle-aged men. This is a major change from the pre-1948 days, when the elders sat at the helm of the Hawarith structure. To maintain respect toward their elders, however, the Hawariths created a consulting committee made up of the older generation living in Kuwait. It is composed of six elderly individuals whose respect, age, and family allegiance have entitled them to be consulted in all important matters related to the affairs of the Kuwait Hawariths. Their role is basically as interpreters of the tribal code. They provide advice and remind the young of the traditional ways. According to Jamil Dursiyah, "The fund's Board of Directors, the Founding Committee, and the Consulting Committee all together amount to an ᶜAshira [tribal] Council in the Kuwaiti diaspora."[56]

151

In every sense, the Hawariths have survived the displacement experience and have been quite successful in protecting their social cohesion. In so doing, they have become better equipped to face the psychological, social, and economic effects of their exile.

The Funds in Perspective

All of these funds and associations have become an additional force to influence and mold informal village and town ties. They contribute to strengthened solidarity at every level. In fact, the funds' functions in welfare and education, marriage, death, and other village and town occasions imbue the informal structure of relations with momentum and strength and an enhanced ability for regeneration. When a fund-raising party brings all of the Jerusalemites of Kuwait together or when children gather to sing for Jerusalem, the entire informal structure, that is, the extended network, that makes up Jerusalem in Kuwait is strengthened. The same goes for the annual meeting of a fund's general assembly or called meetings to decide on action to resolve a particular crisis. In short, every fund activity is helpful to the cohesiveness of the network of that particular town or village. The fact that the existence of a fund and its legitimacy are based on town and village ties guarantees the continuity of these ties. All fund activities are directed at building community continuity through supporting fellow members of the original Palestinian family and village.

A dialectical relation of survival therefore exists. The informal village or town network produces the fund, and the fund, by limiting its scope of activity to these ties, provides them with additional strength and continuity. As the relation progresses, the informal structure draws in more people from the village, even those on the sidelines who initially lacked interest. These associations tighten and formalize the network of the town or village, arouse interest in it, and impart to it a sense of solidarity much more than a marriage, a death, or a feast can. Purposeful action aimed at the survival of these village and town ties is making an important contribution to the politics of survival.

Palestinian Politics and the Social Structure

All of these cases involve village and town leaders who start the process of association formation. Every group has individuals who are more influential, who have a higher interest in social and political activity. They are the ones who initiate the formation of village and town associations and promote unity within the group. Once they initiate a project, they put their credibility behind it and bring to it the support of most of their family members. Usually age, ability to convince and to lead a group discussion, and willingness to provide some services to those in need by cultivating whatever connections they have are the characteristics of those who play a leading role in town and village affairs. A college education is an increasingly important asset to leaders of these associations. Teachers, professionals, and others with higher education become prime movers of their town or village.

The village or town leaders can unite the community in the face of crises or decision. During a misunderstanding, they are the first to be called upon, and when marriage is contemplated or death occurs, they are the first to be consulted. Their views are held in high esteem and are a motivating and directing force in the village or town network in Kuwait.

Although their power does not rest on any traditional claims and their role is not comparable to that played by their counterparts in the former village or neighborhood, these informally determined leaders are an important uniting force in Palestinian town and village relationships in Kuwait. Some of the resources they have are usually dedicated to fulfilling their overall role.

Most of the individuals who become members of the fund councils or who are presidents or general secretaries of village or town associations and funds are of this caliber. Through their ability to gain the trust of the society through this respect of personal ties, they have succeeded in forming effective associations and useful funds in the midst of a complex diaspora.

The political focus of these associations is also very important. Many of the initiators of village funds in Kuwait are Palestinian nationalists. The majority of the initiators of the associations are either members of the PLO. or have been politically active in the past. Among those who have headed the associations are former political prisoners, such as Dr. Subhi Gaushih, who spent three years (1969 to 1971) in an Israeli jail in the West Bank. Others are former Palestinian guerrillas in Jordan or Lebanon. Many of the village or town associations have their annual meeting at the PLO office in Kuwait. They often invite PLO speakers during the annual fund-raising parties. They are an integral part of Palestinian nationalism.

These political and community leaders are united in their belief in the need for the survival of village and town ties. Although they are genuinely interested in meeting the economic challenges of the diaspora, they also realize the political significance of the persistence of their community. To them, this is all part of the overall challenge of Palestinian national survival. Village and town persistence helps keep alive issues of identity and roots.

153

Fund organizers, therefore, are not imprisoned by their microbonds, as a traditional village leader would be. They know the importance of village and town ties and have made a conscious decision to work toward the realization of the survival potential of these relationships. But the role of those who lead the village and town associations in Kuwait has also linked them to the wider stream of Palestinian politics and society.

Yet the link of village and town association members to the diverse political orientations in the wider Palestinian political spectrum has not jeopardized village or town unity. Fund organizers have successfully maintained unity within their particular community at times when divisions existed at the wider political level.

The village and town associations, such as those of Hebron and al-Malhah, are composed of members of diverse political orientations. It seems that the long Palestinian experience of confronting the disparate forces that shaped their destiny has provided them with the strength to keep their families and village relationships separate from the strains of political differences. Probably out of self-defense and an immediate need to withstand the ongoing assault on their nation, they have learned to meet together simply as people who have a common interest.[57] According to Ali al-Hasan, a community leader who has had an important impact on Palestinian activism as well as on funds in Kuwait,

> I have always been amazed at this level of separation. In the fund meeting, they all aggressively pursue their common defensive needs. Fatah, popular front, democratic front, and Islamic meet as relatives, friends, and townspeople. Once the meeting ends, they are political competitors, each pursuing actively a particular political orientation in Palestinian ranks.[58]

This is yet another proof of how powerful the nonideological orientation of family and village relationships in the Middle East can be. While the family and village contain "within themselves all shades of political and professional commitments,"[59] they remain committed to their cohesiveness and bonds of solidarity as a community regardless of internal political differences.

As political focus has affected the nature of community associations, so the strength of village and town relationships has a powerful effect on Palestinian political institutions, such as the PLO. Political associations are frequently influenced by village and town ties. In some cases, individuals from one region, town, or village have composed the majority of the employees of a particular PLO office or department. A director of an office may, in order to enhance his position in the institution

154

or among his fellow townspeople, try to recruit members of his village or region for his office. Furthermore, there are many cases that suggest that individuals have been elected in unions and other PLO institutions not only because of political views but also because of regional, town, or village affiliation.

Although the leadership of the PLO has not encouraged these informal influences, it has been sensitive to their existence. It has followed a policy aimed at maintaining a workable balance. National integration is basic to its philosophy and its effectiveness as a pan-Palestinian institution. Its representative status stems from its ability to balance the varied demands stemming from all sectors of Palestinian society. As long as the informal structures complement the formal institution, the whole range of village and regional ties can be integrated in the PLO thus adding to the strength and survivability of Palestinian nationalism.

Conclusion

Over the years, the informal structure of the Palestinians in Kuwait has maintained the momentum for the re-establishment of Palestinian microbonds of solidarity. Once these ties were established through the family, the momentum simultaneously stimulated village and town ties. Once ties had become solid at the village and town levels, that is, once the village and town came to exist informally as a superstructure in Kuwait, they constituted, in addition to the family, a system of survival and support. But as the complex diaspora intensified its pressures and the members of villages and towns increased in Kuwait, more formal mechanisms were needed for the survival of the informal network. This led to the rise of village and town associations. They sprang up to meet the economic and social welfare needs of the people. They also reinforced the informal system and network at every level. This may be their most important contribution to the continued survival of the Palestinian villages and towns in Kuwait.

Variation in educational levels, trading experiences, and skills, as well as variation in family cohesiveness and levels of primordial loyalties, have had their effect on the formation of town and village associations. Some villages were quick to form strong, viable associations; others were slow. Yet in this as in every strategy of survival employed, the few active village and town networks served as models of action for the rest, hence expanding the phenomena of village and town networks in Kuwait. This expansion of village and town associations in Kuwait has provided an additional bonding which gives the Palestinian society its especially persistent solidarity.

NOTES

1. Janet Abu-Lughod, "Migrant Adjustment to City Life: The Egyptian Case," American Journal of Sociology 67, no. 1 (July 1961):31.

2. Ibid., p. 26.

3. David Jacobson, "Mobility, Continuity, and Urban Social Organization," Man 6 (December 1971):639.

4. Interview with Rabah al-Natshih, Kuwait, summer 1985.

5. Alexander Scholch, "European Penetration and the Economic Development of Palestine, 1856-1882," in Studies in the Economic and Social History of Palestine in the 19th and 20th Centuries, ed. Roger Owen (Carbondale: Southern Illinois University Press, 1982), pp. 51-52.

6. Estimate provided by the Hebron University Graduate Union in Kuwait.

7. Interview with three members of the administrative council of Hebron's University Graduate Union in Kuwait: Dr. Hamdi Hammuri, president; Muhammad A. Milhim, vice-president; ᶜAbd al-Majid al-Natshih, secretary, Kuwait, summer 1985.

8. Interview with ᶜAbd al-Majid al-Natshih, Kuwait, summer 1985.

9. Interview with Dr. Hamdi Hammuri, Muhammad Milhim, and ᶜAbd al-Majid al-Natshih, Kuwait, summer 1985.

10. See T. Farah, F. al-Salem, and M. K. al-Salem, "Arab Labour Migration: Arab Migrants in Kuwait," in Sociology of Developing Societies: The Middle East, ed. Talal Asad and Roger Owen (New York: Monthly Review Press, 1983), pp. 42-53.

11. Ibid., note 1, p. 232.

12. The account of the establishment of the fund was provided by ᶜAbd al-Majid al-Natshih. It was confirmed by lawyer Muhammad A. Milhim and Dr. H. Hammuri.

13. Sanduq al-Khalil al-Khayri: al-Nizam al-'Asasi [The Hebron Charitable Fund: The Charter], (1980), p. 12.

14. Ibid., pp. 20-21.

15. Ibid., p. 21.

16. Interview with ᶜAbd al-Majid al-Natshih, Kuwait, summer 1985.

17. Al-Nizam al'Asasi li-Jamᶜiyat rabitat al-jamiᶜiyyin Bi-muhafazat al-Khalil: firᶜ al-Kuwayt [The Charter of the University Graduate Union of the Hebron district: The Kuwait Chapter], p. 3.

18. Muhammad ᶜAyash Milhim, "Rabitat al-jamiᶜiyyin fi muhafazat al-Khalil fi al-watan Wa al-mahjar" ["The University Graduate

Union of the Hebron District in the Diaspora and the Homeland"], in Rabitat al-jam^ciyyin fi muhafazat al-Khalil: Masiratuha Khilal Thalathin ^cAm, aylul 1953 ila aylul 1983 [The University Graduate Union of the Hebron District: Its Accomplishments in Thirty Years, September 1953-September 1983] (Amman: University Graduate Union), p. 114.

19. ^cAbd al-Khaliq Yaghmur, Introduction, The University Graduate Union of the Hebron District, p. 3.

20. Rajab Mustafa al-Tamimi, The University Graduate Union of the Hebron District, p. 109 (Figure, p. 13).

21. The University Graduate Union of the Hebron District, pp. 11-15.

22. Ibid., p. 15.

23. Ibid., pp. 17-25.

24. Ibid., pp. 23-24.

25. Ibid., pp. 28-29.

26. Ibid., p. 30.

27. For example, the league reissued the classic Biladuna Philistine [Palestine Our Country] by Mustafa M. al-Dabbagh.

28. The University Graduate Union of the Hebron District, p. 33.

29. Ibid., p. 115.

30. Interview with ^cAbd al-Ilah Qasim, cofounder of the Singil Association and the investigator of the Mirqab Police Station during the early 1960s.

31. The accounts of the Jerusalem Fund were provided by Dr. Subhi Gaushih, the fund's president, Kuwait, summer 1985.

32. Through the fund's lists and by relying on figures provided by Jerusalemites in Kuwait, the fund's administrative council has concluded that fifteen thousand is the approximate number of Jerusalemites in Kuwait. The figure includes those who were displaced from West Jerusalem in 1948.

33. Interview with ^cAdli al-Titi, president of the Nablus Fund and its Zakat committee, Kuwait, summer 1985.

34. Interview with Husni Zu^crub of Khan-Unis (Gaza), who is active in establishing a Khana-Unis Fund and in PLO institutions and unions in Kuwait, summer 1985.

35. There are no reliable statistics on the population from the Gaza district in Kuwait. Most of those interviewed cited fifty thousand to sixty thousand as acceptable. PLO estimates provided by Salim al-Za^cnun (Abul-Adib) confirmed the estimate. Za^cnun is Fatah's representative to the Gulf States. He is a member of Fatah's Central Committee and deputy to the chairman of the Palestine National Council.

36. Interview with Husni Zu^crub, Kuwait, summer 1985.

37. Interview with Salim al-Za‘nun (Abul-Adib), Kuwait, summer 1985.

38. Ibid.

39. Interview with Husni Zu‘rub, Kuwait, summer 1985.

40. Interview with Dr. Raja Sumrayn, Kuwait, summer 1985. See also Harry Levin (1948), "The Attack on the Arab Village Kolonia, April 12, 1948," in From Haven to Conquest: Readings in Zionism and the Palestine Problem until 1948, ed. Walid Khalidi (Beirut: Institute for Palestine Studies, 1971), pp. 767-770.

41. Interview with Dr. Raja Sumrayn, Palestinian poet and cofounder of the General Assembly of the Village of Qalonya, Kuwait, summer 1985.

42. The account of the creation of the Qalonya Fund is based on extensive interviews with Dr. Raja Sumrayn, Kuwait, summer 1985.

43. Interview with ‘Abd al-Ilah Qasim, cofounder of the Singil association, Kuwait, summer 1985.

44. Based on a taped interview conducted by Dr. Raja Sumrayn with Hajj Muhammad Sumrayn, a pre-1948 village mukhtar, and Hajj Muhammad Matar of Qalonya.

45. Ibid.

46. The first mukhtars of villages in Palestine appeared after 1864 as a result of an Ottoman law requiring that villages be linked with the authorities through mukhtars. In most cases, the mukhtar or mukhtars from a village represented the family balance and the most influential families in a village. Before that villages were solely ruled by shaykhs, that is, the old men of the village. See Gabriel Baer, "The Economic and Social Position of the Village Mukhtar in Palestine," in The Palestinians in the Middle East Conflict ed. Gabriel Ben-Dor (Ramat Gan: Turtledove Publishing, 1978), pp. 101-117.

47. Interview with Dr. Raja Sumrayn, Kuwait, summer 1985.

48. The account of al-Malhah is provided by Ibrahim Safi, son of the former village mukhtar (between approximately 1926 and 1943). Safi is cofounder of the al-Malhah Fund in Kuwait . Interview, Kuwait, summer 1985.

49. The accounts on Tarshiha were provided by Muhammad Samarah of Tarshiha. He is at present director of the Office of Assistant to the Kuwait Accounting Diwan (council).

50. According to ‘Abd al-Rahman, Palestinians have in recent years received on the average seventy-five of the highest hundred scores in both the scientific and literary high school exams. In 1979-1980, they made eighty-two of the highest scores: As‘ad ‘Abd al-Rahman, Educational Attainment among the Palestinian Community in Kuwait (Paper presented to TEAM International as part of a study on the

"Economic and Social Situation and Potential of the Palestinian Arab People," presented in March 1983 to the United Nations Economic Commission for West Asia) (Beirut, November 1981), p. 20. I found that this trend has continued. In 1983-1984, forty-eight of the highest fifty scores belonged to Palestinians. This achievement is not necessarily due to any characteristic unique to the Palestinians, but rather to circumstances that force diaspora and exiled people to invest heavily in education. See also Shamlan Y. Alessa, The Manpower Problem in Kuwait (London: Kegan Paul International, 1981), p. 110; James Markham, "Palestinians, People in Crisis Are Scattered and Divided," New York Times (February 19, 1978).

51. Interview with Muhammad Abu-Unis, deputy to the director of the ᶜAwdah sports club, a Hawarith-run club in Kuwait, Kuwait, summer 1985.

52. Interview with Jamil Dursiyah, cofounder of the ᶜAwdah Club, the Hawarith Fund, folklore bands, and spokesman for the Hawariths of Kuwait, Kuwait, summer 1985. Dursiyah came to Kuwait at the age of seventeen in 1953 on the underground railroad.

53. Ibid.

54. Ibid.

55. The account in the rest of this section was provided by Jamil Dursiyah and leading members of the Hawarith Fund and of the ᶜAwdah Club, notably, Muhammad Abu-Unis (Abu Ghalib) and Saᶜd ᶜArash. Kuwait, summer 1985.

56. Interview with Jamil Dursiyah, Kuwait, summer 1985.

57. In every interview conducted with members of village funds and associations in Kuwait, this theme was asserted.

58. Interview with Ali al-Hasan, Kuwait, summer 1985.

59. James Bill and Carl Leiden, Politics in the Middle East 2d ed. (Boston: Little, Brown and Co., 1984), p. 87.

9

New Crisis in the Diaspora

Since 1948, Kuwait has become a haven for many Palestinians. It presented to them, as did the Gulf and many other Arab countries, a set of opportunities that proved vital to their survival. The dismemberment of Palestine and the dispersion of its people coincided with the oil boom and the ambitious development programs in Kuwait and the Arab world. In Kuwait, Palestinians provided (and still provide) labor, skills, and know-how and had a decisive impact on the country's developmental process. In return, they found in Kuwait protection, employment, mobility, and the opportunity to reknit the social fabric. A reciprocal arrangement evolved.

The fact that post-1948 Palestinian nationalism, expressed in the activities of Fatah in the early 1960s, developed some of its embryonic organizational structures in Kuwait testifies to the importance of Kuwait and the Gulf to the rising Palestinian social, economic, and political structures in the diaspora. It is in areas and countries where Palestinians were able to address some of their familial and physical needs that they could shift to satisfying political aspirations expressed in their need for self-determination and return. From the beginning, Palestinian leaders, and therefore the PLO, made a conscious decision not to interfere in the internal politics of Kuwait and the Gulf. They also agreed not to have a military presence in Kuwait or the rest of the Gulf. This was acceptable because Kuwait and the Gulf states share no borders with Israel.

But by the mid- to late-1970s, new developments started to affect Palestinians and Kuwaitis in Kuwait. Such developments were simultaneously taking place in many other Arab states. In Kuwait, the mobility of the 1950s and 1960s was ending. In the 1950s, 1960s, and

1970s, Kuwait, like the rest of the Gulf, had experienced rapid growth that relied on nonindigenous labor. Thus it welcomed Palestinians at first. By the mid-1970s, the process had reversed. In Kuwait and the Gulf, with infrastructural development nearing completion, the indigenous Kuwaiti middle-class growing in size and strength, and a mounting economic crisis, the situation was the most serious it had been in three decades and touched both nationals and expatriates. The crisis, still in its early phase, is a result of the process that transformed the Kuwaitis and most of the indigenous populations of the Gulf into local minorities.[1]

The dilemmas facing the nationals and the expatriates, of which the Palestinians are the most numerous, were created during the rapid development stemming from the unprecedented oil boom. As the oil boom slowed the contradictions inherent in the developmental process of the preceding decades laid the groundwork for increased localism, resulting in a set of laws and regulations aimed at reducing the number of expatriates. In Kuwait, this has affected all Palestinians (except the two thousand or so who have been naturalized).[2] As a result, Palestinians today face new challenges in housing, rent, residence, retirement, and local schooling. Increased restrictions force them to live in a state of continuing crisis.[3] In the words of Saᶜid Khuri, co-owner and cofounder of Consolidated Contractors Company (C.C.C.),

> During the days when we lost our homeland and were displaced, we found a developing Arab world in need of our efforts. We seized the opportunity and found jobs that permitted many of us to lead a decent life. Now I worry about the new generations of Palestinians, as I see a closed Arab world facing them. Unemployment has hit this generation in frightening proportions. When the Palestinians lost their homeland, their property, and all forms of security, the only security that attracted them became their investment in education. So each of them sacrificed greatly and went as far as putting all of their life savings into educating their children on the college level. Today, as parents accomplish the mission of educating their children, they discover that education is not the vehicle it used to be. The result is disastrous to the family and all its members.[4]

The question is where do the Palestinians go from here. Most of those who carry Jordanian citizenship (at least two-thirds of the community in Kuwait) have never lived in Jordan. They are from the West Bank or are related to the refugees who were displaced in 1948 to the

West Bank. Most of them cannot go to the West Bank except for short visits due to Israeli occupation policy. As there are problems with Kuwait's absorptive capacity, there are also problems with Jordan's absorptive capacity. To limit the flow, Jordan has begun to draft young people into its army. Usually, young Palestinians who were born and reared in Kuwait are not enthusiastic about being drafted into Jordan's army.

The rest of the community, the literally stateless one-quarter, face a worse dilemma. Lebanese travel documents usually are not renewed by the Lebanese government. Those with Syrian travel documents, particularly the young, are required to register for the draft in Syria, even though they have never lived or been citizens there. Those who have Egyptian travel documents (about sixty thousand in Kuwait) may visit Egypt on a visa but cannot work there. Most of these are from Gaza (either originally, or refugees who were expelled there during the war of 1948), but cannot return there because of Israeli occupation and restrictions. All stateless Palestinians with travel documents have greater difficulty traveling from one country to another, and any permission to travel is accompanied by more severe restrictions.[5]

Having limited choices and having to move at the age of retirement are fears that haunt every Palestinian family. This anxiety afflicts both the young, born and reared in Kuwait, and the old, who have had to move so many times already. Being forced to retire in a place where they do not have the same networks of friends and relationships they have built up over the years in Kuwait seems a harsh final blow in a life already fraught with the frustrations of displacement.

The fact that none of the acquired cultural and political freedoms of the earlier period were lost and that open channels continued to exist between local Palestinians and PLO leaders, on one hand, and Kuwaiti leaders, on the other, has helped to at least partially address some of the problems. For instance, in 1984, Kuwait permitted nonworking widows and their children a form of permanent residency. Furthermore, Kuwait is still considering the possibility of providing a form of permanent residency to Palestinians who have been in the country since the early 1950s.

These problems are not the sole responsibility of one Arab state. After World War II, each Arab state had so many developmental tasks to accomplish, problems to address, ethnic or religious groups to integrate, that their systems became heavily overloaded. By the 1980s, the systems had become acccumulatively burdened because of their failure to address many of the problems of the previous decades.

Under conditions of scarcity and instability, it is the stateless who are the first to be left out. In the last few years, different Arab states have competed with regard to restrictions (mostly subtle regulations) that would

163

show that each is not the best place for Palestinians to seek work, education, or residence. The events in Lebanon since 1982 and the constant massacres taking place in the Palestinian camps have added to the fears of Arab states trying to avoid a further influx of Palestinians from Lebanon. Furthermore, the situation in the West Bank and Gaza, that is, lack of solutions to the Arab-Israeli conflict and, creeping Israeli annexation, has added to their fears of a possible new wave of refugees and the possibility that the Palestinians in their midst are more permanent than thought in earlier decades.

This competition over nonresponsibility, which neither addresses the problems at hand nor diffuses them, adds to the sufferings, the sense of crisis, and helplessness among the Palestinians. While the Palestinians have been among the first after 1948 to sow the seeds of development in the region, they are the last to reap the benefits. Their ability to come a long way since the days of their near total destruction in 1948 has not yet earned them even basic civil rights, let alone political rights. The rights to secure residence, equal employment, and education are still unaddressed in most of the Arab world. The right not to be discriminated against, deported, restricted from travel, or have one's acquired citizenship or travel documents revoked are rights far from being achieved by the Palestinians.

This condition is similar to the one that created the post-1948 politics of family survival. The dilemmas of 1987 are extensions and recurrences of those of 1948. The Palestinian family, like the Palestinian people, continues, therefore, to be involved in a process of survival and crisis management on every level. The intensification of problems the diaspora has created renew the pain and confusion of displacement. The young, like their displaced parents before them, are now seeking new opportunities in other diasporas. The family, village, and town networks will have to cope, once again, with the discouraging reality of exile. The ability of the stateless community to deal creatively with the necessity to restructure their society will once again be tested.

Family, Village, and Town Ties in the New Crisis

How has the Palestinian family reacted to this crisis since 1980? What is the possible impact of the new crisis on the Palestinian family, town, and village network in Kuwait? What means will the family employ to confront the rising challenges? To answer these questions one must analyze the patterns of family behavior since 1976, and particularly since 1980. By understanding the 1980-1985 period, future trends may be better appreciated.

164

All along, the Palestinian case in Kuwait has suggested that any increase in the crisis level transforms the extended family network and even the most dormant relationships into an expanded effective family and social network. Any decrease in the crisis level has the opposite effect. Therefore, the more severe and abrupt the crisis, the more effective family and social ties become. And the more effective these ties become, the more important are changes and redefinitions of function and role. Hence, family functions expand. One can deduce, therefore, that the longer the diaspora lasts, the more creative the family and the basic social structure will become in facing its challenges.

Since the crisis of the late seventies, family and social networks have reacted in line with their past role and importance in the stages of Palestinian diaspora survival. Family and personal town and village social relationships are as basic in this last stage as they were immediately after 1948.

The main response to the recent crisis has been the formation of village and family funds. The effective and extended family and social networks in Kuwait were already in need of an institutionalized form to expand their functions and to increase stability and effectiveness in family, village, and town relationships. Through the funds, associations, centers, or clubs that have developed, the family, village, or town has created the formal structure that it needs to protect its relationships and to respond effectively to the crisis. Support becomes more institutionalized. Even meetings and encounters on the village level become formalized as a result of efforts by the fund or center. Purposeful action aimed at continuously protecting the village, town, or family network becomes an established goal, a national as well as a local need. The club or the fund becomes, in itself, a central mechanism by which family and village ties are promoted and strengthened. It symbolizes permanence in a prolonged and increasingly complex diaspora.

But it must be noted that the Palestinians have not become prisoners of their microbonds of solidarity. In fact, family and village ties, though basic to a stateless population, can provide solutions only up to a certain point. Such ties become a prerequisite for the rise of formal institutions and structures. Since the early 1960s and particularly since 1967, the Palestinians have also created in the diaspora many non-family based cultural, educational, economic, and political institutions that perform essential tasks and functions. PLO institutions alone in Kuwait and the diaspora cover a whole range of activities and community services: the general unions of Palestinian women, teachers, students, artists, egineers, doctors and pharmacists, writers and journalists, for example.[6] Other non-PLO, privately owned institutes have been essential to diaspora survival, for example, the Fund for Palestinian Higher Education, and the

lfare Society. Since new institutions evolved in the 1960s in the
ontext of national integration, the relationships between the micro and
macro levels of solidarity have become closely intertwined. Therefore, at
this stage, the primordial ties represent the core, the underpinnings of
Palestinian survival; but they are supplemented and reinforced by the
formal instrumentalities (see figure 4) of the Palestinian community.

Figure 4: Micro-Macro Relationships

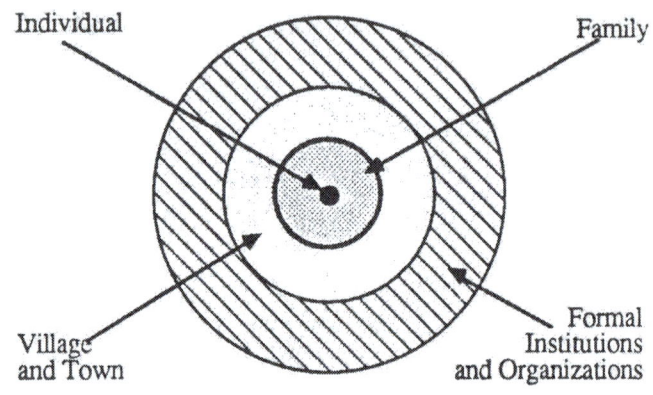

In this context, the well-publicized and far-reaching community
project of the General Union of Palestinian Women of the PLO in Kuwait,
recently took on the burden of putting in private schools over one
thousand Palestinian children from limited income families living in
Kuwait. The present program of the Women's Union costs $500,000
annually and is paid for by the well-to-do members of the Palestinian
community in Kuwait.[7] The membership of the union is derived from
Palestinian women hailing from many different towns and villages, thus
transcending the primordial ties.

Increased Nationalism

Another trend gaining momementum and shaping the Palestinian
response to crisis and diaspora conditions is the increased and deepened

166

emotional attachment to Palestine. Tibawi's Palestinian Zionism of the 1960s was only one episode in a long, cyclical reaction to the post-1948 era.[8] At present, in the midst of pressures engulfing Palestinian life and society, salvation is increasingly perceived in return to the homeland and establishment of statehood. Palestinians in Kuwait find themselves in a more direct relationship to the homeland. In the years to come, the strength of this drive to return will be much greater than any experienced to date.

The need to "return," by itself, has become part of the anatomy of exile. Though most Palestinians exiled in 1948 are emotionally attached to their former towns and villages, it is their exclusion from the homeland and the denial of their right to return that frustrates them most. By seeing Jews from the Soviet Union or the United States emigrate under Israel's law of return, while they, the native-born, cannot, their obsession becomes more determined. The lack of Israeli and Jewish recognition of Palestinian suffering, loss, and hardships since 1948 exacerbates the problem.[9] In essence, this insistence on physical return, symbolized by retaining the key to the house and the deed to the land, is, by itself, an insistence on return to the world map, an expression of the need to offically exist.[10]

Forty years after their displacement, the Palestinians are desperate for a place, a state, a homeland that could provide them with the grounding to affirm their right to exist They want a nation, a government that can find ways to address the problems resulting from decades of conflict, exile, and dispossession. Until such ground is found, the family, among other important socioeconomic and political diaspora institutions, will conceptually carry, in its pocket as it were, the burdens of a displaced and exiled nation and the vision belonging to a recognized nation with a real place on the earth.

NOTES

1. In Kuwait, of a total population of 1.709 million, 1.025 are non-Kuwaiti (Ministry of Planning, Central Statistical Office, Kuwait, Monthly Digest of Statistics, April 1985). In 1975, in the United Arab Emirates, citizens composed 15 percent of the population, Qatars 18.9 percent, Saudi Arabians 57 percent, and Bahrainians 60.4 percent (J. S. Birks and C. A. Sinclair, International Migration and Development in the Arab Region [Geneva: ILO, 1980:132]).

2. See ᶜAbdul-Ra'uf ᶜAbd al-ᶜAziz al-Jardawi al-Hijrah WalᶜUzzlah al-'Ijtimaᶜiyah fi al-Mujtamaᶜ al-Kuwayti: Dirasah Sūsulugiyah [Migration and Social Isolation in Kuwaiti Society: A

167

Sociological Study] (Kuwait: Sharikat Al-Rubay^can lil-Nashr wa al-Tawzi^c, 1984), p. 42.

3. See "Palestinians at the Age of 60 and the Nightmare of Retirement," Al-'Anba (Kuwaiti daily) (June 27, 1985):17; "A Journey into Palestinian Concerns in Kuwait," al-'Anba (August 1, 1984). Also see al-'Anba for August 2, 1984; "The Palestinians in Kuwait," al-Rai' al-^cAm (Kuwaiti Daily) (March 30, 1985); Hawl Qanun al-Ijarat (on the rent law) al-Watan (Kuwaiti daily) (June 18, 1983); al-Watan (July 12, 1983); Badr Abdulla al-Mutawa^c, "Qanun al-Ijarat wa'-Atharuh ^cala al-Wala' wa al-Intima' " ["The Rent Law and Its Effect on Loyalty and Belonging"], al-Watan (March 19, 1984). For views of Palestinian residents, see al-Rai' al-^cAm (Kuwait) (March 11 & 13, 1984). See also Eric Rouleau, "The Palestinian Diaspora of the Gulf," MERIP Reports 132 (May 1985):13-15; Pamela Ann Smith, Palestine and the Palestinians 1876-1983 (New York: St. Martin's Press, 1984).

4. Interview with Sa^cid Khuri, Kuwait, summer 1985.

5. For a report that investigates the overall status of Palestinians with travel documents, see Khawla Nazzal, in al-Watan (August 14, 20, and 27, 1984).

6. For a pioneering and recent study on such institutions, see Laurie Brand, Building the Bridge of Return: Palestinian Corporate Mobilization in Egypt, Kuwait and Jordan (Ph.D. dissertation, New York: Columbia University Graduate School of Arts and Sciences, 1985).

7. Based on interviews with Salwa Abu-Khadra, the secretary general of the General Union of Palestinian Woman, Siham Sukkar, president of the Kuwait chapter of the union, Siham Abu-Ghazalah, secretary of the Tradition Committee, and Siham Khalil, secretary of the Social Committee. I am indebted to Siham Khalil for taking me to meet families who have been getting support through the schooling project and other projects of the union.

8. A. L. Tibawi, "Visions of Return: The Palestine Arab Refugees in Arabic Poetry and Art," Middle East Journal 7, no. 5 (Autumn 1967):507-526.

9. David K. Shipler, Arab and Jew: Wounded Spirits in a Promised Land (New York: Times Books, 1986), pp. 63-64.

10

Conclusion

The uprooting and dispersal in 1948 resulting from Israeli occupation of Palestine threatened to destroy the entire fabric of Palestinian life. The social networks and bonds of solidarity that held society together were suddenly subjected to enormous strain and dislocation. By the end of 1948, as a result of the destruction of Palestine's body politic and its social and civic macrostructures, and because of the dislocation of society's microbonds, no Palestinian society existed geographically.

But the strength of the pre-1948 family and village relationships proved decisive to the post-1948 revival of Palestinian society. The sinews of the social system remained in place even though they had undergone great stress and strain. Hence, the informal fundamental apparatus comprising family, neighborhood, village, town, and friendship provided the basis for a new and different Palestinian superstructure. Without the family and the other basic social relationships, Palestinian society would have been totally fragmented and almost nonexistent after 1948.

To the earlycomer Palestinians from both the intelligentsia and the peasantry, Kuwait offered opportunity for the economic and physical survival of individuals and families. The first priority of the earlycomers was to relieve their families of their suffering. They had to provide their parents, brothers, and sisters with the necessities of life. They also wanted to continue the education of their brothers and sisters, which had been interrupted by the war. Those pioneers became the bridgehead of the Palestinian community in Kuwait. Their move facilitated the migration of many other members of their scattered families and friends. By finding a

169

place to live they started the arduous process of reknitting the raveled social and physical threads of the family. The Palestinians who came to Kuwait immediately after the exodus and during the 1950s provided the roots for a new and different superstructure in the diaspora.

The new structure was based on the relocation in Kuwait of sections of every Palestinian family. Family networks were formed. These networks served many important functions, but, in essence, they held together the informal personal and professional relationships that could have been destroyed in the wake of the dispersion.

Since 1948, the networks have come to mirror the needs and new conditions of the Palestinians. The Kuwait case seems to indicate that the family and village networks gave order and meaning to post-1948 Palestinian society. But to reflect the realities of an exiled population, the family had to become a less rigid formation. Family networks had, therefore, to include much broader ties than pre-1948 society permitted. The family also had to absorb many changes in a short period and socialize its young in ways helpful to their ability to face the challenges of statelessness. A high priority was placed on education, hard work, and competition.

The Palestinians who came to Kuwait discovered that many of the same values, habits, relationships, and way of life that had given them a sense of direction and protection in the original village or town could also exist in the new environment. Even the dialects, feuds, poetry, and dances survived. Marriage and divorce, disputes and dispute resolution, death and burial, birth and celebration are all conducted in an atmosphere that reminds the Palestinians of the former village or town.

This has had a strong impact on the continuity of Palestinian family networks. But it was basic, as well, to the recreation of former village and town networks so vital to diaspora survival. These networks, based on hometown and family ties, perform recreational, social, political and economic tasks. The network, both in its familial and social forms (village and town), became especially important on both the local and the cross-national levels during the normal events of the family life cycle, that is, during marriage, death of spouse, birth of a child, children going to school, or children leaving home.

Underlying the whole system are three important components. The first is reciprocity in relationships, services, and commitments. Each person is expected to reciprocate services received by the individual or family with equivalent services to the person or family who has given services or support.

The second factor underlying the network's success is the set of expectations based on previous knowledge of modes of behavior of kin and fellow townspeople. In fact, what creates the clusters in settlement, business, and marriage is the fact that traditions create a system of predictable governing behavior.[1] As a result of these evolving networks, the city becomes a reflection of the former towns and villages, as if each had been uprooted and replanted in a section of the new city, or a sector of the economy. The network itself is an extended form of the closer, face-to-face daily relations of the village.

The third factor underlying the network's success is the intensity of the Palestinians' need to survive in the diaspora under conditions characterized by dispossession and crisis. As this study demonstrates, crisis and statelessness imbued family, town, and village relationships with zeal, strength, and cohesiveness. They also contributed to a special mythical relationship between Palestinians and their homeland.

The family and village networks will remain in the foreseeable future basic to individual and group existence. They will continue to be the basic means of helping the Palestinians preserve and protect their history, connectedness, social and economic security. They are basic to the ability to keep every community a part of a wider number of networks spread out through Palestine, Jordan, Kuwait, and the rest of the diaspora. As statelessness and dispersion continue, the family and the total network of traditional ties will serve as the basic mechanism to keep the group from disintegrating. The recent formalism in village and town ties is intended consciously to preserve these ties and their functions across space and time.

The success of Palestinians from all villages, towns, and strata in building nonfamilial formal institutions and structures is also vital to their survival. Such institutions are increasingly visible as they cover a range of concerns and interests (educational, academic, cultural, philanthropic, political, social, athletic).

Statelessness in the Palestinian experience, therefore, has been confronted by the structures that reinforce the family and the social network. The next decade may witness not only increasingly cohesive family, town, and village networks, but also the continued evolution and expansion of institutions designed to support a stateless society in a prolonged and challenging state of exile. Whatever is built, added, or created, the continuity of family, village, and town ties remains one of the central, most fundamental impulse in the preservation of Palestinian society.

NOTES

1. David Jacobson, "Mobility, Continuity, and Urban Social Organization," Man 6 (December 1971):630-644.

Bibliography

^cAbd al-Rahman, As^cad, <u>al-'Awda^c al-ta^climiyah lil-jaliyah al-filistinyah fi al-Kuwayt [Educational Attainment Among the Palestinian Community in Kuwait]</u> Paper presented to TEAM International, part of a study on the "Economic and Social Situation and Potential of the Palestinian Arab People," presented in March 1983 to the United Nations Economic Commission for West Asia, (Beirut: November, 1981).

_____, "al-Ittihadat wa al-Jam^ciyat al-sha^cbiyah al-Filastinyah fi al-Kuwayt" ["Palestinian Mass Associations and Unions in Kuwait"] unpublished paper, 1984.

Abraham, Sameer Y.; Nabeel Abraham; and Barbara Aswad, "The Southend: An Arab Muslim Working-Class Community," In <u>Arabs in the New World</u>, edited by Abraham, Sameer Y. and Nabeel Abraham, pp. 164-184.

Abu-Lughod, Ibrahim, The Demographic Transformation of Palestine: Essays on the Origin and Development of the Arab-Israeli-Conflict, Evanston, Ill.: Northwestern University Press, 1971.

_____, "Educating a Community in Exile: The Palestinian Experience" <u>Journal of Palestine Studies</u> 11, no. 3 (Spring 1973):94-111.

Abu-Lughod, Janet, <u>Cairo: 1,001 Years of the City Victorious</u>, Princeton: Princeton University Press, 1971.

_____, "The Demographic Transformation of Palestine" In <u>The Transformation of Palestine, Essays on the Origin and Development of the Arab-Israeli Conflict</u>, edited by Abu-Lughod,

Ibrahim, pp. 139-163. Evanston, Ill.: Northwestern University Press, 1971.

_____, "The Growth of Arab Cities," Middle East Year Book, London: 1 C Magazines, 1980.

_____, "Migrant Adjustment to City Life: The Egyptian Case" American Journal of Sociology 67, no. 1 (July 1961): 22-32.

_____, "Problems and Policy Implications of Middle Eastern Urbanization," Studies on Development Problems in Selected Countries of the Middle East , Beirut: United Nations Economic and Social Office, 1972.

_____, "Urbanization and Social Change in the Arab World," Ekistics 50 (May/June 1983):223-231.

_____, "Varieties of Urban Experience: Contrast, Coexistence, and Coalescence in Cairo," In Middle Eastern Cities, edited by Lapidus, Ira M., pp. 159-187, Berkeley and Los Angeles: University of California Press, 1969.

Aldous, Joan, "Urbanization, the Extended Family, and Kinship Ties in West Africa," in Urbanism in World Perspective, edited by Fava, Ylvia Fleis, pp. 297-305.

Alessa, Shamlan Y., The Manpower Problem in Kuwait, London: Kegan Paul International, 1981.

Ammar, Hamed, Growing up in an Egyptian Village: Silwa, Province of Aswan. New York: Octagon Books, 1954.

_____, "The Social Organization of the Community," Readings in Arab Middle Eastern Society and Cultures, edited by Lutfiyya, Abdulla M. and Charles W. Churchill, pp. 109-134. The Hague: Mouton, 1970.

Anderson, Michael, Family Structure in Nineteenth-Century Lancashire, England. Cambridge: Cambridge University Press, 1971.

Anthropological Quarterly 12, no. 1 (January 1974), entitled "Visiting Patterns and Social Dynamics in Eastern Mediterranean Communities."

Antoun, Richard T., "Pertinent Variables in the Environment of Middle Eastern Village Politics: A Comparative Analysis," In Rural Politics and Social Change in the Middle East, edited by Antoun, Richard and Iliya Harik, pp. 118-162. Bloomington: Indiana University Press, 1972.

Arendt, Hannah, The Origins of Totalitarianism, 5th ed. San Diego: Harcourt Brace Jovanovich, 1973.

Avitsur, Shimuel, "The Influence of Western Technology on the Economy of Palestine during the Nineteenth Century", In Studies on Palestine during the Ottoman Period, edited by Ma^{c}oz, Moshe, pp. 485-495. Jerusalem: Magners Press, 1975.

174

Ayyoub, Samir M., Al-Bina' al-Tabaqi lil-filistiniyin fi-lubnan [The Class Structure of Palestinians in Lebanon]. Beirut: Beirut Arab University, 1978.

Baer, Gabriel, "The Economic and Social Position of the Village Mikhtar in Palestine," In The Palestinians in the Middle East Conflict, edited by Ben-Dor, Gabriel, pp. 101-117. Ramat Gan, Israel: Turtledove Publishing, 1978.

al-Balad, Ibn, (pseud) "al-Philistinyin fi al-Kuwayt" ["The Palestinians in Kuwait"], al-Ra'i al-ᶜAm, (Kuwaiti Daily) (March 30, 1985).

Barakat, Halim, "The Arab Family and the Challenge of Social Transformation," In Women and the Family in the Middle East: New Voices and Change, edited by Fernea, Elizabeth Warnock. Austin: University of Texas Press, 1985.

Barns, J.A, "Class and Committees in the Norwegian Island Parish," Human Relations 7 (1954):39-58.

Bates, Daniel, Amal Rassam, People and Cultures of the Middle East. Englewood Cliffs, N.J.: Prentice-Hall, 1983.

Beatty, Ilene, "The Land of Canaan," in From Heaven to Conquest: Readings in Zionism and the Palestine Problem Until 1948, ed. Walid Khalidi, Beirut: Institute for Palestine Studies, 1971, pp. 3-23.

Benevisti, Meron, Conflicts and Contradictions. New York: Villard Books, 1986.

Bill, James A., and Robert L. Hardgrave, Jr. Comparative Politics: The Quest for Theory, 2nd ed. Washington, D.C.: University Press of America, 1981.

Bill, James A., and Carl Leiden, Politics in the Middle East, 2nd ed. Boston: Little, Brown and Company, 1984.

Birks, J.S., and C. A. Sinclair, International Migration and Development in the Arab Region. Geneva: ILO, 1980.

Boswell, D.M., "Personal Crises and the Mobilization of the Social Network," In Social Networks in Urban Situations: Analyses of Personal Relationships in Central African Towns, edited by Mitchell, J. Clyde, pp. 245-296. Manchester: Manchester University Press, 1969.

Bott, Elizabeth, Family and Social Network. London: Tavistock Publications, 1957.

_____, "Urban Families: Conjugal Roles and Social Networks," Human Relations 8 (1956):345-384.

Brand, Laurie, "Building the Bridge of Return: Palestinian Corporate Mobilization in Egypt, Kuwait, and Jordan," Columbia University, Graduate School of Arts and Sciences, 1985.

175

Brenner, Reuven, and Nicholas Kiefer, "The Economics of the Diaspora: Discrimination and Occupational Structure," Economic Development and Cultural Change 29, 3 (April 1981):517-534.

Brooks, Hugh C., and Yassin El-Ayout, eds., Refugees South of the Sahara: An African Dilemma. Westport: Negro Universities Press, 1970.

Butterworth, Douglas, and John K. Chance, Latin American Urbanization: Urbanization in Developing Countries. Cambridge: Cambridge University Press, 1981.

Childers, Erskine, "The Other Exodus," The Spectator (May 12, 1961):672-675.

_____, "The Worldless Wish: From Citizens to Refugees," The Transformation of Palestine: Essays on the Origin and Development of the Arab-Israeli Conflict, edited by Abu-Lughod, Ibrahim, Evanston, Ill.: Northwestern University Press, 1971, pp. 165-202.

el-Daghestani, K., "The Evolution of the Moslem Family in the Middle Eastern Countries," In Readings in Arab Middle Eastern Societies and Culture, edited by Lutfiyya, Abdulla M. and Charles W. Churchill,pp. 554-566. The Hague: Mouton, 1970.

Dewey, Richard, "The Rural-Urban Continuum: Real but Relatively Unimportant," American Journal of Sociology 66 (July 1960):60-66.

Durkheim, Emile, The Division of Labor in Society. Glencoe, Ill.: Free Press, 1949.

Eban, Abba, Heritage: Civilization and the Jews. New York: Summit Books, 1984.

_____, My People: The Story of the Jews. New York: Behrman House, and Random House, 1968.

Eickelman, Dale, The Middle East: An Anthropological Approach Princeton, N. J.: Prentice-Hall, 1981.

Elkabir, Yassin Ali, "The Study of Urbanization in the Arab World: A Theoretical Perspective," Ekistics 50 (May/June 1983):232-236.

Epstein, A. L., "The Network and Urban Social Organization," In Social Networks in Urban Situations: Analyses of Personal Relationships in Central African Towns, edited by Mitchell, J. Clyde, pp. 77-116. Manchester: University of Manchester Press, 1969.

Farah, Tawfiq, "Political Socialization of Palestinian Children in Kuwait,"Journal of Palestine Studies 6, no. 4 (Summer 1977):90-102.

_____, "al-Tanshi'ah al-wataniyah lil-atfal al-filistiniyin fi Qatar" ["National Socialization of Palestinian Children in Qatar"],

Majalat Dirasat al-Khalij wa al-Jazirah al-ᶜArabiyah (July 19, 1979):43-60.

Farah, T., F. al-Salem, and M. K. al-Salem, "Arab Labour Migration: Arab Migrants in Kuwait," In Sociology of Developing Societies: The Middle East, edited by Asad, Talal and Roger Owen, pp. 42-53. New York: Monthly Review Press, 1983.

Fernea, Elizabeth W., "A Mirror Image," Discovery, Research and Scholarship at the University of Texas at Austin (Spring 1984), pp. 17-21.

_____, Women and the Family in the Middle East: New Voices of Change, Austin: University of Texas Press, 1985.

"Fhilistiniyin fi sin al-sittin wa kabus 'usmuh al-taqa ᶜud" ["Palestinians at the Age of 60 and the Nightmare of Retirement"], in al-Anba' (Kuwaiti daily) (June 27, 1985), p. 17.

Flapan, Simha, "Israelis and Palestinians: Can They Make Peace?" Journal of Palestine Studies 15, no. 1, 57 (Autumn 1985):19-42.

Furlong, Geoffrey, Palestine is My Country: The Story of Musa Alami, London: Murray, 1969.

Gans, Herbert J., The Urban Villagers. New York: Free Press, 1962.

Geertz, Hildred, "The Meaning of Family Ties," In Meaning and Order in Moroccan Society: Three Essays in Cultural Analysis, edited by Geertz, Clifford; Hildred Geertz; and Lawrence Rosen, pp. 315-379. Cambridge: Cambridge University Press, 1979.

Geertz, Hildred, and Clifford Geertz, Kinship in Bali. Chicago and London: University of Chicago Press, 1975.

Glubb, John Bagot, Peace in the Holy Land, London: Hodder and Stoughton, 1971.

Goldscheider, Calvin, and Alan S. Zuckerman, The Transformation of the Jews. Chicago: University of Chicago Press, 1984.

Graham-Brown, Sarah, Education, Repression and Liberation: Palestinians. London, United Kingdom: World University Service, 1984.

_____, Palestinians and Their Society 1880-1946: A Photographic Essay. London: Quartet Books, 1980.

_____, "The Political Economy of Jabal Nablus, 1920-1948," In Studies in the Economic and Social History of Palestine in the Nineteenth and Twentieth Century, edited by Owen, Roger, pp. 88-176. Carbondale: Southern Illinois University Press, 1982.

Granqvist, Hilma, Birth and Childhood among the Arabs: Studies in a Muhammadan Village in Palestine. Helsingfors: Soderstrom and Co. Forlagsaktiebolag, 1947.

177

_____, Marriage Conditions in a Palestinian Village. Vol. 2, Helsingfors: Societas Scientiarum Fennica. Commentations Humanarum Litterarum 3.8, 1931.

_____, Marriage Conditions in a Palestinian Village. Helsingfors: Societas Scientiarum Fennica. Commentations Humanarum Litterarum 6.8, 1935.

_____, Muslim Death and Burial: Arab Customs and Traditions Studied in a Village in Jordan. Helsinki: Societas Scientiarum Fennica. Commentations Humanarum Lifterarum, 34.1, 1965.

Gugler, Josef, and William G. Flanagan, Urbanization and Social Change in West Africa. Cambridge: Cambridge University Press, 1978.

Gulick, John, Social Strucure and Cultural Change in a Lebanese Village. New York: Warner-Green Foundation, 1955.

_____, "Village and City: Cultural Continuities in Twentieth Century Middle Eastern Cultures," In Middle Eastern Cities, edited by Lapidus, Ira M., pp. 122-158. Berkeley: University of California Press, 1969.

Haddad, Yvonne, "Palestinian Women: Patterns of Legitimation and Domination," In The Sociology of the Palestinians, edited by Nakleh, Khalil and Elia Zureik, New York: St. Martin's Press, 1980, pp. 147-175.

Hallaj, Muhammad, "The Mission of Palestinian Higher Education," Journal of Palestine Studies 9, no. 4, 36 (Summer 1980):76-95.

Halpern, Manfred, "Four Contrasting Repertoires of Human Relations in Islam," In Psychological Dimensions of Near Eastern Studies, edited by Brown, L. Carl and Norman Itzkowitz, pp. 66-102. Princeton: Darwin Press, 1977.

Hareven, Tamara K., "Family Time and Historical Time," Daedalus 106, no. 2 (Spring 1977):57-70.

Harries-Jones, P., "'Home-Boy Ties' and Political Organization in a Copperbelt Township," In Social Networks in Urban Situations: Analyses of Personal Relationships in Central African Towns, edited by Mitchell, J. Clyde, pp. 297-347. Manchester: Manchester University Press, 1969.

Hart, Alan, Arafat: Terrorist or Peacemaker? London: Sidgwick and Jackson, 1984.

al-Hassan, Bilal, "al-Filastiniyun fi al-Kuwayt" ["The Palestinians in Kuwait: Statistical Study"], Palestine Monograph No. 97. Beirut: Palestine Liberation Organization Research Center, 1974.

Hawl Qanun al-Ijarat (on the rent law) al-watan (Kuwaiti daily) (June 18, 1983); al-watan (Kuwaiti daily) (July 12, 1983).

Hijjawi, Sulafa, "al-filastinyun fi Lubnan" ["The Palestinians in Lebanon"], Journal of the Center for Palestine Studies, no. 22 (May/June 1977). Baghdad.

Hirabayashi, James; William Willard; and Luis Kemnitzer, "Pan Indianism in the Urban Setting," In The Anthropology of Urban Environment, edited by Weaver, Thomas and Douglas White, pp. 77-87. Washington, D.C.: Society for Applied Anthropology, 1972.

Hirst, David, The Gun and the Olive Branch: The Roots of Violence in the Middle East, 2d ed. London: Futura Macdonald and Co., 1978.

Holbern, Louise W., Refugees: A Problem of Our Time. The Work of the United Nations High Commission for Refugees, 1951-1972, Vol. 1 and 2. Metuchen, N.J.: Scarecrow Press, 1975.

Hurani, Hani, "Muqaddimat Nushu' al-tabaqah al-ᶜamilah wa-al-harakah al-naqabiyah fi al-Urdun: 1950-1947" ["Introductions in the Rise of the Working Class and the Union Movement in Jordan: 1950-1957"], Shu'un Filistiniyah 85 (December 1978):79-98.

Ismael, Jacqueline S., Kuwait: Social Change in Historical Perspective. New York: Syracuse University Press, 1982.

Jacobson, David, "Mobility, Continuity, and Urban Social Organization," Man 6 (December 1971):630-644.

al-Jardawi, ᶜAbdul-Ra'uf ᶜAbd al-ᶜAziz, al-Hijrah WalᶜUzzlah al-'Ijtimaᶜiyah fi al-Mujtamaᶜ al-Kuwayti: Dirasah Susulugiyah (Migration and Social Isolation in Kuwaiti Society: A Sociological Study). Kuwait: Sharikat Al-Rubayᶜan lil-Nashr w'a al-Tawziᶜ, 1984.

al-Jasim, Najat ᶜAbd al-Qadir, Al-Tatawur al-Siyasi wal-Iqtisadi Lil-Kuwayt Bayn al-Harbayn: 1914-1939 [The Political and Economic Evolution in Kuwait during the Interwar Period, 1914-1939]. Kuwait: Kuwait University, 1973.

"Jawlah fi ihtimamat al-filistinyin fi al-Kuwayt"l, ["A Journey into Palestinian Concerns in Kuwait"], in al-'Anba' (August 1, 1984). Also al-Anba' for August 2, 1984.

Kanafani, Ghassan, Men in the Sun and Other Palestinian Stories, translated by Hilary Kilpatrick. Washington, D.C.: Three Continents Press, 1978.

Key, William H., "Rural-Urban Social Participation," In Urbanism in World Perspective: A Reader, edited by Fava, Sylvia Fleis, pp. 305-312. New York: Thomas Y. Crowell Company, 1968.

Khalaf, Samir, and Emile Shawayri, "Family Firms and Industrial Development: The Lebanese Case," Economic Development and Cultural Change 15 (October 1966):59-69.

Khalidi, Walid. ed., <u>Before Their Diaspora: A Photographic History of the Palestinians 1876-1948</u>. Washington, D.C.: Institute of Palestine Studies, 1984.

_____, ed., <u>From Heaven to Conquest: Readings in Zionism and the Palestine Problem until 1948</u>. Beirut: Institute for Palestine Studies, 1971.

_____, "Plan Dalet," <u>The Arab World</u> (October-November 1969):15-20.

_____, "What Made the Palestinians Leave?" <u>Middle East Forum</u> in Beirut, 1959. London: Arab Office of Information, 1963.

Khuri, Fuad I., "Kinship, Emigration and Trade Partnership among the Lebanese of West Africa," <u>Africa</u> 35 (January 1965):385-395.

_____, "A Profile of Family Associations in Two Suburbs of Beirut,"In <u>Mediterranean Family Structures</u> edited by Peristiany, J. G., pp. 81-100. Cambridge: Cambridge University Press, 1976.

_____, <u>From Village to Suburb</u>. Chicago: University of Chicago Press, 1975.

al-Khususi, Badriddine A., <u>Dirasat fi Tarikh al-Kuwayt al-Ijtimaci wa al-Iqtisadi fi al-ᶜAsr al-Hadith</u>. [<u>Studies in the Socioeconomic History of Kuwait in the Modern Age</u>] 2d ed. Kuwait: That-al-Salasil, 1983.

Kuroda, Alice, and Yasumasa Kuroda, <u>Palestinians without Palestine: A Study of Poli Socialization among Palestinian Youths</u>. Washington, D.C.: University Press of America, 1978.

Kuroda, Yasumasa, and Alice Kuroda, "Personal Political Involvement of Palestinian Youths," <u>Middle East Forum</u> (Summer 1971):51-66.

Kuroda, Yasumasa, "Young Palestinian Commandos in Political Socialization Perspective," <u>Middle East Journal</u> (Summer 1972):253-270.

Kuwait Planning Council. Central Statistical Office. <u>Population Census 1975</u>.

_____, <u>Monthly Digest of Statistics</u>, Vol. 1, no. 4 (April 1985).

Levin, Harry, "The Attack on the Arab Village of Kolonia: April 12, 1948," In <u>From Haven to Conquest: Readings in Zionism and the Palestine Problem until 1948</u>, edited by Khalidi, Walid, pp. 767-770. Beirut: The Institute for Palestine Studies, 1971.

Lewis, Oscar, <u>Life in a Mexican Village: Tepoztlan Restudied</u>. Urbana: University of Illinois Press, 1951.

_____, "Urbanization without Breakdown: A Case Study," <u>Scientific Monthly</u> 75 (July 1952):31-41.

Loescher, Gilbert D., and John A. Scanlan, "The Global Refugee Problem: U.S. and World Response," <u>Annals of the American Academy of Political Science</u> 467 (May 1983):1-253.

Lomnitz, Larissa, "Migration and Network in Latin America," seminar on new directions of urban research, Institute of Latin American Studies, University of Texas at Austin, May 16-18, 1974.

_____, Networks and Marginality: Life in a Mexican Shantytown. New York: Academic Press, 1977.

Lutfiyya, Abdulla M., Baytin, a Jordanian Village: A Study of Social Institutions and Social Change in a Folk Community. London: Mouton, 1966.

Manneh, Abu, "The Rise of the Sanjak of Jerusalem in the Late 19th Century," In The Palestinians and the Middle East Conflict, edited by Ben-Dor, Gabriel, pp. 21-32. Ramat Gan, Israel: Turtledove Publications, 1978.

Mansour, Sylvie, "Identity among Palestinian Youth: Male and Female Differentials," Journal of Palestine Studies 6, no. 4 (Summer 1977):71-89.

Markham, James, "Palestinians, People in Crisis are Scattered and Divided," New York Times, February 19, 1978.

Maslow, A. H., (1943) "A Theory of Human Motivation," In Classics of Public Administration, edited by Shafritz, Jay M. and Albert C. Hyde, pp. 80-95. Oak Park, Ill.: Moore Publishing Company, 1978.

Massarueh, Abdul Salam y., "The Palestinians: Exiles in the Diaspora," Middle East Insight 4, no. 6 (1986).

Mayer, Adrian, "The Significance of Quasi-Groups in the Study of Complex Societies," In The Social Anthropology of Complex Societies, edited by Banton, Michael, pp. 97-122. New York: Tavistock Publications, 1966.

McLaughlin, Virginia Y., "Patterns of Work and Family Organ-ization: Buffalo's Italians," Journal of Interdisciplinary History 2 (Autumn 1971):299-314.

Migdal, Joel S., "State and Society in a Society without a State," In The Palestinians and the Middle East Conflict, edited by Ben-Dor, Gabriel, pp. 377-400. Haifa: Institute of Middle Eastern Studies, University of Haifa, 1978.

Milhim, Muhammad Ayash, "Rabitat al-jami^{c}iyyin fi muhafazat al-Khalil fi al-watan Wa al-mahjar" ("The University Graduate Union of the Hebron District in the Diaspora and the Homeland") In Rabitat al-jam^{c}iyyin fi muhafazat al-Khalil: Masiratuha Khilal Thalathin ^{c}Am, aylul 1953 ila aylul 1983 (The University Graduate Union of the Hebron District: Its Accomplishments in Thirty Years, September 1953-September 1983), pp. 114-115. Amman, Jordan: University Graduates Union.

181

Mitchell, J. Clyde, ed., Social Networks in Urban Situations. Manchester: Manchester University Press, 1969.

Morris, Benny, "The Harvest of 1948 and the Creation of the Palestinian Refugee Problem," Middle East Journal 40, no. 4 (Autumn 1986):671-685.

_____, "Operation Dani and the Palestinian Exodus from Lydda and Ramle in 1948," The Middle East Journal 40, no. 1 (Winter 1986):82-109.

Muhammad, Wajih Yassin, "al Takayuf al-ijtima^{c}i lil-usrah al-Falastiniyah al-Muhajirah ila al-Kuwayt" ["Social Adaptation of the Palestinian Migrant Family to Kuwait"]. M.A. thesis, Kuwait University, 1978.

Mundus, Hani, al-^{c}Amal wa al-^{c}Ummal fi al-Mukhayam al-Falastini: Bahth maydani ^{c}an mukhayam Tal-al-Za^{c}tar. [Labor and Workers in Palestinian Refugee Camps: A Field Study on the Tal Al-Za^{c}tar Refugee Camp]. Palestine Books no. 51. Beirut: Palestine Liberation Organization Research Center, 1974.

al-Mutawa^c, Badr Abdulla, "Qanun al-Ijarat wa'-Atharuh ^{c}ala al-Wala' wa al-Intima' " ("The Rent Law and its Effect on Loyalty and Belonging,"), al-watan, (Kuwaiti daily) (March 19, 1984).

Nakhleh, Khalil, and Elia Zureik, The Sociology of the Palestinians. New York: St. Martin's Press, 1980.

Nazzal, Khawla [On Palestinians with Travel Documents] al-watan (Kuwaiti daily) (August 14, 20, and 27, 1984).

Nazzal, Nafez, The Palestinian Exodus from Galilee, 1948. Beirut: Institute of Palestine Studies, 1978.

Needham, Rodney,"Polythetic Classification: Convergence and Consequences", Man (N.S.), 10, no. 3 (September 1975):349-369.

al-Nizam al'Asasi li-Jam^{c}iyat rabitat al-jami^{c}iyyin Bi-muhafazat al-Khalil: fir^c al-Kuwayt (The Charter of the University Graduate Union of the Hebron district: The Kuwait Chapter).

Plascov, Avi, "The Palestinians of Jordan's Border," In Studies in the Economic and Social History of Palestine in the 19th and 20th Centuries edited by Owen, Roger, Carbondale: Southern Illinois University Press, 1982, pp. 203-241.

_____, The Palestinian Refugees in Jordan, 1948-1957. London: Frank Press and Company, 1981.

Peretz, D.; A. M. Wilson; and R. J. Ward, A Palestine Entity. Washington, D.C.: Middle East Institute, 1970.

Peretz, Don, "Palestinian Social Stratification: The Political Implications," Journal of Palestine Studies 7, no. 1 (Autumn 1977):48-74.

182

Qutub, Ishaq Y., "Urbanization in Contemporary Arab Gulf States," Ekistics 50 (May/June 1983):170-182.

Radcliffe-Brown, Alfred R., Structure and Function in Primitive Societies. New York: Free Press, 1969.

al-Rahman, As^cad Abd, "al-'Awda^c al--ta^climiyah lil Jaliyah al-filistinyah fi al-Kuwayt" ["The Educational Attainment among the Palestinian Community in Kuwait"] Paper presented to the Economic Committee for West Asia, United Nations, Beirut, November 1981.

Rapaport, Rhona, "Normal Crisis, Family Structure and Mental Health," Family Process 2 (1963):68-86.

Redfield, Robert, (1947) "The Folk Society," In Classic Essays on the Culture of Cities, edited by Sennett, Richard, pp. 180-205. Princeton, N.J.: Prentice-Hall, 1969.

de Reyner, Jacques, "Dair Yassin: April 10, 1948," In From Heaven to Conquest: Readings in Zionism and the Palestine Problem until 1948, edited by Khalidi, Walid, pp. 761-766. Beirut: Institute for Palestine Studies, 1971.

Roudy, John, "Dynamics of Land Alienation", In The Transfor-mation of Palestine, Essays on the Origins and the Development of the Arab-Israeli Conflict, edited by Abu-Lughod, Ibrahim, pp. 119-139. Evanston, Ill.: Northwestern University Press, 1971.

Rouleau, Eric, "The Palestinian Diaspora of the Gulf," MERIP Reports 132 (May 1985):13-15.

Rugh, Andrea B., Family in Contemporary Egypt. Syracuse, N. Y.: Syracuse University Press, 1984.

Said, Edward W. After the Last Sky: Palestinian Lives, with photographs by Jean Mohr, New York: Pantheon Books, 1986.

Sakhnini, I., "al-filastiniyun fi al-Iraq" ["The Palestinians in Iraq"], Shu'un Filastiniyah, no. 13 (September 1972):90-116.

Salisbury, Richard F., and Mary E. Salisbury, "The Rural Oriented Strategy of Urban Adaptation: Siamese Migrants in Port Moresby," In The Anthropology of Urban Environments, edited by Weaver, Thomas and Douglas White, pp. 59-68. Washington, D.C.: Society for Applied Anthropology, 1972.

Sanduq al-Khalil al-Khayri: al-Nizam al-'Asasi (The Hebron Charitable Fund: The Charter) 1980.

Sarhan, Basim, "al-^cA'ilah wa-all-Qarabah ^cInd al-filistiniyin Fi al-Kuwayt: Natai'j 'awwaliyah libahth ijtima^ci" ["Family and Kinship among the Palestinians in Kuwait: Preliminary Results of Sociological Research"] (Paper presented to al-Ma^chad al-^cArabi lil-Takhtit al-'Iqtisadi Wa-al-Ijtima'i, Kuwait, 1976).

Sayigh, Rosemary, "The Palestinian Experience: Integration and Non-Integration in the Arab Ghourba," Arab Studies Quarterly 1, no. 2 (Spring 1979): 96-112.

_____,"The Palestinian Experience Viewed as Socialization" M.A. thesis, American University of Beirut, 1976.

_____, Palestinians: From Peasants to Revolutionaries. London: Zed Press, 1979.

_____, "Sources of Palestinian Nationalism: A Study of a Palestinian Camp in Lebanon," Journal of Palestine Studies 6, no. 4 (Summer 1977):17-40.

Schneider, David N., American Kinship: A Cultural Account Modern Societies Series. Englewood Cliffs, N.J.: Prentice-Hall, 1968.

Scholch, Alexander, "European Penetration and the Economic Development of Palestine, 1856-82," In Studies in the Economic and Social History of Palestine, edited by Owen, Roger, pp. 10-87. Carbondale: Southern Illinois University Press, 1982.

Sengstol, Mary C., "Detroit's Iraqi-Chaldeans: A Conflicting Con-ception of Identity," In Arabs in the New World: Studies on Arab-American Communities, edited by Abraham, Sameer Y. and Nabeel Abraham, pp. 136-146. Detroit, Mich.: Wayne State University Center for Urban Studies, 1983.

Shaath, Nabeel, "High Level Palestinian Manpower," Journal of Palestine Studies 1, no. 2 (Winter 1972):80-95.

Shhab, Salih Jasim, Tarikh al-Ta'Lim Fi al-Kuwayt wa al-Khalij 'Ayam Zaman [History of Education in Kuwait and the Gulf during the Old Days], Vol I. Kuwait, 1984.

Shippler, David K., Arab and Jew: Wounded Spirits in a Promised Land, New York: Times Book, 1986.

Simpson, John Hope, The Refugee Problem. Oxford: Institute of International Affairs, 1939.

Smelser, Neil, Social Change in the Industrial Revolution: An Application of Theory to the British Cotton Industry. Chicago: University of Chicago Press, 1959.

Smith, Pamela Ann, Palestine and the Palestinians: 1876-1983. New York: St. Martin's Press, 1984.

_____, "The Palestinian Diaspora, 1948-1985," Journal of Palestine Studies 15, no. 3, issue 59 (Spring 1986):90-108.

Spradley, James P., (1969) "Adaptive Strategies of Urban Nomads. The Ethnoscience of Tramp Culture," In The Anthropology of Urban Environments, edited by Weaver, Thomas and Douglas White, pp. 21-38. Washington, D.C.: Society for Applied Anthropology.

Springborg, Robert, Family, Power and Politics: Sayed Bey Marei--His Clan, Clients, and Cohorts. Philadelphia: University of Pennsylvania Press, 1982.

Stewart, Charles, "The Urban-Rural Dichotomy: Concepts and Uses," The American Journal of Sociology 64 (September 1958):151-158.

Stirling, Paul, Turkish Village. New York: John Wiley and Sons, 1965.

"A Survey of Palestine," Vol. 1 and 2, Anglo-American Committee of Inquiry, Palestine: The Government Printer, 1946.

al-Tamimi, Rajab Mustafa, "Rabitat al-jamiᶜiyyin fi muhafazat al-Khalil fi al-watan Wa al-mahjar" ("The University Graduate Union of the Hebron District in the Diaspora and the Homeland") In Rabitat al-jamᶜiyyin fi muhafazat al-Khalil: Masiratuha Khilal Thalathin ᶜAm, aylul 1953 ila aylul 1983 (The University Graduate Union of the Hebron District: Its Accomplishments in Thirty Years, September 1953-September 1983), pp. 109-113. Amman, Jordan: University Graduates Union.

Tannous, Afif I., "Group Behavior in the Village Community of Lebanon," Readings in Arab Middle Eastern Society and Cultures, edited by Lutfiyya, Abdulla M. and Charles W. Churchill, pp. 89-108. 1942 reprint, The Hague: Mouton, 1970.

Team International. "The Economic and Social Situation and Potential of the Palestinian Arab People in the Region of Western Asia." Presented to the United Nations Economic Commission for West Asia, 1983.

Tibawi, A. L., "Visions of Return: The Palestine Arab Refugees in Arabic Poetry and Art," Middle East Journal 7, no. 5 (Autumn 1976):507-526.

Tonnies, Ferdinand, Community and Society. New York: Harper Torchbooks, 1963.

Waxman, Chaim I., America's Jews in Transition. Philadelphia: Temple University Press, 1983.

Weber, Max, The Theory of Social and Economic Organization. New York: Free Press, 1947.

Webster's Third New International Dictionary of the English Language Unabridged. Massachusetts: G. and C. Merriam Company, Publishers, 1961.

Wirth, Louis, "Urbanism as a Way of Life," In Classic Essays on the Culture of Cities, edited by Sennett, Richard, pp. 143-164. 1938 reprint, Princeton, N.J.: Prentice-Hall, 1969.

Wrigley, Anthony, "Reflections on the History of the Family," Daedalus 106, no. 2 (Spring 1977):71-85.

Yaghmur, ᶜAbd al-Khaliq, Introduction, "Rabitat al-jamiᶜiyyin fi muhafazat al-Khalil fi al-watan Wa al-mahjar" ("The University

Graduate Union of the Hebron District in the Diaspora and the Homeland") In <u>Rabitat al-jam^ciyyin fi muhafazat al-Khalil: Masiratuha Khilal Thalathin ^cAm, aylul 1953 ila aylul 1983</u> (<u>The University Graduate Union of the Hebron District: Its Accomplishments in Thirty Years, September 1953-September 1983</u>), pp. 3-5. Amman, Jordan: University Graduates Union.

Yassin, ^cAbd al-Qadir, "al-Tatawwur al-Sina^ci fi Fhilistin hita am 1948 ["The Evolution of Industry in Palestine until 1948"], <u>Shu'un Philistiniyah</u>, no. 80 (July 1978):81-98.

Yusuf, Muhsin D., "The Potential Impact of Palestinian Education on a Palestinian State," <u>Journal of Palestine Studies</u> 8, no. 4 (Summer 1979):70-93.

188

189

191

193

194

Printed in Great Britain
by Amazon

13205442R00122